الاستنباط من البحر العميق

AL- ISTINBĀTU MIN AL BAHRI AL A'MÌQ

DROPS FROM THE DEEP OCEAN

REFLECTIONS ON THE QUR'AN

Effects of Attitudes in Guidance

with a focus on

- ▶ Contemporary Renderings
- ▶ Psychological Explorations
- ▶ Western Discourses
- ▶ Lexical Analysis

VOLUME 1

Dr. M. Yunus Kumek

Address to the Islamic Religious Scholars & Philosophers

Medina House
publishing

Cover Photo by Y. Kumek, Alexandria, Egypt, January 12, 2019.

Medina House ͨ

publishing

www.medinahouse.org
170 Manhattan Ave, Po. Box 63
New York 14215
contact@medinahouse.org

Copyright © 2021 by Medina House ͨ Publishing

ISBN 978-1-950979-18-9

Published in the United States of America.

Table of Contents

VOLUME 1

VOLUME 1

Intention and Introduction

بِسْمِ اللهِ الرَّحْمَنِ الرَّحِيمِ ¹

الْحَمْدُ لِلّهِ رَبِّ الْعَالَمِينَ ²

اللَّهُمَّ صَلِّ عَلَى سَيِّدِنَا وَ حَبِيْبِنَا وَ مَوْلَانَا مُحَمَّدٍ ³

The intention of writing and compiling drops from the Deep Ocean of the Qurãn is to benefit myself and others moving towards purifying our hearts and minds of diseases in our contemporary time. The cure is found in the Qurãn. As the viruses change forms and shapes, and adjust and adapt to the conditions of time and place, the diseases of the heart and mind, in our times, can change with the globalized world of internet, communication, and information sharing. Although the Qurãn has all the keys to cure any disease, I believe, it is important to express and communicate these drops from the ocean in a way in which people are able to understand and implement. In other words, it is important to look, review, and deduce meanings from the Qurãn with the formalized and structuralized disciplines of natural sciences such as physics, math, chemistry, biology, and anatomy, as well as the social and humanitarian sciences of anthropology, psychology, history, political science, education, arts, communication, language, and religion. Therefore, whether we like it or not, there is an existing language of communication dictated by the changes, norms, and cultures of time and place. Even if we fix the time and look at the communication at a certain time frame, the language of communication should change according to different audiences, such as age groups, professions, educational levels, genders, cultures, and geopolitical locations. As an example, one can review in our contemporary time the language of the books for the subjects of K-12 learners compared to college students. Or, the example of the language of the academic books compared to popular books of the same subject, which can have an entirely different mode of language to relay the knowledge to the appropriate reader.

---

1. In the name of Allah the Most Compassionate, the Most Merciful.
2. All praise is due to Allah, Lord of both worlds.
3. Oh Allah, send peace on our master, our beloved, Muhammed ﷺ.

In this perspective, this compilation assumes the reader is already familiar with the classical exegetical sciences of the Qurãn. It also assumes that the reader knows and is familiar with the classical interpretation of the verses. Therefore, as these drops of a little knowledge inspired from the ocean of the Qurãn, it rarely brings forth the classical approaches for the meanings of the Qurãn. Rather, it tries to focus on a few contemporary scholars' perspectives with additional possible interpretations. When someone knows and presents something, it is a discovery of a reality that is already there. If the person does not know or does know, the reality, the existing knowledge, and the science, i'lm, are still there. Therefore, the title of this book is al-istinbãt, which is making deductions and discovering to know what is already there. The author's and the people's discovery do not alter the reality of the knowledge in the ocean of the Qurãn.

Therefore, I take full blame if there are any errors about these renderings due to my ignorance and ask Allah's forgiveness, the Most Merciful; Amìn. If there is anything good or beneficial, that is from the Fadl (grace) of Allah, but definitely not from me.

If there is anyone who would benefit with me from these drops of the ocean, I would feel that inshAllah, I may take a step to remove some of my selfishness inshAllah to share what I benefit with my others. May Allah guide me and all of us to the true understanding of this beautiful religion; Amìn.

Dr. Muhammad Yunus Kumek
Lecturer in Islamic Studies
Harvard Divinity School
Fall 2019

Usûl-u Tafsìr (Exegetical Method)

It is important to follow the salaf, the prior canonized scholarship in their methodology, usûl, when bringing new approaches within existing approaches. In other words, one cannot build or bring an approach for a subject unless there is a proper literature review. One of the methods that is important not to describe the batil, the evil and ugly, explicitly not to leave any traces of undesired descriptions in the minds and hearts (1) especially at our time where this notion of adab, respect, to the sacred is increasingly being lost.

Having a proper adab when this sacred knowledge is presented, written or discussed, is the key in these sciences of sacred knowledge. This approach brings the true, sincere, and genuine learning and tawfîk, help, of Allah ﷻ, inshAllah, and then the acceptance of people with the will of Allah ﷻ. Having proper adab to the approaches of the salaf, although one may not agree, is very critical. The approach of looking at this science as an academic article or a book that can be a freely criticized venue can be a reductionist approach of misunderstood Western scholarship by even some of the Muslims in academia. One should have proper adab/ respect, of understanding the Qurãn, with knowing who the Sender is, the content, style, trans-time, and transnational and trans-generation perspectives. Therefore, the approaches of academic scholarship may not find much value in the classical accepted canonized methodology of the exegesis of the Qurãn unless this adab is preserved by especially Muslim academicians working in the universities. As for the non-Muslims' renderings about the Qurãn and Islamic sciences, if it is done humbly, genuinely, and ethically, then it may bring some perspectives to the scholarship as well. For example, the Arabic language translation to English by Hans Wehr is a useful piece and used by Muslim scholars.

When I was a postdoctoral fellow at Harvard Divinity School, I was attending the courses taught by both Muslims and non-Muslims. In one of the courses taught by a Muslim professor, I was also bringing my perspectives in the class to balance the Western perspectives with the traditional scholarship for the adab and respect of the previous scholars' (the salaf) renderings. The professor then mentioned that in his own experience in Europe, there were students coming to European universities from Muslim countries and they were very sensitive about the concept of adab and respect. According to the professor's observation, later, these students tuned down the Western approaches of looking at the scholarship. Although it can be appropriate to tune down with the notions of empathy and social context, normalizing in one's mind that having no adab or respect is fine, or that maybe it is too much for the academic environment, can be a major deviation in the embodiment of the Islamic sciences of Divinity. One can give different examples of teachings in American and European teaching environments. Nowadays, in the universities in Muslim countries, there has been an increasing trend to popularize criticizing and disagreeing with the salaf without any proper emphatic respect and scholarly literature review. In my opinion, this is an avenue for some people in academia to show their "bold scholarship," unlike to those who can critique but follow certain steps of methodology (usûl) in that field and respectfully contribute to and expand the field with new approaches and perspectives. Today some of the academic Islamic scholarship stems from people who identify themselves as Muslims, while they do not know much about the basics of classical methods (usûl), which have been established for over a thousand years ago. I do not find this approach "scholarship or bold scholarship" because there is no proper literature review, and methodology but naïve approaches of the novice or arrogant approaches of the ignorant. Therefore, most of the time in these types of lectures, conferences, or gatherings people can deduce artificial knowledge of Islamic scholarship compared to the ethnographic, historical, or phenomenological approaches from the practice. I believe this is the **main reason** why there is a disconnect between the academia and practice.

In the eyes of some of the Sufis, Muslim mystics, due to overwhelming love of Allah ﷻ, everything other than Allah ﷻis blocked. It doesn't mean that these Sufis don't love anyone else. At that level, forcing the notions of tawhid to rationalize can be artificial but not natural. In that perspective, it is common to see this notion or approach among some of the Muslim academicians and philosophers in the field of theology and divinity, to force these limits of tawhid and they end up with the false and mixed ideas of reality with a problem. This happened in the past and is happening today. Many books are written in this field of approximating the core principles of tawhid and aqidah with the methodology of philosophy, due to only using the mind and reason. These books are mostly deviated from the core principles of tawhid due to forcing the limits of tawhid with human mind and without any proper adab due to mostly lacking practice of these thinkers. I say thinkers here because religion is not only thinking but living and experiencing, especially in Islam. Therefore, the practicing person can bring perspectives due to his or her experience with the notion of adab when rationalizing the core concepts in aqidah (2). In another words, the practice can guide the person with the process of mind and reason even though the person may fall sometimes into traps of mind. Oppositely, in some of the lectures or books a person can find very interesting exegetical or Tafsìr related analysis of the Qurān and other sacred texts but due to lack of adab, Allah ﷻ does not make these analyses to be widely accepted by people, to be known or popularized but they are lost in the years of the history. In other words, although there are some correct and interesting analysis of the points of tafsìr in some discourses or among some groups, due to lack of adab and positive respectful attitude, their genius true ideas are buried and lost due to lack of adab to the sacred, I believe, الله اعلم, Allah ﷻ knows the best.

Surprisingly, in my experience of attending the lectures of some of the non-Muslim well-intentioned scholars at Harvard who have genuine empathy of understanding this phenomenology and historical data of Islam, I have found more respectful and scholarly attitude of methodology similar to the traditional teachings of salaf. For example, I have found, Dr. J. Cesari very genuine, scholarly at the same time trying to understand and analyze critically some of the approaches in the Islamic scholarship and phenomenology. I have found Dr. J. Baberson very genuine and scholarly in that perspective with the perspectives of Islamic law. I had some disagreements with possibly some of their content knowledge but I found their usûl, methodology, well intentioned towards learning and using the prior established methodologies.

As some of the scholars mention that being insider in a group can prevent certain learnings due to arrogance and being outsider can help see certain phenomenological perspectives better. As the Prophet (ﷺ) mentions "teach the ones who are not present here, possibly they may have a better understanding (3)." One of the traditional important approaches to the Qurān and all natural phenomena is with the reference point of its Divine source. In other words, disconnecting the Qurān and creation from the Divine Source and approaching it only as a rational discourse as suggested with the traditional field of philosophy can be an issue. In other words, the framework of everything and all creation has a purpose with reference to the Creator, Allah ﷻ, is a key element. This understanding gives a holistic and a whole meaning as the main core of the solving a jigsaw puzzle. This can also truly explain why the humans have weaknesses and needs unlike the discourses of philosophy. When classical philosophy disconnects the meanings and structure from the Creator, it gives value to the beings due their self-existence. Then, it can cover the intrinsic nature of humanness about weakness and need. This, then implicitly and explicitly discourages people from practice and worship which is the key to discharge the person's spirituality in their relationship with the Divine.

It is important to realize that as we are moving towards the era of "holistic" approaches in different sciences, divinity itself should primarily adapt this approach as the source of considering everything as a whole and an entire piece but at the same time holy and holistic. Holistic medicine, holistic education, holistic etc. The word holistic in its real sense can entail different perspectives from different disciplines. It may entail ethnography and phenomenology from anthropology, and psychology. It may entail grounded theory from education.

It is important to realize that when one is analyzing a text one can get a better understanding of it and its relevance to the entire text. As the person looks at each piece separately, it can be generally difficult to understand the full message of the author. In other words, each paragraph, or sentence cannot reflect the entire message of the book. However, the Qurān is not like that. The Qurān's each verse, each section or each chapter can completely reflect the full entire message of the Book. This style is considered one of the miracles of the Qurān among many others. One can call this as ijaz or balagah, as a technical term. The scholars have written thousands of books just to reflect on this perspective of the Qurān among the Qurān's many other perspectives.

There have been many exegetical books written with many volumes with different focuses. For example, when one does not understand a word or when one wants to search the literature on a verse, as an example of a methodology, here are some of the books of the classical exegetical, tafsìr author names that one can try to review: Maqaatil, Yahya ibn Salam, Al-hawari, At-Tabari, Ibn Abi Hatim, Al-Maturidi, As-Samarkandi, Ibn Abi Zamnin, As –Salabi, Makki, At-Tawusi, Al-

Qusayri, Al-Wahidi, As-Sama'ni, Al-Bagawi, Az-Zamahshari, Ibn-A'tiyyah, At-Tabursi, Ibn Jawzi, Al-Fakhri Razi, Al-Qurtubi, Al-Baydawi, An-Nasafi, Al-Khazani, Ibn-Kasir, An-Nisaburi, Ibn A'dil, Al-Buqai', Jalaladdin Suyuti, Abu Suud, Al-Mazhari, Ibn Ajibah, As-Shawkani, Al-Awsi, Ibn Ashur, Ibrahim Al-Qatani, As-Sha'rawi, and Sayyid Tantawi . In my literature review, there are names that I did not include in above authors because I don't refer to them much. I also did not include some of the contemporary authors that I much frequently refer to in this list. The above authors mostly are from the early periods of first 300-400 years after the Prophet Muhammad ﷺ. For each one line, verse of the Qurãn, average total pages written in the above list of books are around 30 pages. If one makes the calculation with the number of verses and with the assumption of an average size book of 300 pages, one can realize that there were approximately minimum of 1000 books written only on exegesis in the early times that I to try to incorporate some of them. In other words, one should not forget that the above calculation is only based on the authors and books that I mostly use. There are many other books written starting from the early periods of 700 AD. I think, the reason is that it is very critical to understand what the early scholars understand from the Qurãn. A text can reflect the language, culture, practices, and norms of the individuals and the society at a specific time and place. Thus, in the early generations, the perspectives of the first addressees of the Qurãn with its language, content and style are supremely critical in order to interpret with different understandings for later generations in different places and time.

Therefore, it will be totally illogical, unmethodical and nonacademic approach if one ignores all current available information and puts one's own opinion about the verses of the Qurãn. This does not mean that there are no new avenues and understandings in the Qurãn with the change of time, culture and norms. Yes, there is, but one should follow the proper steps of doing the literature review and within the established literature and framework then, one can develop and bring perspectives for our contemporary time. This book also uses the approaches and commentaries of two of my teachers, the contemporary shayhqayn. One already passed way and may Allah ﷻ give long life to the other one who is alive with afiyah and achievements of khayr.

It is important to approach to the Qurãn with the suggested methodology mentioned in the Qurãn itself first. In other words, the

Qurãn acknowledges and classifies the two main types of verses in the Qurãn al-muhkam, the explicit ones and al-mutashabih, the implicit ones as mentioned in Sûrah Al-Imrãn [3:7]. There is an agreement among the scholars about the essence of muhkam, the explicit verses. In other words, the muhkam verses are clear and explicit. According to the scholars, the other interpretations of these muhkam verses, clear verses, other than the explicit canonized teachings is considered deviation or kufr. This methodology is applied also in the science of hadith for the most authenticed levels of hadith, al-mutawatir.

One may ask the hikmah, wisdom, of the muhkam and mutasabbih verses in the Qurãn. The Qurãn uses different styles for different level audiences so that everyone can have a benefit from it.

The implicit ones can have clear metaphors, similes, and figurative language compared to the explicit ones. One of the reasons of this figurative language is to approximate the intended meanings to the human mind at different times, contexts, cultures, individual and/or communal cases. One can always argue that when there is a communication of the Transcendent Reality with humans, there will be always reductionism in its meanings. Therefore, there will always be room for error and misinterpretation. This is the reality of the limits of language and the human mind. For example, in the case of one's communication with a child, it is also important to understand what the child understands in regard to what the parent explains about any topic.

There can be other categories in the ayah such as with the new disciplines of science such as physics, math, biology, or chemistry or with the social sciences some of them can be revisited to be interpreted with this new expertise.

Accordingly, the practice of the Prophet ﷺ, the hadith and the sunnah brings a very key and meaningful value in the application of the Qurãn. Because, the Prophet was immediately corrected and guided by Allah ﷻ in different cases if there was any question in the application of the verses in the realities of life. In other words, the Prophet ﷺ received revelation what Allah ﷻ wants in establishing the teachings of the religion, the structure and the order. This brings the importance of studying the science of sababi nuzûl, the reasons of revelation, for each verse. It is important to study in which case, context, time, and person for which the verse was revealed. From this, one can look into how to extend the meanings to different contexts and times.

With the notion of sabab nuzûl, I also want to mention one misinterpreted discussion that the Qurān can be interpreted according to what the person is looking for and therefore, sabab nuzûl is very important. One may apply here this discourse to any text, but, especially to the scriptures. This discussion is generally presented to prevent misinterpretations of the Qurān. The arguments can go further about the language being literal versus figurative and with other fine details. But, one should not forget that the Qurān is an interactive and a live Divine Book from Allah ﷻ. There should be the personal connection for each individual with the Qurān. One can say that there is an individualized personal sabab-nuzûl for each person from the Qurān depending on the need of the person. One should get inspirations, guidance, and conversations from the Qurān in a genuine reading. Therefore, these two approaches should be balanced with intention, knowledge and personal relevance. First approach is understanding the Qurān with its initial reason of revelation to the Prophet. The second approach is reading the Qurān daily as a personal relevance encounter. Yes, it is true that a person with a not genuine intention can misinterpret the Qurān. But, a sincere person is encouraged to engage with the Qurān regularly for one's need with knowledge and personal relevance. Because, sometimes by emphasizing the concepts of initial or literal sabab nuzûl then other forms of the problems of misinterpretation can occur such as making the Qurān only for the intellectuals. This approach by itself can distance the others to establish connection in day to day discourse. Yes, the original sabab-nuzûl to the Prophet ﷺ is the key and founding pillar but this argument should not be used to estrange the person for personal sabab nuzûl to each person every day at the point of personal relevance.

The early Muslims, sahabah, were witnessing all these new revelations, and at the same time living and observing the Prophet in different applications of the Quranic verses in practical life encounters. As the first encounters of the Quranic language, the early Muslims, sahabah, were trying to contextualize the meanings of the revelation with their mind by observing the Prophet ﷺ. One should also remember that the early Muslims were very adept in language. Some of the commodities of language were memorizing thousand lines of poems, discussions on literature of words, styles and genres etc. This brings another step of an established methodology in studying the Qurān is the importance of reviewing the understandings about the meanings and their applications in the life of the early Muslims. Lastly, it is important to look at all the literature reviews of the new understandings at different times and different regions of Muslim culture about the interpretation of the Qurãn until our contemporary times.

As one can summarize from this a brief introduction for a *general methodology of literature review* in approaching and understanding the Qurãn is from

1. The Qurãn itself,
2. The reasons for revelation, sababi nuzûl
3. The Prophet's practices and applications, the hadith and the Sunnah
4. The early Muslims understandings, reasoning and applications, the sahabah (the first generation), tabeen (second generation) and taba-tabeen (third generation)
5. The remaining historical literature review at different times and different regions of Muslim culture about the interpretation of the Qurãn until our contemporary time.

If one skips this above methodology, it is very normal and inevitable to make mistakes and errors. From academic perspective of methodology, it is not scientific or rational to remove this methodology when one is reviewing the Qurãn. This methodology is already there. It has been established and used for centuries. It is not fair and logical to blind oneself to all the rich intellectual and relevant data because the Qurãn is accessible and a popular Book for everyone. In other words, it is encouraged to use the Qurãn in everyday life, read it and benefit from it. At the same time, it is important to properly understand and apply the knowledge with a genuine method.

After completing the general methodology of literature, then the person can focus on the studied verse or ayah to entangle the meanings through specific methodology of focus by:

1. Reviewing and analyzing, the siyãq and sibãq, the prior and later verses to deduce intended meanings.
2. Analyzing and reviewing different recitation of the words with the schools of qirãah.

3. Linguistic analysis of each word and deducing different possible meanings with I'rab, vowel and consonant renderings

In the above specific methodology for the case one, normative scholarly and legally interpretations and exegesis of Qurān, contextual (*siyāq and sibāq*[4]) previous and subsequent understandings of the verses are paramount (4). One of the methodologies in this perspective is that if it fits in the context of siyāq and sibāq and then, this is understood to be the desired and explicit meaning in the usûl, methodology.

Secondly, one should also realize that there is the existence of the science of recitation called qirāah. As the Arabic have structured on vowels with its letters, it has also consonants denoted by signs called harakahs. The Quranic consonants, harakahs are marked in the entire Qurān by considering and mimicking the recitation of the Prophet originally revealed to him with their implied meanings. Occasionally, in some cases, the minor differences of recitation of these harakahs, letters and words have structured and established the different schools of recitation, qirāah in the Islamic scholarship. The number of these schools are ranging from seven to thirteen according to Jalaladdin Suyuti (rh) (5). Why this is important is that the science of recitation also brings sometimes additional possible interpretation in exegetical meanings of the Qurān. Therefore, one can also add this perspective to the above list in the classical established methodology of the Quranic exegesis. In other words, reviewing different schools of recitation can bring some perspectives in the interpretation of the Qurān. This is one of the methods followed by all established scholars of tafsìr as part of their literature review historically.

Thirdly, one should not underestimate the complexity of the Arabic language with its history, structure and styles unlike other languages. Similes, allegories, embedded meanings in one word, connection with other words in the sentence, if a word is skipped, the implications of changing the sentence structure, or instead of putting subject first putting object can have implied and different meanings in interpretations. Therefore, there are only specialized tafsirs, classical exegetical volumes analyzing the Qurān only linguistically. One of these

---

4. Siyq and sibq are is a term to indicate the methodology in the Quranic exegesis for understanding the contextual meaning of the analyzed verse by examining the prior and following verses.

examples is the book of Zamakshari. There are contemporary popular
ones as well called tafsirul i'rãb which is the exegesis of the Qurãn based
on grammar. Exegetical scholars refer also to these linguistic intricacies
of the Qurãn to deduce intended meanings. One should also refer to this
along with other perspectives in the listed methodology above.

Interpreting the Qurãn and making tafsìr according to the maqãsid,
purpose, is important. What is maqãsid? Maqãsid can be for some the
immediate meanings of the muhkam, explicit, verses. There are always
implicit meanings next to the maqãsid. In this perspective, it may be
important to ask some questions such as: what is the objective of the
person when someone is doing the tafsìr? Who will be the audience of
this tafsìr? What is the maqsadu al-sharia'h, the explicit goal of the Qurãn
according to the specific audience? The answers of these questions can
also help the interpreter early in the process of writing so that there is
a purpose of interpreting and after the above brief methodologies can
follow inshAllah.

Lastly, to remind and emphasize this point that one should remember
in any of the renderings of the Qurãn, one should primarily consider the
initial and primary meanings through the methodology of muffasirun.
In this methodology, the understanding of riwãyah, narrations as
explained by Rasulullah ﷺ with their sabab nuzûl[5], and early salaf of the
sahabah and tabiû'n precedes the engagements of dirãyah, using other
analysis in the contexts of intellect, time and context.

What is the Qurãn?

The Qurãn is the explanation of the universe. The Qurãn is the translator
of the meanings of the different signs in one's personal and social life.
The Qurãn is the translator of the meanings of the different signs in the
nature, universe, galaxies, in the known and unknown dimensions. The
Qurãn is the explanation of the seen and unseen and mystical and literal
realities. The Qurãn is the opener of the secrecies of Allah ﷻ on the earth
and in the skies. The Qurãn is the explanation of the personal experiences
and social encounters. The Qurãn is the language of the unseen world
in the seen world of ours. The Qurãn is the reflection and explanation

---

5. Reason for narration.

of the favors, Mercy and Caring of Allah ﷻ on humans. The Qurān is the pillar of Islam. The Qurān is the map of the afterlife. The Qurān is the explanation of the Names, and Attributes of Allah ﷻ. The Qurān is the teacher of the humans. The Qurān is the water and food of Islam. The Qurān is the essence of humanity. The Qurān is the real guidance of humanity for peace. The Qurān is a book of guidance, a book of prayer, a book of wisdom, a book of worship, a book of invitation, a book of chant, and a book of reflection and critical thinking. The Qurān is the book of compilation of all other books that contain the essentials for the person's spiritual and emotional needs. The Qurān is the source of all the branches of different paths followed by different prophets, messengers, saints and friends of Allah ﷻ. The Qurān is the Word of Allah ﷻ. The Qurān is the declaration of the Allah ﷻ as the Creator of everything. The Qurān is the address of Allah ﷻ who is the Creator of the earth, galaxies, universes, and skies. The Qurān is the mutual conversation with the perspective of Rububiyah, upbringing, teaching and guidance of Allah ﷻ. The Qurān is the eternal sermon with the Perfect Authority of Allah ﷻ. The Qurān is the Favor of the Most Merciful due to the Divine Infinite Mercy. The Qurān is a Divine Favor, Kindness, and Sympathy from the Creator to the creation. The Qurān is the communication from the Most High and Exalted with some secret codes.

Therefore, the title of "the Word of God" has always and will always be given to the Qurān.

The Qurān is the final Book of Allah ﷻ. Therefore, the Qurān includes all the previous Books sent by Allah ﷻ. Therefore, the Qurān encompasses all the previous Books without any darkness of skepticism and doubts. The Qurān is with certainty the revelation from Allah ﷻ. The objective of the Qurān is the eternal happiness and peace. The inside of the Qurān is guidance. The front of the Qurān is the required light of belief. The back of the Qurān is the proof with certainty. The right side of the Qurān is the submission of the heart and conscience. The left side of the Qurān is the acceptance and surrender of the mind, intellect, reason and logic. The fruit of the Qurān is the mercy of Allah ﷻ and happiness and peace in this world and afterlife. The Qurān is the Divine Revelation signified and engaged by the angels, humans, jinns, animals, stones, clouds, mountains, animate, and inanimate beings.

The Qurān inspires the person depending on the need of the person. Therefore, sabab nuzûl, reason for revelation, is still active at a personal level although in its specific case to the Prophet was over. What I mean by this is that the Qurãn is an interactive sacred book. The Qurãn opens itself to the person according to the need, time, place and context of the person. Therefore, it is not a classical book written in the past and its teachings are over and not valid today. Oppositely, depending on the need, the Qurãn can mean different to a person living in the West, versus in the East. The Qurãn can mean different to a woman than a man. The Qurãn can mean to a person if the person knows how to approach to it with genuine need and with the intention of benefitting from it. Even, this happened during the time of the sahabahs. For example, when the Prophet passed away everyone was at shock. Until Abu Bakr ra came and read the verse of the Qurãn regarding the mortality of the Prophet Muhammad 🕮 as well. At that time, Omar ra mentioned a famous statement of his: "When I heard this verse from Abu Bakr as if it was revealed at that time and I did not know about it, but I knew that verse before (3)." This is an example of personal sabab nuzûl depending on the need, time, context and place.

The Qurãn emphasizes according to scholars (1) especially four themes:

1. Tawhid: The correct and true belief, knowledge and practice to establish a relationship with Allah 🕮 Who is One and Unique.
2. Nubuwwah: The correct and true knowledge and practice about the role and purpose of the messengers and the prophets sent by Allah 🕮.
3. Hashir: The correct and true knowledge and practice about the resurrection, afterlife and accountability after death.
4. Adalah and Ibadah: The correct and true knowledge and practice about justice, ethics, morality and worship.

1

Sûrah Fātiha

بِسْمِ اللهِ الرَّحْمَنِ الرَّحِيمِ {الفاتحة/1}

الْحَمْدُ لِلّهِ رَبِّ الْعَالَمِينَ {الفاتحة/2} الرَّحْمنِ الرَّحِيمِ {الفاتحة/3} مَلِكِ يَوْمِ الدِّينِ {الفاتحة/4} إِيَّاكَ نَعْبُدُ وإِيَّاكَ نَسْتَعِينُ {الفاتحة/5} اهدِنَا الصِّرَاطَ المُسْتَقِيمَ {الفاتحة/6} صِرَاطَ الَّذِينَ أَنْعَمتَ عَلَيهِمْ غَيرِ المَغضُوبِ عَلَيهِمْ وَلاَ الضَّالِّينَ {الفاتحة/7}[6]

In our western understanding of writing a book or an article entails writing an introduction or an abstract. This Sûrah brings all the concepts that would be detailed in the entire Qurān later: mainly the specific four themes mentioned above as tawhid, nubuwwah, hashir, adalah and ibadah. In this perspective, this Sûrah has in it all the embedded means with inclusivity and generalizability with implanted dense meanings. One can call this in classical sciences of tafāsir, the style of baraat istidlal, introducing a topic that would be explained in detail later. As one can see this style at its utmost level in this Sûrah, this style is constantly carried in the Qurān in different chapters as well.

The chapter of opening, Sûrah Fātiha is critical. It is similar to a master key that can be used for anything to open any doors. Therefore, it is the most read chapter in the practice, repeated constantly with the engagements of its meanings and with the engagements of its use as a prayer.

Below is a quote for the commentary of this Sûrah as:

The name of this chapter is called the Opening. This is the first chapter of the Qurān, short in length but dense in meaning according to the scholars. Therefore, this chapter is critical in practice. It is repeated every day in the prayers. Some of the scholars think that this short chapter has the essential meaning of the Qurān. In of the narrations, there was a person who was sick

---

6. [1:1] With the name of Allah, the All-Merciful, the Very-Merciful. [1:2] Praise belongs to Allah, the Lord of all the worlds. [1:3] The All-Merciful, the Very Merciful. [1:4] The Master of the Day of Requital. [1:5] You alone do we worship, and from You alone do we seek help. [1:6] Take us on the straight path. [1:7] The path of those on whom You have bestowed Your Grace, not of those who have incurred Your wrath, nor of those who have gone astray.

during the time of early followers. A friend of the Prophet read
these seven lines chapter to the sick and blew on his body and the
person was cured. The incident was reported to the Prophet. The
Prophet smiled and said "the chapter of Opening is a cure." [Some
of the scholars explain that God is teaching us how to pray to God
in this short chapter as well. The first four lines explain who God is.
Second two lines explain the person's mental and spiritual position
in prayer. Last four lines are the prayer itself. In other words, in
the first lines, God explains the Divine Self. In the second part, the
person places his or her position in the relationship with God, and
then finally, the person asks from God about one's most important
needs in a very condensed form in everyday life (6) (7).

[1]

Before the first phrase of بِسْمِ اللهِ الرَّحْمَنِ الرَّحِيمِ[7], the word قل addressing the
Prophet is hidden. The word قل in the entire Qurān is one of the proofs
of the prophethood of Rasulullah ﷺ. In other words, Allah ﷻ is ordering
the Prophet to share the revelation with the word قل which can translate
as "say" or "inform." Because if the Prophet was not a messenger than
he would not have the responsibility of messengership. The Qurān, as
the true revelation, Allah ﷻ is instructing Rasulullah ﷺ in the Qurān
with the word قل. The phrase الرَّحْمَن[8] denotes structure and justice and
the phrase الرَّحِيم denotes accountability after death and the existence of
afterlife.

Lafzu Mubarak, الله, Allah, includes all the names and attributes
of Allah ﷻ. Ar-Rahmān and Ar-Rahīm can signify how Allah ﷻ
immediately introduces the Divine Self to us with love, mercy and
caring.

According to some scholars, الله, Allah, is named as Lafzu Jalal. There
are different names of Allah ﷻ that some scholars would like to list under
two main Attributes of Allah ﷻ.

One is Al-Jalal. This Name of Allah ﷻ necessitates structure, order,
meaning, justice, accountability, awe and majesty. The other is Al-Jamal.
This Name of Allah ﷻ includes love, caring, beauty, reward, forbearing
and mercy. In this perspective, the scholars give further examples.

---

7. In the name of Allah, The Most Compassionate, The Most Merciful.
8. The Most Compassionate.

One of the proofs of the akhirah is الرَّحْمنِ الرَّحِيمِ[9]. Because, if there is a ni'mah, a bounty from Allah ﷻ it really becomes a bounty and pleasure if the person knows and understands that he or she will have this infinitely. In other words, reasoning and thinking death without afterlife makes all the bounties poison because they are going to end. If the person knows it is just a sample given in this world but given eternally and infinitely later in the afterlife, then it becomes a real bounty. Therefore, the names of Ar-Rahmān and Ar-Rahìm is Loving, Caring, Merciful and the Most Merciful. They imply the eternal afterlife to transform the poison of death into real bounty, nimah from Allah ﷻ, الله اعلم[10].

[2]

الْحَمْدُ لِلَّهِ رَبِّ الْعَالَمِينَ [11] {الفاتحة/2}

The expression الْحَمْدُ لِلَّه[12] has ل,Laam for specificity of Hamd, the real appreciation, gratitude, and thanking only but only for Allah ﷻ.

In this perspective, the word رَبِّ[13] can signify that as the person seeks guidance from Allah then Allah ﷻ gives guidance as the Rabb, the one who gives tarbiya, nourishment, hidāyah and guidance. Everything in the universe is under guidance, system and order with the word Rabb as mentioned Rabbul Alamin. The only exception to this is humans and jinns who have free choice with their kasb. But as soon as they show signs of inclination, intention and struggle towards guidance which we can call it acquirement or kasb as a technical word, then Allah ﷻ guides them as the Rabb as mentioned with Rabbul Alamin.

One should remember that Allah ﷻ creates everything and Allah ﷻ is the Real Cause. Humans and Jinns are given free will and free choice. They are not under force or compulsion to make a decision. Due to their kasb, acquirement, inclination and struggle of their usage of free will and free choice, Allah ﷻ creates the action what they want. One should remember Allah ﷻ mentions that the Divine Mercy, Caring and Fadl is

---

9. The Most Compassionate, The Most Merciful.
10. Allah knows best.
11. All praise is due to Allah, Lord of both worlds.
12. All praise is due to Allah.
13. Lord.

more beyond than the Divine Justice and Accountability as mentioned in below in the phrase [14] كَتَبَ عَلَى نَفْسِهِ الرَّحْمَةَ:

قُل لِّمَن مَّا فِي السَّمَاوَاتِ وَالأَرْضِ قُل لِلَّهِ كَتَبَ عَلَى نَفْسِهِ الرَّحْمَةَ لَيَجْمَعَنَّكُمْ إِلَى يَوْمِ الْقِيَامَةِ لاَ رَيْبَ فِيهِ الَّذِينَ خَسِرُواْ أَنفُسَهُمْ فَهُمْ لاَ يُؤْمِنُونَ} [15] {الأنعام/12

وَإِذَا جَاءكَ الَّذِينَ يُؤْمِنُونَ بِآيَاتِنَا فَقُلْ سَلاَمٌ عَلَيْكُمْ كَتَبَ رَبُّكُمْ عَلَى نَفْسِهِ الرَّحْمَةَ أَنَّهُ مَن عَمِلَ مِنكُمْ سُوءًا بِجَهَالَةٍ ثُمَّ تَابَ مِن بَعْدِهِ وَأَصْلَحَ فَأَنَّهُ غَفُورٌ رَّحِيمٌ} [16] {الأنعام/54

Therefore, a lot of times a person may be asking constantly an evil outcome with his or her free will and free choice but Allah ﷻ can be delaying the outcome of what the person is asking due to the Infinite Divine Mercy and Fadl. If it is the justice the person immediately should face the constant insistence of one on evil renderings. It is interesting to note that both verses about Allah ﷻ's Mercy and Fadl both mentioned in the Sûrah An'am which is the chapter of Bounties. In other words, Allah ﷻ's treating the creation with utmost Mercy and Fadl is another bounty from Allah ﷻ. If Allah ﷻ treated creation with what they deserved they would be doomed to punishment and severe deserved recompense. This bounty itself necessitates Hamd, appreciation and recognition by the creation, humans.

Allah ﷻ takes care of all the systems and structures perfectly. So, in this perspective, there is nothing to be worried about, the earth and all the systems in the universe such as humans keeping the galaxies in order and structure. Everything is under guidance, system and order with perfect structure as mentioned in the expression of Rabbul Alamin. Allah ﷻ takes care of them as the Rabbul Alamin. The approach of grandfather of the Prophet ﷺ towards destruction of Kabah by Abraha can be an example of this as well.

---

14. Who has willed upon Himself the law of grace and mercy
15. 6:12 Say: "Unto whom belongs all that is in the heavens and on earth?" Say: "Unto God, who has willed upon Himself the law of grace and mercy." He will assuredly gather you all together on the Day of Resurrection, [the coming of] which is beyond all doubt: yet those who have squandered their own selves—it is they who refuse to believe [in Him],
16. (6:54) And when those who believe in Our messages come unto thee, say: "Peace be upon you. Your Sustainer has willed upon Himself the law of grace and mercy—so that if any of you does a bad deed out of ignorance, and thereafter repents and lives righteously, He shall be [found] much-forgiving, a dispenser of grace."

So, these ungrounded fears about external affairs can defocus the person about his or her purpose and goal in one's life. The person in this perspective should really worry about the imān, belief and practice of oneself first. Because the person has the free choice to appreciate or not, to believe or not, or to do good or evil. As one establishes this, then one can go beyond oneself as the role models and prophets did such as Ibrahim as or al-Mustafa ﷺ did. Then, one can start informing about this appreciation of Allah ﷻ from the immediate relatives, and other people.

The ethics, justice and morality should follow the imān, belief. We are born in a structure, order, and perfect nature. These have their intrinsic qualities of ethics, justice and morality. We are not responsible of the order of the stars, galaxies, and planets. Allah ﷻ takes care of them as the Rabbul Alamin. We are not responsible of the system of sun's orbit or moon's rotation. We find them in a perfect order and structure. Allah ﷻ takes care of them as the Rabbul Alamin. We observe them and get meaning from them. We are not responsible of the systems and structure of the ants, birds, cells in our bodies, bacteria or viruses. Allah ﷻ takes care of them as the Rabbul Alamin. We find the perfect structure and order in them. We observe them and get meaning from them. When we are born our first and primary responsibility is to recognize this perfectness, system, structure and order and recognize Allah ﷻ who takes care of them as the Rabbul Alamin. In this perspective, the phrase, له الملك و له الحمد[17] can signify that Allah ﷻ owns and takes care of everything but everything as the Rabbul Alamin. This phrase is constantly chanted as a form of dhikr in a Muslim's life to remind this reality.

In this perspective, the structure, order and the perfect system in nature that we find ourselves are given, and are in the most just, ethical and moral dispositions. Our position as humans is not to break this system as mentioned fasadull ardu bi ma kasabat aydi nass in Sûrah Rum. Our position is to recognize, and appreciate all this perfectness given to us by Rabbul Alamin. This is the imān, belief through observation, mind and reason. This imān is solidified and triangulated with the Qurān and other divine scriptures. This imān is solidified and triangulated with the messengers, prophets and saints of God. This imān is solidified and triangulated with internal and external experiences in life. This imān is

---

17. To Him is the kingdom, and to Him is all praise.

solidified and triangulated with practice, prayer and worship. So, one can see that imān and belief is not stagnant but it has a lot of avenues to grasp onto it. After all these avenues, if a person is still heedless to all these signs then the kufr becomes the biggest crime, and the most unethical, unjust and immoral oppression. Therefore, kufr is the biggest unjust crime and disposition in Islam. The definition of kufr is not truly recognizing all these avenues and not recognizing and appreciating the Creator. Then, other types of injustice, immoral and unethical behavior follows in which all are introduced by humans either in their relation with other humans or in their relation with other beings and nature to break the given system by Allah ﷻ.

In this perspective, one can visit the role of humans on earth as mentioned with khalìfah in the Qurãn:

ثُمَّ جَعَلْنَاكُمْ خَلَائِفَ فِي الْأَرْضِ مِن بَعْدِهِم لِنَنظُرَ كَيْفَ تَعْمَلُونَ {يونس/14}[18]

فَكَذَّبُوهُ فَنَجَّيْنَاهُ وَمَن مَّعَهُ فِي الْفُلْكِ وَجَعَلْنَاهُمْ خَلَائِفَ وَأَغْرَقْنَا الَّذِينَ كَذَّبُواْ بِآيَاتِنَا فَانظُرْ كَيْفَ كَانَ عَاقِبَةُ الْمُنذَرِينَ {يونس/73}[19]

وَهُوَ الَّذِي جَعَلَكُمْ خَلَائِفَ الْأَرْضِ وَرَفَعَ بَعْضَكُمْ فَوْقَ بَعْضٍ دَرَجَاتٍ لِّيَبْلُوَكُمْ فِي مَا آتَاكُمْ إِنَّ رَبَّكَ سَرِيعُ الْعِقَابِ وَإِنَّهُ لَغَفُورٌ رَّحِيمٌ {الأنعام/165}[20]

هُوَ الَّذِي جَعَلَكُمْ خَلَائِفَ فِي الْأَرْضِ فَمَن كَفَرَ فَعَلَيْهِ كُفْرُهُ وَلَا يَزِيدُ الْكَافِرِينَ كُفْرُهُمْ عِندَ رَبِّهِمْ إِلَّا مَقْتًا وَلَا يَزِيدُ الْكَافِرِينَ كُفْرُهُمْ إِلَّا خَسَارًا {فاطر/39}[21]

As mentioned in the above ayahs, the responsibility of khalìfah is mentioned with the word جَعَلَ[22]. In other words, this is a given attribute by Allah ﷻ besides the creation of humans. Khalìfah is an external and

---

18. (10:14) And thereupon We made you their successors on earth, so that We might behold how you act.
19. And yet they gave him the lie! And so We saved him and all who stood by him, in the ark, and made them inherit [the earth],94 the while We caused those who gave the lie to Our messages to drown: 95 behold, then, what happened in the end to those people who had been warned [in vain]!
20. 6:165 For, He it is who has made you inherit the earth, and has raised some of you by degrees above others, so that He might try you by means of what He has bestowed upon you.
21. (35:39) He it is who has made you inherit the earth. Hence, he who is bent on denying the truth [of God's oneness and uniqueness ought to know that] this denial of his will fall back upon him: for their [persistent] denial of this truth does but add to the deniers' loathsomeness in their Sustainer's sight and, thus, their denial of this truth does but add to the deniers' loss.
22. Made.

expected attribute of a human as a responsibility. With the free choice of humans, some can fulfill this responsibility and some may not. The discussions about the word جَعَلَ comes later in this book that how it is used in the Qurãn to signify the attribute of responsibility. Allah ﷻ created humans and gave the responsibility of khalīfah as an attribute to humans as the word جَعَلَ implies.

One can also review the Qurãn with the perspective of the word الْحَقَّ which can imply structure and order in all creation, universe and expected attitude of justice, structure and order as the responsible, khalīfah, from a person in worldly dealings. For example,

وَهُوَ الَّذِي خَلَقَ السَّمَاوَاتِ وَالأَرْضَ بِالْحَقِّ وَيَوْمَ يَقُولُ كُن فَيَكُونُ قَوْلُهُ الْحَقُّ وَلَهُ الْمُلْكُ يَوْمَ يُنفَخُ فِي الصُّوَرِ عَالِمُ الْغَيْبِ وَالشَّهَادَةِ وَهُوَ الْحَكِيمُ الْخَبِيرُ {الأنعام/73}[23]

In the above expression, Allah ﷻ created everything bil haqq. In the broder context, this word can mean also the structure, order, and the truth how Allah ﷻ defines and describes. For example,

كَمَا أَخْرَجَكَ رَبُّكَ مِن بَيْتِكَ بِالْحَقِّ وَإِنَّ فَرِيقاً مِّنَ الْمُؤْمِنِينَ لَكَارِهُونَ {الأنفال/5} يُجَادِلُونَكَ فِي الْحَقِّ بَعْدَمَا تَبَيَّنَ كَأَنَّمَا يُسَاقُونَ إِلَى الْمَوْتِ وَهُم يَنظُرُونَ {الأنفال/6} وَإِذْ يَعِدُكُمُ اللّهُ إِحْدَى الطَّائِفَتِيْنِ أَنَّهَا لَكُمْ وَتَوَدُّونَ أَنَّ غَيْرَ ذَاتِ الشَّوْكَةِ تَكُونُ لَكُمْ وَيُرِيدُ اللّهُ أَن يُحِقَّ الْحَقَّ بِكَلِمَاتِهِ وَيَقْطَعَ دَابِرَ الْكَافِرِينَ {الأنفال/7} لِيُحِقَّ الْحَقَّ وَيُبْطِلَ الْبَاطِلَ وَلَوْ كَرِهَ الْمُجْرِمُونَ {الأنفال/8}[24]

In the above case, Allah ﷻ defines what al-haqq is. Sometimes, it may not be what we want or see as al haqq. But one can see the creation, the universe, already has its structure and order. In the limited responsibility

---

23. 6:73 And He it is who has created the heavens and the earth in accordance with [an inner] truth"—and whenever He says, "Be," His word comes true; and His will be the dominion on the Day when the trumpet [of resurrection] is blown. He knows all that is beyond the reach of a created being's perception, as well as all that can be witnessed by a creature's senses or mind: for He alone is truly wise, all-aware.

24. 8:5 EVEN AS thy Sustainer brought thee forth from thy home [to fight] in the cause of the truth, although some of the believers were averse to it, (8:6) [so, too,] they would argue with thee about the truth [itself] after it had become manifest—just as if they were being driven towards death and beheld it with their very eyes. 8:7 And, lo, God gave you the promise that one of the two [enemy] hosts would fall to you: and you would have liked to seize the less powerful one, whereas it was God's will to prove the truth to be true in accordance with His words, and to wipe out the last remnant of those who denied the truth—(8:8) so that He might prove the truth to be true and the false to be false, however hateful this might be to those who were lost in sin.

of khalîfah, humans are expected to assure this structure, and order how Allah ﷺ describes, [25]اعلم الله. Therefore, Allah ﷺ takes care of them as the Rabbul A'lamin.

The expression الْعَالَمِينَ[26] can signify galaxies, universes, stars, world, skies, other dimensions as well as other systems unknown to humans. According to some scholars, there are eighteen thousand different systems, universes or dimensions (1). The word الْعَالَمِينَ is conjugated in the language in its plural form similar to the beings who have mind, uqala, like humans, for example:

إِذْ قَالَ يُوسُفُ لِأَبِيهِ يَا أَبَتِ إِنِّي رَأَيْتُ أَحَدَ عَشَرَ كَوْكَبًا وَالشَّمْسَ وَالْقَمَرَ رَأَيْتُهُمْ لِي سَاجِدِينَ {يوسف/4}[27]

As mentioned in the Qurãn that the skies, stars and other beings make tasbih, glorification of Allah ﷺ and take different positions for the sins, evil and oppression of humans especially when they don't recognize and appreciate Rabbul Alamin, for example:

تَكَادُ السَّمَاوَاتُ يَتَفَطَّرْنَ مِن فَوْقِهِنَّ وَالْمَلَائِكَةُ يُسَبِّحُونَ بِحَمْدِ رَبِّهِمْ وَيَسْتَغْفِرُونَ لِمَن فِي الْأَرْضِ أَلَا إِنَّ اللَّهَ هُوَ الْغَفُورُ الرَّحِيمُ {الشورى/5} وَالَّذِينَ اتَّخَذُوا مِن دُونِهِ أَوْلِيَاءَ اللَّهُ حَفِيظٌ عَلَيْهِمْ وَمَا أَنتَ عَلَيْهِم بِوَكِيلٍ {الشورى/6}

The skies are almost going to explode with the signs of thunder due to humans disrespectful and unappreciative behavior, words, and attitudes in their relationship with Rabbul Alamin. The disrespectful and unappreciative words that they say when they talk about their Creator. All the beings and creation witness about this and take positions. In that regards, the angels make dua to Allah ﷺ for the ignorance of humans for their words and attitudes. However, Allah ﷺ is aware and constantly watching them in their evil affairs, giving them the chance, time and respite over and over. Therefore, the plural form is similar to this uqala with mind to these beings such as skies, [28]اعلم الله.

---

25. Allah knows best.
26. Both worlds.
27. 12:4 LO! Thus spoke Joseph unto his father: "O my father! Behold, I saw [in a dream] eleven stars, as well as the sun and the moon: I saw them prostrate themselves before me!"
28. Allah knows best.

[3]

الرَّحْمنِ الرَّحِيمِ [29] {الفاتحة/3}

As the Sûrah starts with this expression, the same expression comes again immediately to emphasize the Kind, Caring, Loving treatment of Allah ﷻ which is the Divine Infinite Mercy, Rahmah.

[4]

مَلِكِ يَوْمِ الدِّينِ [30] {الفاتحة/4}

In the above verse, the word يَوْم can signify the cycles of time: second, minute, hour, day, year and periods. After the period cycles of lifespan of the humans and the life span of earth and universe, there is the span of meeting Day or Period with Allah ﷻ in Hashir, in the Day of Judgment. One of the meanings of this verse allude to the Owner of the Day of Religion. In this perspective, from the creation of humans till the end of days, humans are in the struggle, choice and pursue of religions. Allah ﷻ is now telling, exposing and revealing the people's pursuits and choices as the Owner of the Day of Religion. Allah ﷻ ends all the arguments about the religion and reveals all the discourses of humans in their lifespan. In another perspective, there are many names of the Day of Accountability. As Sûrah Fātiha is a similar to the introduction the Qurān, the general and short style with inclusivity is preferred in an abstract. Similarly, the choice of "the Day of Religion" can give inclusivity and generalizability to other names about this Day mentioned in the Qurān. Each of the specific names can allude different perspectives that would occur that Day, [31] الله اعلم.

Lastly, the day is not a human understanding one day but so and so long as the tafasirs interpret (8).[32] اللهم اهدنا الصراط المستقيم امين

[5]

إِيَّاكَ نَعْبُدُ وإِيَّاكَ نَسْتَعِينُ [33] {الفاتحة/5}

---

29. The Entirely Merciful, the Especially Merciful.
30. Sovereign of the Day of Recompense.
31. Allah knows best.
32. Guide us to the straight path.
33. It is You we worship and You we ask for help.

The word إِيَّاكَ[34] is a very personal pronoun in the above verse that can signify the importance of understanding the meanings when one is reciting the Qurãn, especially, in the sciences of balagah. This may mean that "Oh Allah, I am worshipping to You as if I see You" especially with the repetition of the pronouns كَ, You.

إِيَّاكَ نَعْبُدُ وإِيَّاكَ نَسْتَعِينُ [35]{الفاتحة/5}

The plural pronoun in نَعْبُدُ[36] can signify different parts of the human body. The classical interpretation is that, jamaah, congregations of all believers and creation are asking and praying to Allah together. Also, when the person is praying, doing ibadah to Allah, this is not possible unless there is the tawfik and iane, the activation of the help of Allah, therefore it is إِيَّاكَ نَعْبُدُ وإِيَّاكَ نَسْتَعِينُ. In other words, the person can be praying, إِيَّاكَ نَعْبُدُ[37], to achieve the help, iane and tawfik of Allah by وإِيَّاكَ نَسْتَعِينُ[38]. Therefore, in of the hadith (9) Rasulullah mentions that the person prays, the fard and the nawafil and Allah becomes this person's hand and feet figuratively as if Allah is helping this person, with iane and tawfik due to this person's closeness to Allah with the ibadah, worship. As a result, this is given to this person by Allah.

The phrase وإِيَّاكَ نَسْتَعِينُ in إِيَّاكَ can signify removing all the humiliating perspectives of sabab which are reasons and means and then, directly asking from Allah about one's needs. The person does not consider any means or causes but believes and knows that Allah can do anything beyond the natural laws.

The word نَعْبُدُ is in present and future tense to signify the continuity of the worship. If it was expressed in the past tense and then, asking iane, help from Allah, can imply some arrogance which can mean that "I did my worship and I am asking now."

The full expression of إِيَّاكَ نَعْبُدُ وإِيَّاكَ نَسْتَعِينُ[39] can also signify the intention of the person. Although the person cannot fully achieve what he or she intends, Allah can reward the person according to one's intention. Because it is in future and present tense not in the past.

---

34. It is you.
35. It is You we worship and You we ask for help.
36. We worship.
37. It is you we worship.
38. And You we ask for help.
39. It is You we worship and You we ask for help.

[6]

اهدِنَا الصِّرَاطَ المُستَقِيمَ ⁴⁰ {الفاتحة/6}

The word الصِّرَاطَ[41] is used instead of other words such as at-tariq or as-sabil. This word can imply a path of a highway that once the person enters it then, it is very difficult to leave. Also, here, the question of what is the truth and falsehood is present. Therefore, the Prophet ﷺ used to make dua to Allah ﷻ for Allah ﷻ to show the truth (al-haqq) and the batil, the falsehood to the person (10) (11). In this perspective, the middle way, sirat al mustaqim, instead of one extreme or another extreme such as Ifrād or tafrìd but the wasat or middle way is preferred. The person is asking and praying to Allah ﷻ constantly to be guided to the middle way, as-sirat al Mustaqim. The below chart can explain this concept:

Ability	Extreme 1 (Ifrād)	Extreme 2 (Tafrìd)	Middle Way (Wasad)
Desires	Having no desire for anything	Having extreme desire, going over limits	Balance: Knowing the limits of permissible and impermissible for good, and ethical (Ex: Halal & Haram)
Anger	No Anger	Extreme anger leading to oppression	Courage: Anger for Justice and for ethical
Mind	Using no logic	Using logic to mix the truth and falsehood such as demagogy or some political discourses	Wisdom: Using logic with wisdom for good and ethical action
Belief	No Belief: Not recognizing the self as a created being and not recognizing and appreciating the Creator	Mixing the Creator and created. For example: figurative language in scriptures	Unity, Oneness, Uniqueness of the Creator from the created.

Figure 1   Middle Way, Examples of Sirat al Mustaqim

---

40. Guide us to the straight path.
41. Path.

[7]

صِرَاطَ الَّذِينَ أَنعَمتَ عَلَيهِم غَيرِ المَغضُوبِ عَلَيهِم وَلاَ الضَّالِّينَ {الفاتحة/7[42]}

The expression صِرَاطَ الَّذِينَ أَنعَمتَ عَلَيهِم[43], the ones who Allah ﷻ gave blessings, is explained in another verse of the Qurān as the prophets and messengers of Allah ﷻ, awliya, friends, of Allah ﷻ, and other people of salihin on the path. In this regards, the word عَلَيهِم[44] can signify the difficulties and hardships on the shoulders of these role models: prophets, the friends of Allah ﷻ, and the people who are with ethics, justice, fairness and appreciation. These people are on the correct and true path but it has its own difficulties, challenges and trials as mentioned with the word عَلَيهِم, الله اعلم. All the prophets of Allah ﷻ have the same belief about Allah ﷻ, tawhid, about the essence of the divine rules and about the essence of worship to Allah ﷻ. The divine rules or laws have the essence of bringing justice, ethics and removing oppression. The essence of worship has the essence of remembering Allah ﷻ regularly with humbleness and appreciation. If one asks why all the scriptures or divine books are not exactly the same but their essence are the same? The answer would be that in different seasons a person may wear different clothing, a thick cloth to be protected from the harsh cold of the winter and a thin cloth to cover oneself and sometimes protect oneself from the deadly sun light in a desert. Although they may have detail differences but if one switches the clothing type wearing a thin cloth in the cold winter and a thick cloth in a very hot day, then it can possibly be deadly. Similarly, some of the teachings of some scriptures such as the Tawrah can be valid at a certain time and with specific group of people. In this regard, the Qurān has the position of contemporizing these Divine teachings.

The expression غَيرِ المَغضُوبِ عَلَيهِم وَلَا الضَّالِّينَ[45] has the state, maqam, of firar to Allah ﷻ. The person does not have a guarantee from the above cases being al magdub or ad-dalin. Therefore, the person should have always this intrinsic fear for these possibilities in one's relation with Allah. Therefore, the person should constantly ask istia'na, tawfik, help from Allah ﷻ as mentioned in the earlier parts of this Sûrah.

---

42. The path of those upon whom You have bestowed favor, not of those who have evoked [Your] anger or of those who are astray.
43. The path of those upon whom You have bestowed favor.
44. Upon them.
45. Not of those who have evoked [Your] anger or of those who are astray.

The notion of firar, escaping to Allah ﷻ mentioned in different parts of the Qurān, such as [51:50]. A person can make a firar with the expression of غَيْرِ الْمَغْضُوبِ عَلَيْهِمْ وَلَا الضَّالِّينَ from all the fears and overwhelming anxieties to Allah ﷻ. If this is achieved and then it is the state of tawakkul. If the person makes tawakkul as a permanent trait of oneself, then it becomes as the station of tawakkul.

The expression of غَيْرِ الْمَغْضُوبِ عَلَيْهِمْ وَلَا الضَّالِّينَ was classically identified in tafsir as Jews and Christians. I think it is important to look at the qualities rather than the groups. Because, the purpose of the Qurān is not to alienate people from the Divine Message but rather reviewing the qualities of people for personal relevance. In other words, there is no group mentioned in the verse but the quality. In this perspective, when religion is used as a divisive tool at our times of mixed global multicultural and multi-religious engagements, this type of interpretations should be strictly avoided. On the other hand, the quality of الْمَغْضُوبِ عَلَيْهِمْ[46] can refer the notions in the Qurān for a person who knows but does not have a good and positive attitude. Alternatively, الضَّالِّينَ[47] can be a person who has a positive attitude with no or wrong knowledge. So, the table pictures this as:

Personal Approach	الْمَغْضُوبِ عَلَيْهِمْ	الضَّالِّينَ
Attitude	Negative	Positive
Knowledge	Positive	Negative

Table 2   The effect of attitude and knowledge in guidance

In this perspective, negative attitude can entail arrogance, jealousy, rejection, narrow mindedness, opposing to change and etc. Positive attitudes can entail humbleness, humility, caring, acceptance, open mindedness, willing to change and etc. Positive knowledge can entail the correct, genuine, logical and authentic knowledge about Allah ﷻ and practice. Negative knowledge can entail the incorrect, untrue, irrational, inauthentic, and fictitious knowledge about Allah ﷻ and practice. Table 2 shows the effect of attitude and knowledge in guidance in this perspective. This can be in any individual or a group.

---

46. Those who have evoked [Your] anger.
47. Who are astray.

In the expression غَيرِ المَغضُوبِ عَلَيهِمْ وَلَا الضَّالِّينَ [48], the word المَغضُوب is isim-maful which may imply continuity. Therefore, if a person changes one attitude of arrogance then there is the door of forgiveness being open for the person. Alternatively, as in this case if the quality does not change with continuity with المَغضُوب, isim maful then, the gadab of Allah ﷻ is on this person or people. Oppositely, the people of الضَّالِّينَ is presented with ism-fail, which may not be as continuous as ismi maful. In other ways, if one finds the correct true knowledge of Allah ﷻ and changes her or himself, then الضَّالِّينَ as ismi-fail can imply a temporary state compared to ismi maful state which is a continuous state.

2

Sûrah Baqarah

Rasulullah ﷺ mentioned everything has its peak, the peak of the Qurãn is Sûrah Baqarah, sinamul Qurãn (9) (252). This Sûrah in detail explains what is meant in the introductory and opening Sûrah of Fãtiha. As the introduction and abstract is very brief as in in the case of Sûrah Fãtiha, the following chapter, Sûrah Baqarah, is expected to be longer and explains in detail the introduction and the abstract. This is the longest chapter, the Sûrah in the entire Qurãn.

[1]

الم

Huruf-muqatta is really interesting, novel and ground-breaking as one considers the styles of the literature in that society and today. There are one to few letters of Arabic in the beginning of some chapters of the Qurãn generally referred as huruf-muqatta. No one knows their true meanings except Allah ﷻ. Therefore, all are possible meanings about these letters and all are interpretations that there are no literal meanings. In the Quranic exegesis, tafasir, there are literal, explicit meanings and figurative, implicit meanings. It is also interesting to note that the Arabic reading rules are not applied in the recitation of these letters. In other words, one reads the name of the letters instead of how these should

---

48. Not of those who have evoked [Your] anger or of those who are astray.

be pronounced according to the sounds from these letters in Arabic alphabet. For example, in the case of الم, one should normally read this as i'lm, or u'lm or other possible versions depending on harakas as an Arabic word. Rather, it is read with the name of the letters in Arabic alphabet as Alif, Laam, Meem, and there is some unknown elongation applied which is not in the name of the letters themselves. So, all these are ground-breaking and novel as a style and content. Therefore, some of the scholars are in the opinion that the Qurān has been challenging all the experts of the language, and literature with simple looking but complicated structures in order to show that this Scripture, the Qurān has a Divine Origin.

The wisdom of these letters are to remind the humans of their limitations in their knowledge according to some scholars. Abu Bakir ra mentions that Allah has some secrecies in each Divine scripture and huruf-muqatta are those ones in the Qurān (8).

On another perspective, Ahlu tasawwuf, the people of mystical sciences, Sufism, gave special meanings to these letters. They have even given meanings and interpretations to the portions and dots of these letters. Such as, the letter alif is interpreted to signify the name of Allah .

It is interesting to note that there are 29 letters in Arabic language. There are 29 surahs, chapters of the Qurān, which start with these codified secret letters, harf muqatta. If one counts hemze and alif as one letter, the number of total letters are 28, where there are 14 shamsi and 14 qamari letters. The total number of harf-muqatta in the Qurān is 14 as well. One can analyze further with the Arabic letter system of which one of these letters are strong, light and other types of letters in their relationship with numbers. There is some analysis about how many of these letters are strong, light and other types to further interpret some possible renderings.

Some of the scholars believe that this is another proof for the prophethood of the Messenger Muhammad and that the Qurān is from Allah . Because, the above type of arguments are only for the ones who are really expert in the languages and its styles. Considering the society and the Messenger, they were not intellectuals, and formally educated in the language which means the word ummi refers to the title of the Prophet. Ummi means who did not have any formal education.

It is known that when a person writes a text, he or she is affected by the previous texts. The style of hurufu muqatta was and is still unique and ground breaking and it can be another proof that the Qurãn did not use other styles and it has a Divine origin.

It is important to realize that people benefit from the Qurãn according to the need. In this perspective, sometimes a letter, a word, a verse as a sentence, and a few verses as a paragraph can suffice for the person in one's daily, hourly or even sometimes minutely intakes from the Qurãn. As the person is dynamically and non-stop thinking except maybe in sleeping, the encounters of feelings, sadness, joys, and sometimes heedless moments can be disturbed and balanced with these teachings. Therefore, the Qurãn itself instructs as in Sûrah Muzzamil,

إِنَّ رَبَّكَ يَعْلَمُ أَنَّكَ تَقُومُ أَدْنَى مِن ثُلُثَيِ اللَّيْلِ وَنِصْفَهُ وَثُلُثَهُ وَطَائِفَةٌ مِّنَ الَّذِينَ مَعَكَ وَاللَّهُ يُقَدِّرُ اللَّيْلَ وَالنَّهَارَ عَلِمَ أَن لَّن تُحْصُوهُ فَتَابَ عَلَيْكُمْ فَاقْرَؤُوا مَا تَيَسَّرَ مِنَ الْقُرْآنِ عَلِمَ أَن سَيَكُونُ مِنكُم مَّرْضَى وَآخَرُونَ يَضْرِبُونَ فِي الْأَرْضِ يَبْتَغُونَ مِن فَضْلِ اللَّهِ وَآخَرُونَ يُقَاتِلُونَ فِي سَبِيلِ اللَّهِ فَاقْرَؤُوا مَا تَيَسَّرَ مِنْهُ وَأَقِيمُوا الصَّلَاةَ وَآتُوا الزَّكَاةَ وَأَقْرِضُوا اللَّهَ قَرْضًا حَسَنًا وَمَا تُقَدِّمُوا لِأَنفُسِكُم مِّنْ خَيْرٍ تَجِدُوهُ عِندَ اللَّهِ هُوَ خَيْرًا وَأَعْظَمَ أَجْرًا وَاسْتَغْفِرُوا اللَّهَ إِنَّ اللَّهَ غَفُورٌ رَّحِيمٌ {المزمل/20}[49]

to read whatever you can. The expression فَاقْرَؤُوا مَا تَيَسَّرَ مِنَ الْقُرْآنِ[50] is repeated twice in this Sûrah, chapter, to instruct to hold the portion of the Qurãn in one's daily and constant encounters even it could be a page or a few lines. And, Allah mentions that everyone's schedule is different but the key is the struggle of reading every day and constantly even it may be small.

As humans are constituted from simple elements such as hydrogen or oxygen, languages are constituted from simple letters such as A or B or other letters of the alphabet. In this perspective, the Qurãn starts

---

49. 73:20 BEHOLD, [O Prophet,] thy Sustainer knows that thou keepest awake [in prayer] nearly two-thirds of the night, or one-half of it, or a third of it, together with some of those who follow thee. And God who determines the measure of night and day, is aware that you would never grudge it: and therefore He turns towards you in His grace. Recite, then, as much of the Qur'an as you may do with ease. He knows that in time there will be among you sick people, and others who will go about the land in search of God's bounty, and others who will fight in God's cause. Recite, then, [only] as much of it as you may do with ease, and be constant in prayer, and spend in charity, and [thus] lend unto God a goodly loan: for whatever good deed you may offer up in your own behalf, you shall truly find it with God—yea, better, and richer in reward. And [always] seek God's forgiveness: behold, God is much-forgiving, a dispenser of grace!
50. Recite, then, as much of the Qur'an as you may do with ease.

with simple letters such as alif, lām, and mīm, to challenge the humans to bring a similar Qurān if they did think that this Qurān is not original or the word of a human. Humans know the alphabet. They know the letters. In this perspective, the Qurān challenges the humans also to create a human like being similar to Allah ﷻ creates. Humans know the basic elements and all the periodic table but they still cannot create and give life.

[2]

الم [51] ذَلِكَ الْكِتَابُ لاَ رَيْبَ فِيهِ هُدًى لِّلْمُتَّقِينَ

When one reviews each word in the above verse and expression, each expression by itself and together supports the high status of the Qurān and that the Qurān is from Allah ﷻ. So, when one takes each word in the above expression, one can deduce the exalted status of the Qurān and the Qurān is from Allah ﷻ.

The word الْكِتَابُ[52] signifies specificity and the Qurān's high status. Compared to other books from Allah ﷻ, the Qurān can have the highest status due to its inclusivity. In other words, there is no rankings among the Kalam of Allah ﷻ and the Divine Books or Scriptures in their original form. But, due to the Qurān's inclusivity that the Qurān mentions and explains the other sacred books sent from Allah ﷻ as a final book and it has the compilation of the all other books in their essence. Therefore, some scholars can mention that Qurān has a higher status, الله اعلم. It is also due to the fact that the Qurān explains other books such as Torah and Bible and elevates their lost status among their followers. So, one can make the similitude of the Qurān of a father with its inclusivity of their children. The Qurān in that sense protects the Bible and Torah and asks their followers to give their due respect, الله اعلم. When one reviews the verses of the Qurān about Bible and Torah, one can easily and clearly see these perspectives of the Qurān for other sacred texts. In addition, the word الْكِتَابُ can imply that this book is sent through a prophet who is ummi, not a person of a book meaning that he ﷺ is not intellectual or

---

51. 2:1 Alif. Lam. Mim. 2:2 HIS DIVINE WRIT—let there be no doubt about it is [meant to be] a guidance for all the God-conscious
52. The book.

a writer, but is bringing a divine message from Allah ﷻ because writing books are generally associated with intellectuals.

Zalika, ذَلِكَ, in Arabic is composed of three letters, "za, lam, and kaf". The word "here" to indicate nearness for the letter "za"; noble indicating distance and highness for the letter "lam" and the letter "kaf" indicating "a personal book, for you" with the pronoun "ka." English translations use the word "that" to translate this word to imply respect for far distance which is in Arabic but English does not carry this meaning with the word "that" most of the time.

ذَلِكَ الْكِتَابُ لاَ رَيْبَ فِيهِ هُدًى لِّلْمُتَّقِينَ {البقرة/2} [53]

The expression لاَ رَيْبَ فِيهِ [54] alerts the reader not to view and approach to this Book, the Qurān as an ordinary book, an essay or story but with the focus of view and perspective that there is no rayb in it, there is no doubt in this book and the Qurān is from Allah ﷻ.

[3]

الَّذِينَ يُؤْمِنُونَ بِالْغَيْبِ وَيُقِيمُونَ الصَّلاةَ وَمِمَّا رَزَقْنَاهُمْ يُنفِقُونَ {البقرة/3} [55]

One can view the expression يُؤْمِنُونَ بِالْغَيْبِ [56] as the constant effort of increasing the imān, the belief through the effort of believing in al-gayb, the unseen. Instead of المومنين[57], the expression الَّذِينَ يُؤْمِنُونَ is used to signify the importance of renewing one's imān through amal, knowledge, and struggle. In that perspective, the gayb can become known from one's belief through knowledge and practice as a continuous struggle. In other words, the imān comes first with الَّذِينَ يُؤْمِنُونَ بِالْغَيْبِ. Then this imān, belief is solidified with amal with وَيُقِيمُونَ الصَّلاةَ وَمِمَّا رَزَقْنَاهُمْ يُنفِقُونَ[58].

---

53. 2:2 HIS DIVINE WRIT—let there be no doubt about it is [meant to be] a guidance for all the God—conscious
54. Let there be no doubt.
55. (2:3) who believe in [the existence of] that which is beyond the reach of human perception, and are constant in prayer, and spend on others out of what We provide for them as sustenance;
56. Who believe in [the existence of] that which is beyond the reach of human perception.
57. The believers.
58. And are constant in prayer, and spend on others out of what We provide for them as sustenance.

The yaqin or certainty of imān can increase. According to some scholars (S.Nu)[1], the word الْمُتَّقِينَ[59] in the previous ayah and this ayah are connected. Some scholars use two technical words takhliya, تخلي and the other one is tahliya تحلي. Takhliya, تخلي means to clean and the other one is tahliya, تحلي, to embellish and to fill. Takhliya is part of the imān to remove what is not. One can call this as tanzih. Also, to make the person abstain from the disliked, falsehood and prohibited. The other one, tahliya, تحلي, is to put what is and one can call this as the true imān. Also, this can mean to replace and embellish with the beautiful, the truth and liked by Allah ﷻ. In more detail, تخلي means leaving the disbelief (shirk), the sins, and everything except Allah ﷻ. After cleaning, the word تحلي can imply putting the belief (imān) as the act of heart, salah (five times prayer or namaz) as the act of body, and zakah (the required charity) as the act of wealth in this verse of the Qurān.

[4]

{ وَالَّذِينَ يُؤْمِنُونَ بِمَا أُنزِلَ إِلَيْكَ وَمَا أُنزِلَ مِن قَبْلِكَ وَبِالْآخِرَةِ هُمْ يُوقِنُونَ {4/البقرة} [60]

The first الَّذِينَ[61] in the third ayah can signify the believers, Muslims from kufr. The second الَّذِينَ in this ayah can signify the previous believers of ahlu kitāb to solidify, clarify, support, strengthen, increase and improve their existing belief. Therefore, if a person accepts and improves their belief from ahlu kitāb, then they can get double reward compared to the person who accepts Islam from other groups according to the hadith (9).

In another perspective, الَّذِينَ يُؤْمِنُونَ بِالْغَيْبِ[62] in the previous ayah is explained here as what is al-ghayb. Al-ghayb, unseen are the previous books that Allah ﷻ revealed that also there is an afterlife and accountability mentioned in the previous scriptures such as Bible and Torah. The expression بِمَا أُنزِلَ إِلَيْكَ[63] can include both the Qurān and hadith, matluw and gayri matluw.

---

59. For the believers.
60. (2:4) And who believe in that which has been bestowed from on high upon thee, [O Prophet,] as well as in that which was bestowed before thy time: for it is they who in their innermost are certain of the life to come!
61. The who.
62. Who believe in [the existence of] that which is beyond the reach of human perception.
63. And who believe in that which has been bestowed from on high upon thee, [O Prophet,].

Here in the expression الَّذِينَ يُؤْمِنُونَ بِالْغَيْبِ[64], imãn, believing in Allah ﷻ, can simply mean believing in the existence of Allah ﷻ. Believing in the Qurãn can mean about the belief that the Qurãn is sent by Allah ﷻ. Belief about afterlife can mean about the belief in the upcoming life after death. This all can include part of the al-ghayb. The Qurãn sets for a believer an attitude of submission and surrender about the unknowns, al-ghayb. Other al-ghayb can be angels, jinn and etc.

It is also very interesting to note that the Qurãn uses يُؤْمِنُون and أُنزِلَ[65] in present, future and past tenses with similar renderings as if signifying the One, Allah ﷻ is beyond time and limits. Both past and present tenses are used. For some other scholars, it can be also to wake up the reader with a very novel and nonstandard style.

Sometimes, the word إِلَيْكَ[66] or عَليكَ[67] is used. In this case of إِلَيْكَ, the taklif of prophethood is given to the Prophet and it is accepted by him with his juz ikhtiyar, choice and acceptance. The word عليك is used for the given responsibility without choice but with the Divine Will. The words إِلَيْكَ or عليك are repeated in the Qurãn with different contexts also to indicate that the responsibility of messengership was not the Prophet's choice but given by Allah ﷻ. The Prophet is a messenger delivering the message of Allah ﷻ to the people.

The expression وَمَا أُنزِلَ مِن قَبْلِكَ[68] can show the inclusivity of the Qurãn. In words, Islam can be imagined as a tree. This tree has roots and branches from the past. It has its fruits in the present and future. In other words, Islam or Muslim is not a technical identity term that just came with the Prophet Muhammad ﷺ. But in their original meaning as the true religion of Allah ﷻ. It has always existed and will exist. In this perspective, the Qurãn with this verse and others is not telling to Christians or Jews to leave their existing religions which were already accompanied with the scriptures such as Bible or Torah from God but it is suggesting and offering them to update their existing beliefs, practices and approaches. Therefore, for the true people of understanding of this message, it is very common to hear expressions or statements as "now, I

---

64. Who believe in [the existence of] that which is beyond the reach of human perception.
65. Bestowed.
66. Upon you.
67. On you.
68. As well as in that which was bestowed before thy time.

am a better and true Christian or Jew," when they view and understand the Quranic suggestions with new updates. In this perspective, some of the contemporary scholars give the example of updates similar to the phones or computer operating systems that the Qurãn comes with already existing message of the Bible and the Torah and updates by still holding and advocating their true value and respect that these scriptures were sent by God. Unfortunately, this perspective is much missing in the application of true dialogue between Muslims and others. Therefore, implicit and explicit identity engagements do not much serve the purpose of sharing, learning and benefitting from each other.

The expression مِن قَبْلِكَ[69] can signify the true prophethood of the Prophet Muhammad, that he is the conclusive and complementary Prophet, that he is the last Prophet, that his message is inclusive and universal and these teachings include the previous prophets and scriptures' teachings. A group or class of people with the same mission and purpose is referred with the expression مِن قَبْلِكَ. The pronoun كَ in this expression refers to the Prophet Muhammad. In this perspective, the expression مِن قَبْلِكَ necessitates the Prophet Muhammad to be from the same group or class of people of the Prophets and Messengers sent by God before. All the proofs that necessitates the messengership of the previous prophets such as Abraham, Moses and Jesus and the previous scriptures such as the Torah and Bible are also proofs for the messengership of the Prophet Muhammad and the Divine origin of the Qurãn.

Humans are advancing in civilization, social life and humanities. It is expected and normal that the last messenger would be all inclusive of these advancements in his traits and mission. As the contemporary life is becoming more and more globalized as a one single town or city, it can be normal and logical that one Prophet for all humanity would suffice compared to many prophets and messengers of previous times with little or no means of communication.

The word يُوقِنُونَ[70] is used for believing in the afterlife with certainty. Before starting the steps of the expected belief in afterlife with certainty, one should review the nature and all creation with a perspective. If one

---

69. Before thy time.
70. Who in their innermost are certain of the life to come!

looks at all universe, the world, day, night and all the excellent system that we are in that there is determined, set and running perfect order and structure. There is a purposeful wisdom in the creation. There is nothing in the universe that is useless, purposeless, and excess. Everything is in perfectness both in quantity and quality. All the scientific disciplines such as math, physics, chemistry, biology, engineering and all others in their expertise and scholarship are the witnesses of this perfection with their discoveries of this perfect order and structure in the universe.

After this brief recapping perspective, it is expected to believe in the afterlife with certainty without any doubt as mentioned in this verse. This can be due to a few reasons[1]:

- ► Due to the Names and Attributes of Allah ﷻ that necessitates this reality.
- ► Due to the system, structure and order in the universe that necessitates this reality.
- ► Due to the Mercy of Allah ﷻ that necessitates this reality.
- ► Due to the essence of the message of the messengers and the prophets that necessitates this reality.
- ► Due to the perfection in the essence of humans that necessitates this reality.
- ► Due to the necessity of human internal faculties being in need of afterlife that necessitates this reality.

If we look at the word يُوقِنُونَ linguistically, this word is in the form of mudari, which is both the present and future tense in English. This can mean that the person should be in constant struggle of reaching to the level of certainty about the afterlife and meeting with Allah ﷻ. In other words, the word, يُوقِنُونَ, can mean that the person struggles in one's life to have yaqin, certainty. There are two important points here. A person should have the desire and goal to reach this certainty about the akhirah, the afterlife. Another point is that the need for having certainty for afterlife cannot allow any type of doubt or skepticism.

It is interesting note that one of the missions of Shaytan is to give doubts about the akhirah in one's believe as stated in Sûrah Sabah, in the below:

وَلَقَدْ صَدَّقَ عَلَيْهِمْ إِبْلِيسُ ظَنَّهُ فَاتَّبَعُوهُ إِلَّا فَرِيقًا مِّنَ الْمُؤْمِنِينَ {سبأ/02}[71] وَمَا كَانَ لَهُ عَلَيْهِم مِّن سُلْطَانٍ إِلَّا لِنَعْلَمَ مَن يُؤْمِنُ بِالْآخِرَةِ مِمَّنْ هُوَ مِنْهَا فِي شَكٍّ وَرَبُّكَ عَلَى كُلِّ شَيْءٍ حَفِيظٌ {سبأ/12}

This can be also evidence that the belief for akhirah comes with yuqinun with certainty that it cannot tolerate any skepticism.

Also, the word شَكّ[72], shakk, in the Qurãn is used for the people when they challenged the prophethood of the prophets when they were sent to a certain group or town. In addition, the same word is used when the true position of Isa as is explained in the Qurãn by Allah ﷻ and mentioning to the reader that the person should not be in shakk, skepticism of humanness of Jesus. In other words, Allah ﷻ mentions in the Qurãn that Isa as is a human and not to be in doubt about it. In some other parts of the Qurãn, the word shakk is also mentioned for the people's perspectives for the books of Allah ﷻ, the shakk, skepticism to the message and invitation of the messengers. Below is an example from Sûrah Naml for the afterlife, akhirah again this attitude of shakk, skepticism:

{[73] بَلِ ادَّارَكَ عِلْمُهُمْ فِي الْآخِرَةِ بَلْ هُمْ فِي شَكٍّ مِّنْهَا بَلْ هُم مِّنْهَا عَمُونَ {النمل/66}

---

71. [34:20] And Iblees had already confirmed through them his assumption, so they followed him, except for a party of believers. [34:21] And he had over them no authority except [it was decreed] that We might make evident who believes in the Hereafter from who is thereof in doubt. And your Lord, over all things, is Guardian.
72. Doubt.
73. (27:66) Nay, their knowledge of the life to come stops short of the truth: nay, they are [often] in doubt as to its reality: nay, they are blind to it.

At the end of Sûrah Saba, there is the general approach of shakk, skepticism, that overviews this concept when the people speculate about the unknowns and unseen, al-gayb:

وَحِيلَ بَيْنَهُمْ وَبَيْنَ مَا يَشْتَهُونَ كَمَا فُعِلَ بِأَشْيَاعِهِم مِّن قَبْلُ إِنَّهُمْ كَانُوا فِي شَكٍّ مُرِيبٍ53
{سبأ/54}74

It is interesting to note that this word is used when Allah ﷻ sends at different times to different people the books, their approach was with this word شَكّ, skepticism. But the Qurãn suggests a treatment of this attitude as well with how and why the Qurãn follows a scientific and rational methodology to establish the authority of authentication.

Another interesting point is that as mentioned in Sûrah Dukhan "bal hum fi shakking yala'bun" shows the concept of ignoring, and trying to enjoy life although there is some type of shakk, skepticism, that is bothering the person from inside possibly from his or her conscience.

If one looks at the two words يُؤْمِنُونَ75 and يُوقِنُونَ, they have two different roots. A person can generally believe in akhirah, afterlife with يُؤْمِنُونَ but the expected goal should be يُوقِنُونَ, the certain belief. Also, it is interesting to note that there is a name of Allah ﷻ Al-Mum'in, the One who gives security. But, there is no name of Allah ﷻ as Al-Muki'in because the word يُوقِنُونَ, includes the possibility of shakk, skepticism, which cannot be used for Allah ﷻ.

Allah ﷻ explains us about the Divine Self. The Prophet explains about Allah ﷻ further and also puts limits on thinking about the Divine Self. For example, it is haram to think about the Essence of Allah ﷻ. This limitation is to tell the humans that realizing the limits is part of the knowledge. When a person is increasing their knowledge about Allah ﷻ, the approach should be certainty with caution of adab about knowing Allah ﷻ. The certainty about the afterlife is also critical in the application of the ethics of personal, family and social relationships. In other words, to implement justice in all personal, family and social

---

74. (34:53) Seeing that aforetime they had been bent on denying the truth, and had been wont to cast scorn, from far away, on something that was beyond the reach of human perception? 34:54 And so, a barrier will be set between them and all that they had [ever] desired, as will be done to such of their kind as lived before their time: for, behold, they [too were lost in doubt amounting to suspicion.
75. Doubt.

interactions, the more the afterlife is detailed in belief then the more certainty of afterlife belief will increase.

In the world, different sciences allude to different conservation laws such as the ones in physics or chemistry. Allah ﷻ created the laws of conservation. In this perspective, Allah ﷻ created everything in the best, the most optimized and efficient manner with conservation laws. This alludes to the fact that nothing is without purpose in the creation of Allah ﷻ. In this perspective, there is significance, substance and earnestness in all the creation of Allah ﷻ. One can review the Qurān with the keys words of باطلا and لعب as mentioned:

مَا خَلَقْتَ هَذَا بَاطِلاً سُبْحَانَكَ [76] in [3:191]. Even, thinking this concept is not right. It can be a sin because the expression سُبْحَانَكَ[77] comes immediately. With this, the conservation of the world with everything inside alludes to the existence of another realm, the afterlife.

One can also view the anatomy of a human, the number of bones and their functions, the number of different nerves and their functions, the number of systems constituting different organs, the number of cells constituting these organs, the units in each cell etc. If one thinks these systems in a human's physical body, how about the spiritual faculties? The soul, emotions, conscience…etc. Actually, this is more complicated. According to many scholars, the real purpose of a human is the discovery of this complicated spiritual faculties through the teachings of the Qurān, hadith, and practice. In this perspective, this adds the real value to the person. Will it be logical that a complicated system of physical and spiritual faculties is destroyed, exterminated and eliminated? No. Because, some of the names of Allah ﷻ such as the Most Merciful, Ar-Rahmān, Ar-Rahìm, Al-Quddus, and Al-Hakim necessitate it.

Humans think and reflect. Thinking of death without any afterlife can make the person suffer. The animals don't have future related concerns or worries. They live the present time. Therefore, Allah ﷻ does not torture the people by the worries of future in their present time of world by them thinking and reflecting about non-existence after death. If non-existence would be the case, then the person would continuously be suffering in the world and knowing and thinking that this person would be terminated from all her or his loved ones.

---

76. You did not create this aimlessly; exalted are You [above such a thing]; then protect us from the punishment of the Fire.
77. Exalted are you.

Humans have very complex internal spiritual faculties. There are a lot of skills that arise from these faculties. There are a lot of thoughts, reflection and inclinations from these skills of a person. This complex system necessitates through the Names of Allah ﷻ such as the Ar-Rahmãn, Most Merciful, Al-Hakim, the Wise, and Al-Quddus, the One who establishes everything perfectly with means and conservation that this complex system should be preserved with mercy, wisdom and perfection after death but not terminated. One can call this as the conservation of the spiritual faculties in the afterlife through the conservation laws that we witness in our everyday lives in the world.

The word بِالآخِرَة can signify that there is one and specific akhirah, afterlife because it comes al-marifah. The current belief of some of the ahlu kitãb, the people of the book about akhirah, afterlife is not the correct one. In other words, the Qurãn is referring to some of the changes that have been happening in the understanding of afterlife in Jewish faith among different groups and sects within the Judaism. Although the Christian understanding of afterlife is more similar to Islam, still the Qurãn is establishing the original correct understanding of afterlife especially with the al marifah of ال, alif and lam. On the other hand, marifah of ال also denotes the existence of afterlife belief in the other scriptures such as in the Bible and the Torah. The expression بِالآخِرَة is used instead of yawm ul Qiyamah or hashr in order to implicitly refer to the first creation and second re-creation with the word بِالآخِرَة. The expression يُوقِنُونَ is used instead of يُؤْمِنُونَ may possibly refer to the doubts about the afterlife for some people. In this perspective, the belief in afterlife should be in certainty with يُوقِنُونَ. Some of the assertions of the people of the book for their beliefs in akhirah cannot be a true belief or imãn if yaqin, certainty is not present.

On another perspective, imãn, knowing or certainty, yaqin from the word يُوقِنُونَ can have three stages:

1. I'lm-by knowledge
2. A'yn-by senses of vision and hearing especially
3. Haqqa-by taste fully

In the first case, for example, a person can hear the suffering of another person such as a sickness or trial. He or she may feel sad and bad. This is knowing by knowledge or intellect. When the person actually sees this person, this is a higher knowledge by witnessing through the senses. The last case is when the person oneself is in this difficulty, suffering or sickness, then this is called the last stage of full knowledge by experience or tasting it. Some people can call this a full sympathy. Some people can call this full certainty.

When one looks the Quranic verses, this style is very vivid. The Qurān first engages the reader with knowledge, reason and mind. Then, it gives the witnessing agents through senses, and vision. The last stage is the full description of sceneries such as Judgement Day, the people of Heaven or Hell, the people's arguments and conversations in different places. The last stage is the experiential stage with knowledge.

In classical approach, one can call this as the fiqh or shariah, the knowledge through reason. The other one is tasawwuf the knowledge through experience. Both should be complementary. They don't contradict but experience and knowledge is the highest stage of yaqin, knowing with certainty. Therefore, the real scholars in the field of religion is always described as not intellectuals but the people of knowledge with taqwa, the real people of experiential knowledge. They know all the regular, legal and apparent sciences of the Qurān, hadith, fiqh and others. But, they live, implement and experience this knowledge. Therefore, this was at the highest level represented by the Prophet ﷺ with the title of "Walking Qurān."

[5]

78{البقرة 5/5} أُوْلَئِكَ عَلَى هُدًى مِّن رَّبِّهِمْ وَأُوْلَئِكَ هُمُ الْمُفْلِحُونَ

The word أُوْلَئِكَ shows an infinite farness at the same time infinite nearness. The word أُوْلَئِكَ can also signify the high and noble state and status of the people with these qualities. Since the beginning of Sûrah Fātiha, the word هُدَى[79] is presented three times. The first one, اهِدِنَا الصِّرَاطَ الْمُسْتَقِيمَ in Sûrah Fātiha, presents the demand and intention, search of the person for hidāyah, guidance. The second one in the second ayah of this Sûrah presents, هُدَى لِّلْمُتَّقِينَ[80] that hidāyah comes with the kasb, effort of the person. These efforts are belief, imān, salah, prayer, zakah, charity

---

78. 2:5 It is they who follow the guidance [which comes] from their Sustainer; and it is they, they who shall attain to a happy state!
79. Guidance.
80. Guidance for those who fear you.

and other obligations. Lastly, Allah ﷺ creates the hidāyah as mentioned here as أُوْلَـٰئِكَ عَلَى هُدًى مِّن رَّبِّهِمْ[81] with the intention and effort of the person, الله اعلم[82].

The expression عَلَى هُدًى[83] has عَلَى instead of any other preposition, harf jar. Each word in this context can picturize something in one's mind. This can signify as if the person can ride the vehicle of hidāyah, guidance as if going on the road with a car with the tawfik and guidance of Allah ﷺ.

The expression مِّن رَّبِّهِمْ[84] can signify that the guidance of each person is given one by one and constantly from their Rabb. In other words, the person's choice with اهدِنَا الصِّرَاطَ الْمُسْتَقِيمَ[85] then the person's inclination and effort with هُدًى لِّلْمُتَّقِينَ is ended with the pleasure, Ridwan of Allah ﷺ with عَلَى هُدًى مِّن رَّبِّهِم.

It is interesting to note that الْمُفْلِحُونَ, the falāh comes with and at the end of the هُدًى hidāyah. In other words, falāh is the result of hidāyah.

There is a relationship between the hidāyah, guidance and the rûh, soul. There is an existence, a life of heaven and paradise in the world when the person has hidāyah from Allah ﷺ. The sweetness, peace and content of the hidāyah in one's conscience, heart, and mind can put the person in a life of Jannah in the world. Although an outsider can view this person as someone living the conditions of evil or torture, this person is in reality in Jannah, heaven, and peace. An example of this is Ibrahim as. As he as was in the fire, he was enjoying the most pleasurable times of his life because he as was guided by Allah ﷺ. One can write an article on this concept and relation of hidāyah and rûh, the guidance and the soul.

In the expression هُدًى مِّن رَّبِّهِمْ, the preposition مِّن does not signify a force for guidance from Allah ﷺ but it signifies that when the person is seeking guidance with a genuine intention for the means of belief and practice, then Allah ﷺ creates guidance for this person. Hidāyah is given by Allah ﷺ as a fadl and mercy for one's effort or kasb as mentioned with hudan lil muttaqìn. They have the effort of having taqwa. In other words, the person puts one's willpower towards this direction seeking guidance, hidāyah.

---

81. It is they who follow the guidance [which comes] from their Sustainer.
82. Allah knows best.
83. On guidance.
84. From your lord.
85. Guide us on the straight path.

أُولَٰئِكَ عَلَىٰ هُدًى مِّن رَّبِّهِمْ وَأُولَٰئِكَ هُمُ الْمُفْلِحُونَ {البقرة/5}

In the above verse as mentioned, falāh can be the result of hidāyah. In addition, one can realize that there are two أُولَٰئِكَ in the above expression. The first أُولَٰئِكَ can refer to the ummi Muslims and the second أُولَٰئِكَ can refer to ahlu kitāb Muslims. In other words, the first one can signify the ones coming from no guidance, ignorance to hidāyah. The second أُولَٰئِكَ are the ones who already have some hidāyah, guidance but it is perfected and completed by the Qurān and the Prophet ﷺ. In this perspective, the second ones become in falāh, happiness and complete satisfaction due to their pitfalls in their religion either due to the changes occurred overtime or due to the lacking necessary updates for the requirements of time.

The first أُولَٰئِكَ can refer to الَّذِينَ يُؤْمِنُونَ بِالْغَيْبِ وَيُقِيمُونَ الصَّلَاةَ وَمِمَّا رَزَقْنَاهُمْ يُنفِقُونَ [86] {البقرة/3} as the Muslims coming from darkness to light, ummi Muslims. The second أُولَٰئِكَ can refer to وَالَّذِينَ يُؤْمِنُونَ بِمَا أُنزِلَ إِلَيْكَ وَمَا أُنزِلَ مِن قَبْلِكَ وَبِالْآخِرَةِ هُمْ يُوقِنُونَ [87] {البقرة/4} of the people of ahlu kitāb, Christians, Jews and others.

In the expression وَأُولَٰئِكَ هُمُ الْمُفْلِحُونَ, the pronoun هُمُ comes between أُولَٰئِكَ and الْمُفْلِحُونَ. This is between mubteda and khabar. If one follows the discussion above, this pronoun can encourage the people of the Book with an emphasis to portrait all the fruits of recognition of Islam, the Qurān and the Prophet that they would be happy, and peaceful in this state of falāh. The case of ahlu kitāb, the people of the book can be similar to a person having a car and the factory sends a recall message for an error or mistake in the car. They can still use the same car. The factory is not telling them to give the car back but the factory is doing the recall for a free update due to safety, and may be other reasons. In the cases of the books of Bible and Tawrah, the reasons of recall can be the errors and changes introduced overtime by people. Also, the Qurān has the inclusivity and contemporizing of for our time till the End of Day as the Scripture of Allah ﷻ because there will not be any other book or messenger sent to people by Allah,[88] والله اعلم.

---

86. Who believe in the unseen, establish prayer, and spend out of what We have provided for them.
87. And who believe in what has been revealed to you, [O Muhammad], and what was revealed before you, and of the Hereafter they are certain [in faith].
88. Allah knows best.

In the expression الْمُفْلِحُونَ[89], the marifah form can signify that being muflihun is at different levels. For some, being muflihun is being saved from Jahannam. For some, it is going to Jannah, and for some, it is seeing Allah ﷻ.

One can also remember that the word Rabb in رَبِّهِمْ[90] can give the meaning of giving sustenance. In this regards, the riziq or sustenance can have two forms, the physical sustenance what we need for our physical bodies and the other is, the spiritual sustenance through guidance, hidāyah.

[6]

إِنَّ الَّذِينَ كَفَرُواْ سَوَاءٌ عَلَيْهِمْ أَأَنذَرْتَهُمْ أَمْ لَمْ تُنذِرْهُمْ لاَ يُؤْمِنُونَ {البقرة 2/6}[91]

The word إِنَّ, according to some scholars, can signify the much zeal of the Prophet that the Prophet was much concerned about the imān of the people and Allah ﷻ made a qasam, swearing and emphasis, to ease the Prophet's ﷺ concern and worry. The sila word الَّذِينَ can signify the multitude and changing form of types of kufr that is adapting according to the situation, time and context. Therefore, one should constantly look one's heart and at the inner faculties if these traces of kufr are present in oneself. In this perspective, there are a lot of great sahabah and wali, the friends of Allah ﷻ, that during their lives and during their times of dying, they were scared and fearful of dying as a kāfir or as a munāfiq. The person may not realize about the shirk or kufr in oneself. It is so intricate and silent and as the Prophet describes of a black ant walking in the dark and no one sees it (12). For a Muslim and a true believer, there is no certainty of being saved and therefore, there should not be any type of arrogance till one dies and meets with Allah ﷻ. At that time, the realities will be shown about one's inner self, nafs. This perspective can always keep the person humble, dynamic and striving on the path. The beginning of the verse إِنَّ الَّذِينَ كَفَرُواْ[92] explains who they are and as the answer comes as the people of لاَ يُؤْمِنُونَ[93]. The expression of إِنَّ الَّذِينَ

---

89. The happy ones.
90. Their Lord.
91. 2:6 BEHOLD, as for those who are bent on denying the truth6—it is all one to them whether thou warnest them or dost not warn them: they will not believe.
92. Indeed those who disbelieve.
93. Who don't believe.

come often in the Qurãn. The word إِنَّ can really bring the attention and focus of the people to the message with emphasis. The word الَّذِينَ is sila, relative pronoun in English, can be in the context of description of the situations, people or cases. For example, one can review these symmetrical cases of descriptions in the beginning verses about the believers with this sila word الَّذِينَ:

الَّذِينَ يُؤْمِنُونَ بِالْغَيْبِ وَيُقِيمُونَ الصَّلاةَ وَمِمَّا رَزَقْنَاهُمْ يُنفِقُونَ 94{البقرة/3}

وَالَّذِينَ يُؤْمِنُونَ بِمَا أُنزِلَ إِلَيْكَ وَمَا أُنزِلَ مِن قَبْلِكَ وَبِالآخِرَةِ هُمْ يُوقِنُونَ 95{البقرة/4}

and oppositely for unbelievers with this sila word الَّذِينَ is used as well:

إِنَّ الَّذِينَ كَفَرُواْ سَوَاءٌ عَلَيْهِمْ أَأَنذَرْتَهُمْ أَمْ لَمْ تُنذِرْهُمْ لاَ يُؤْمِنُونَ 96{البقرة/6}

In both cases, one can see that the sila word الَّذِينَ[97] is used for the description of both the people of imãn and kufr, believers and non-believers. Another category is that munafiqin is not mentioned with this sila word الَّذِينَ in the coming ayahs as it will be explained later that it is important realize this difference.

Imãn and Kufr

Imãn is a light that is the outcome of a humble acceptance and confirmation of all the required parts of the religion with its details, exactness, and precision, brought by Rasulullah ﷺ. Also, it is a light that is the outcome of a humble acceptance of all the unrequired parts of the religion with their general understandings. In this perspective, one can realize that everyone has a different level of understanding and education. Therefore, a person's inability to express the intrinsic exact notions of imãn does not mean that this person does not have imãn, or belief. Because most of the time language is insufficient to describe the fine details of one's emotions and beliefs in one's heart and conscience.

---

94. Who believe in the unseen, establish prayer, and spend out of what We have provided for them,
95. And who believe in what has been revealed to you, [O Muhammad], and what was revealed before you, and of the Hereafter they are certain [in faith].
96. Indeed, those who disbelieve—it is all the same for them whether you warn them or do not warn them—they will not believe.
97. Those who.

There even are a lot good experts and scholars in textual and literature analysis but they can even be sometimes disabled to express some of the fine details in a convoluted piece of a poem. In this perspective, if a person asks a farmer or a villager who may not be much formally educated in a school system about a question of "which direction Allah ﷻ is, then, if this person just says "Allah ﷻ is not in any direction, it is not possible," then this can be a proof of imān in this person's conscience that Allah ﷻ is not bound to any direction. In that perspective, he or she may not elaborate all the proper Names and Attributes of Allah ﷻ with the details of aqāid formalized by for example by Imam Tahawi. But this inability of not expression does not mean that he or she does not have imān or belief.

According to Imam Taftazani (13), imān is a light given from Allah ﷻ to the person's heart due to person's intention of seeking. Then, the person has a meaning and purpose in relevance to all creation and all the universe in their relation with Allah ﷻ. They are all servants and creations of the Creator. With this perspective, the person feels secure, safe and affinity with everything. With this power of imān in the heart and mind, the person can have resistance and stamina to all evil looking incidents, trials and tests. This person knows with the light of imān that all the ugly and good looking incidents have a purpose and meaning and they are the servants of Allah ﷻ. Even, imān gives such a power to the person that this person can see, understand and digest the meanings of things beyond time, past and future.

On the other hand, kufr, disbelief can have different types: persistent kufr, purposeful negligence oriented kufr, and lack of knowledge and ability oriented kufr.

Persistent kufr can detail the people who knows that there is the Creator. They know that Allah ﷻ sent the Qurān and the Prophet ﷺ. But due to mostly identity, position, fame, or wealth related concerns, a person may not accept the message although he or she knows that it is the truth from Rabbul Alamin. As one can evaluate the example of Abu Jahil, Abu Lahab or some of the ahlu kitāb as we know today and in the past. The Qurān mentions that they knew the Prophet and the Qurān similar to their own children.

Kasb can be translated into English with the word of acquirement. Kasb is a word that is constantly repeated in many verses in the Qurān such as:

فَوَيْلٌ لِّلَّذِينَ يَكْتُبُونَ الْكِتَابَ بِأَيْدِيهِمْ ثُمَّ يَقُولُونَ هَذَا مِنْ عِندِ اللهِ لِيَشْتَرُواْ بِهِ ثَمَناً قَلِيلاً فَوَيْلٌ لَّهُم مِّمَّا كَتَبَتْ أَيْدِيهِمْ وَوَيْلٌ لَّهُمْ مِّمَّا يَكْسِبُونَ {البقرة/79}[98]

} وَمَن يَكْسِبْ إِثْمًا فَإِنَّمَا يَكْسِبُهُ عَلَى نَفْسِهِ وَكَانَ اللهُ عَلِيمًا حَكِيمًا {النساء/111}[99] وَمَن يَكْسِبْ خَطِيئَةً أَوْ إِثْمًا ثُمَّ يَرْمِ بِهِ بَرِيئًا فَقَدِ احْتَمَلَ بُهْتَانًا وَإِثْمًا مُّبِينًا {النساء/112}[100]

} وَذَرُواْ ظَاهِرَ الإِثْمِ وَبَاطِنَهُ إِنَّ الَّذِينَ يَكْسِبُونَ الإِثْمَ سَيُجْزَوْنَ بِمَا كَانُواْ يَقْتَرِفُونَ[101] {الأنعام/120}

وَكَذَلِكَ نُوَلِّي بَعْضَ الظَّالِمِينَ بَعْضًا بِمَا كَانُواْ يَكْسِبُونَ {الأنعام/129}[102]

وَلَوْ أَنَّ أَهْلَ الْقُرَى آمَنُواْ وَاتَّقَواْ لَفَتَحْنَا عَلَيْهِم بَرَكَاتٍ مِّنَ السَّمَاء وَالأَرْضِ وَلَكِن كَذَّبُواْ فَأَخَذْنَاهُم بِمَا كَانُواْ يَكْسِبُونَ {الأعراف/96}[103]

فَلْيَضْحَكُواْ قَلِيلاً وَلْيَبْكُواْ كَثِيرًا جَزَاء بِمَا كَانُواْ يَكْسِبُونَ {التوبة/82}[104]

أُوْلَئِكَ مَأْوَاهُمُ النُّارُ بِمَا كَانُواْ يَكْسِبُونَ {يونس/8}

} فَمَا أَغْنَى عَنْهُم مَّا كَانُواْ يَكْسِبُونَ {الحجر/84}[106] [105]

الْيَوْمَ نَخْتِمُ عَلَى أَفْوَاهِهِمْ وَتُكَلِّمُنَا أَيْدِيهِمْ وَتَشْهَدُ أَرْجُلُهُم بِمَا كَانُوا يَكْسِبُونَ {يس/65}[107]

---

98. 2:79 Woe, then, unto those who write down, with their own hands, [something which they claim to be] divine writ, and then say, "This is from God," in order to acquire a trifling gain thereby; woe, then, unto them for what their hands have written, and woe unto them for all that they may have gained!

99. (4:111) for he who commits a sin, commits it only to his own hurt; and God is indeed all-knowing, wise.

100. (4:112) But he who commits a fault or a sin and then throws the blame therefore on an innocent person, burdens himself with the guilt of calumny and [yet another] flagrant sin.

101. 6:120 But abstain from sinning be it open or secret—for, behold, those who commit sins shall be requited for all that they have earned.

102. 6:129 And in this manner do We cause evildoers to seduce one another by means of their (evil) doings.

103. 7:96 Yet if the people of those communities had but attained to faith and been conscious of Us, We would indeed have opened up for them blessings out of heaven and earth: but they gave the lie to the truth—and so We took them to task through what they [themselves] had been doing."

104. (9:82) Let them, then, laugh a little—for they will weep a lot in return for what they have earned.

105. (10:8) Their goal is the fire in return for all [the evil] that they were wont to do.

106. (15:84) And of no avail to them was all [the power] that they had acquired.

107. (36:65) On that Day We shall set a seal on their mouths—but their hands will speak unto Us, and their feet will bear witness to whatever they have earned [in life].

قَدْ قَالَهَا الَّذِينَ مِن قَبْلِهِمْ فَمَا أَغْنَى عَنْهُم مَّا كَانُوا يَكْسِبُونَ ﴿الزمر/50﴾108

أَفَلَمْ يَسِيرُوا فِي الْأَرْضِ فَيَنظُرُوا كَيْفَ كَانَ عَاقِبَةُ الَّذِينَ مِن قَبْلِهِمْ كَانُوا أَكْثَرَ مِنْهُمْ وَأَشَدَّ قُوَّةً وَآثَارًا فِي الْأَرْضِ فَمَا أَغْنَى عَنْهُم مَّا كَانُوا يَكْسِبُونَ ﴿غافر/82﴾109

وَأَمَّا ثَمُودُ فَهَدَيْنَاهُمْ فَاسْتَحَبُّوا الْعَمَى عَلَى الْهُدَى فَأَخَذَتْهُمْ صَاعِقَةُ الْعَذَابِ الْهُونِ بِمَا كَانُوا يَكْسِبُونَ ﴿فصلت/17﴾110

قُل لِّلَّذِينَ آمَنُوا يَغْفِرُوا لِلَّذِينَ لَا يَرْجُونَ أَيَّامَ اللَّهِ لِيَجْزِيَ قَوْمًا بِما كَانُوا يَكْسِبُونَ ﴿الجاثية/14﴾111

كَلَّا بَلْ رَانَ عَلَى قُلُوبِهِم مَّا كَانُوا يَكْسِبُونَ ﴿المطففين/14﴾112

Another with similar to kasb and maybe repeated more in the Qurān is the word يَعْمَلُونَ such as:

تِلْكَ أُمَّةٌ قَدْ خَلَتْ لَهَا مَا كَسَبَتْ وَلَكُم مَّا كَسَبْتُمْ وَلَا تُسْأَلُونَ عَمَّا كَانُوا يَعْمَلُونَ ﴿البقرة/134﴾113

In other words, the person makes an intention and inclination to acquire an action. The seed of acquirement is inclination and intention. The concept of kasb is the intrinsic qualities of free choice and free will in the aqāid. If we can review the two schools of aqāid: Asharites and Maturi, there is a fine line between them and both are very similar. Below diagram shows the process of kasb (acquirement) leading to one's free will within the notions of inclinations in oneself.

---

108. 39:50 The same did say [to themselves many of] those who lived before their time; but of no avail to them was all that they had ever achieved:
109. 40:82 HAVE THEY, then, never journeyed about the earth and beheld what happened in the end to those [deniers of the truth] who lived before their time? More numerous were they, and greater in power than they are, and in the impact which they left on earth: but all that they ever achieved was of no avail to them—
110. 41:17 And as for [the tribe of] Thamud, We offered them guidance, but they chose blindness in preference to guidance: and so the thunderbolt of shameful suffering fell upon them as an outcome of all [the evil] that they had wrought;
111. (45:14) Tell all who have attained to faith that they should forgive those who do not believe in the coming of the Days of God,12 [since it is] for Him [alone] to requite people for whatever they may have earned.
112. 83:14 Nay, but their hearts are corroded by all [the evil] that they were wont to do!
113. 2:134 Now those people have passed away; unto them shall be accounted what they have earned, and unto you, what you have earned; and you will not be, judged on the strength of what they did.

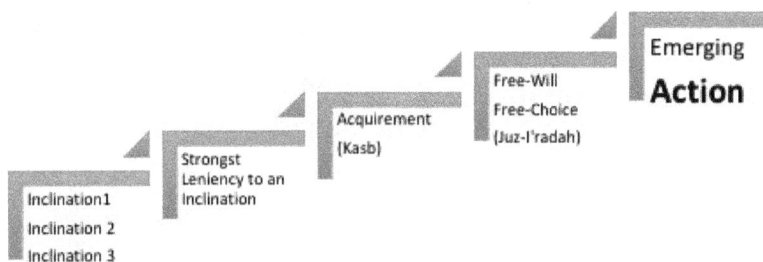

Figure 3   The Process of Inclinations in Oneself Leading to Free Choice and an Emerging Action from the Person

According to the above diagram, the creation of the action by Allah ﷻ emerges from the inclination of the person. One can also replace certain words in their non-technical usage in the common language. In this case, the word intention of the person can best fit to the stage of acquirement or kasb according to the above diagram. Sometimes, one can or cannot identify one's different inclinations for an issue. Then, after the dominant inclination with strongest leniency then, one takes a purposeful, calculated and deliberate step with intention. Thus, the word intention in popular usage can equate the word acquirement (kasb) in the above diagram. Therefore, the word "kasb" is used as a technical word in the fine discourses of aqāid. On the other hand, the word "intention" is used as a more non-technical term but with its general popular usage in all other fields of Islamic sciences such as in hadith or fiqh.

In another perspective, a person in a short span of lifetime can tend to incline their disposition and attach to it. Most of the time, it becomes difficult for humans to change their dispositions. This could be similar to the law of inertia in physics, a force acting against the notion of change. In a positive sense, the specializations in one field can add a value to one's attachment in one disposition. Therefore, in this natural fitrah of humans, if the person does not have regular self-reflection to diagnose constantly where his or her inclinations are with their purpose, then an entire life can be spent in an initial disposition that the person has encountered. The Quranic verses constantly engages the reader with this notion with similar ayahs below:

وَإِذَا قِيلَ لَهُمُ اتَّبِعُوا مَا أَنزَلَ اللَّهُ قَالُوا بَلْ نَتَّبِعُ مَا أَلْفَيْنَا عَلَيْهِ آبَاءَنَا أَوَلَوْ كَانَ آبَاؤُهُمْ لاَ يَعْقِلُونَ شَيْئًا وَلاَ يَهْتَدُونَ {البقرة/170}[114]

وَإِذَا قِيلَ لَهُمْ تَعَالَوْا إِلَى مَا أَنزَلَ اللَّهُ وَإِلَى الرَّسُولِ قَالُوا حَسْبُنَا مَا وَجَدْنَا عَلَيْهِ آبَاءَنَا أَوَلَوْ كَانَ آبَاؤُهُمْ لاَ يَعْلَمُونَ شَيْئًا وَلاَ يَهْتَدُونَ {المائدة/104}[115]

{ قَالُوا وَجَدْنَا آبَاءَنَا لَهَا عَابِدِينَ {الأنبياء/53} قَالَ لَقَدْ كُنتُمْ أَنتُمْ وَآبَاؤُكُمْ فِي ضَلَالٍ مُّبِينٍ {الأنبياء/54}[116]

قَالُوا بَلْ وَجَدْنَا آبَاءَنَا كَذَلِكَ يَفْعَلُونَ {الشعراء/74}[117]

وَإِذَا قِيلَ لَهُمُ اتَّبِعُوا مَا أَنزَلَ اللَّهُ قَالُوا بَلْ نَتَّبِعُ مَا وَجَدْنَا عَلَيْهِ آبَاءَنَا أَوَلَوْ كَانَ الشَّيْطَانُ يَدْعُوهُمْ إِلَى عَذَابِ السَّعِيرِ {لقمان/21}[118]

بَلْ قَالُوا إِنَّا وَجَدْنَا آبَاءَنَا عَلَى أُمَّةٍ وَإِنَّا عَلَى آثَارِهِم مُّهْتَدُونَ {الزخرف/22}[119]

That people don't want to change their given or initial dispositions where they initially find themselves in. One of the key words in here is آبَاءَنَا[120] to reflect their initial or given dispositions or inclinations.

Difficulties and Problems of the Method of Comparison in knowing Allah ﷻ

In the methodology of comparison in human realm, one should know that the person is a creation with endless limitations. Therefore, one cannot use the human realm to fully compare and contrast in order to

---

114. 2:170 But when they are told, "Follow what God has bestowed from on high," some answer, "Nay, we shall follow [only] that which we found our forefathers believing in and doing." Why, even if their forefathers did not use their reason at all, and were devoid of all guidance?

115. (5:104) for when they are told, "Come unto that which God has bestowed from on high, and unto the Apostle"—they answer, "Enough for us is that which we found our forefathers believing in and doing." Why, even though their forefathers knew nothing, and were devoid of all guidance?

116. 21:53 They answered: "We found our forefathers worshipping them." (21:54} Said he: "Indeed, you and your forefathers have obviously gone astray!"

117. 26:74 They exclaimed: "But we found our fore-fathers doing the same!"

118. (31:21) and when such [people] are told to follow that which God has bestowed from on high, they answer, "Nay, we shall follow that which we found our forefathers believing in and doing!" Why—[would you follow your forefathers] even if Satan had invited them unto the suffering of the blazing flame?

119. 43:22 Nay, but they say, "Behold, We found our forefathers agreed on what to believe—and, verily, it is in their footsteps that we find our guidance!"

120. Our forefathers.

know Allah ﷻ. In this perspective, a human's realm can be only an image but not a real tool of comparison with Allah ﷻ, the Infinite Powerful, All-Knowing, Ever Existing and Ever Lasting, al-Hayy[121], al-Qayyum[122], al-A'ziz[123], and al-Hakim[124].

In another perspective, all the funny problems come into existence if one does not realize the difficulties and problems of the method of comparison for knowing Allah ﷻ. Because, one cannot compare Wajibul Wujud, the One Whose existence is Absolute, Always Present and Not Dependent on anything or anyone from the creation whose existence is limited and dependent and possible or not.

In this sense, different formation of creeds within different religions have been representative and stemming from this problematic unrealized complications and difficulties of comparison in understanding. Here are some examples: the case of calling God as father to mean caring, protective or implementing just authority; the case of calling God with a son to give a value or to elevate a human's status because he was special and therefore God sent the son to earth to guide people; the case of thinking God with an attribute of tiredness that now God needs to rest on a day; the case of God does not create the bad, ugly or evil so that there should be Satan responsible or any other gods responsible for this; the case of imaging God with anger, authoritative, androcentric or patriarchal being.

These are all problems stemming mainly due to human problematic understanding of construction or thinking due to comparison, analogy when knowing who Allah ﷻ is. There are billions following these notions without going to the essence with a simple methodology: Allah ﷻ is the Creator. All others are created as Aristotle concludes in his journey of logical deduction (14).

Therefore, La ilaha illa Allah, has first negation what Allah ﷻ is not with the phrase La ilaha. Then, with the phrase "illa Allah ﷻ," the true and genuine understanding of Allah ﷻ follows with the primary guidelines of the Qurān and hadith. Then, reason and experience follow.

One should know where to stop the comparison. In other words, one should be always aware of the limits of comparison and the limits

---

121. The Ever-lasting.
122. The Eternal.
123. The mighty.
124. The Wise.

of thinking. Stopping with adab, respect and etiquette, knowing the limitation of oneself with humbleness are the main tools. Therefore, some Muslims also are trapped in temptations, waswasa, wrong wanderings of mind due to not knowing this adab, the methodology of limits with humbleness and true humility.

The Infinite Divine Will Power of Allah ﷻ encompasses both the cause and result. In other words, sometimes people make mistake by imagining the Divine Will Power of Allah ﷻ, (referred as mashiyyah or irada i kull) as something linear. In other words, in a case of a premise that if this happens then this happens or if this doesn't happen then this does not happen. So, if there is no apparent sabab or cause to humans we can't fully say that the result would not be this. In other words, if a person gets sick by eating food, we cannot say that if he did not eat the food he would not get sick but from the perspective of qadar, destiny and from the point of Ahlu sunnah wa jamah, one can say "we don't know." On the other hand, the group of jabriyya can say ", it doesn't matter, the person would be still sick," giving no effect on the cause, free will or free choice. Oppositely, the group of itizal (mutazilah) would say "no, the person would not be sick", giving full authority to the cause, to the sabab. In other words, making free choice or free will not dependent on the intervention of Allah ﷻ or mashiyyah, or irada i kull.

Another mistake in this approximation of comparison, for example, a person can make a small simple block toy car from wood. Then also, hundreds of people can come together to build a car with complex systems of self-navigation with fuel options of gas or hybrid electric system. For any person observing these two cases, the latter will be more difficult to build and accomplish then the first simple toy wood car. But, for Allah ﷻ, there is no notion of difficulty. All are the same for Allah ﷻ as mentioned:

$$مَّا خَلْقُكُمْ وَلَا بَعْثُكُمْ إِلَّا كَنَفْسٍ وَاحِدَةٍ إِنَّ اللَّهَ سَمِيعٌ بَصِيرٌ {لقمان/28}^{125}$$

---

125. (31:28)Your creation and your resurrection will not be but as that of a single soul. Indeed, Allah is Hearing and Seeing.

One should remember within understanding of kasb, the acquirement and the application of free will and choice, the Real Effective Cause is Allah ﷻ. In other words, Allah ﷻ creates the outcome what the person wants with his choice of inclination, acquirement, intention and action. The laws in nature can assure structure and order to ensure the free will, choice and execution of this in the world of causality. For example, the case of fire not burning Ibrahim as is an example of a reminder to humans that the Real Effective Cause is Allah ﷻ. In other words, the existing structure and order in nature through scientific laws are created by Allah ﷻ. Allah ﷻ can order a scientific law not to work and it won't as in the case of fire with Ibrahim as.

One should remember that the value of a human is according to his or her essence. One 's essence is according to the one's effort and struggle. The worth of one's effort and struggle has the value according to the significant elevated level of one's intention, purpose and goal. One can see this in the below diagram to make it easy to understand.

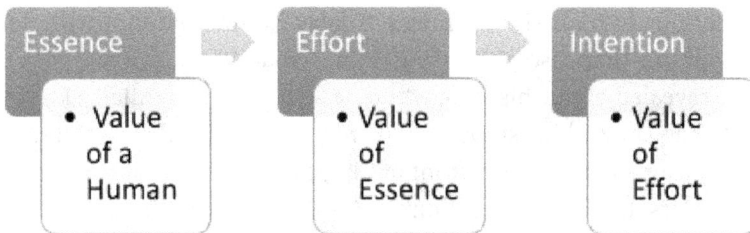

Figure 4   Value of Human in Islam

One should remember the learning process of a person in all above discussions. A person's learning skills mainly are built up on the methodology of comparing and contrasting towards increasing one's knowledge. In other words, a person looks around the objects, beings, incidents and experiences and deduces causalities and results. This is the area where inclinations form. Then, the person intends to execute the inclinations with one's free choice and free will.

On the other hand, Allah ﷻ is not like humans. The person makes a mistake to fully deduce meanings about the Creator, Allah ﷻ by using same methodology of analogy and comparison. This is a major mistake of humans in executing the free will and free choice. In other words, the methodology of comparison and contrast cannot be fully executed with the unseen. It cannot be fully executed to have the true knowledge of Allah ﷻ. Therefore, there is a guidance needed. In this perspective, the scriptures from Allah ﷻ, the Qurān and hadith serves as the key to implement the notion of "guided method of comparison and analogy." In other words, the person can have the true knowledge of Allah ﷻ with the same method of comparison and analogy with the guidance of the Qurān and the hadith and by understanding and normalizing the limits of comparison for the unseen and for especially Allah ﷻ. The discussion here mainly underlines rationalizing the limits of execution of free will and free choice.

In this perspective, a person not aware of this, cannot rationalize fully the notion that the One, Allah ﷻ, knows all the inner dynamically changing feelings of a person in the heart, continuously showering thoughts in the mind, forming inclinations, and actions in secret and in public.

The category of خَتَمَ أللّٰہ عَلَى قُلُوبِهِمْ[126] can entail the cases that due to their kasb, acquierment and choice, that they won't change their position of belief due to their stubbornness. Allah ﷻ knows that they will die in that state. In that case, the case of Abu Lahab was a miracle that the Sûrah revealed about his kufr while he was alive and Allah ﷻ knew it. Abu Lahab showed his stubbornness not to change although there was a clear proof and miracle in front of him, the Prophet. As mentioned by the scholars, to disprove the Qurān, Abu Lahab could have even acted to believe the Prophet but he didn't, subhanAllah. The Qurān proved his position while he was alive.

One should remember that Allah ﷻ creates everything and Allah ﷻ is the Real Cause. Humans and Jinns are given free will and free choice. Due to their kasb, acquierment, inclination and struggle of their usage of free will and free choice, Allah ﷻ creates the action what they want.

One should also remember Allah ﷻ mentions that the Divine Mercy, Caring and Fadl is more beyond than the Divine Justice and Accountability as mentioned in below in the phrase كَتَبَ عَلَى نَفْسِهِ الرَّحْمَةَ[127]:

---

126. Allah has set a seal upon their hearts.
127. Who has willed upon Himself the law of grace and mercy.

قُل لِّمَن مَّا فِي السَّمَاوَاتِ وَالأَرْضِ قُل لِلَّهِ كَتَبَ عَلَى نَفْسِهِ الرَّحْمَةَ لَيَجْمَعَنَّكُمْ إِلَى يَوْمِ الْقِيَامَةِ لاَ رَيْبَ فِيهِ الَّذِينَ خَسِرُواْ أَنفُسَهُمْ فَهُمْ لاَ يُؤْمِنُونَ {الأنعام/12}[128]

وَإِذَا جَاءكَ الَّذِينَ يُؤْمِنُونَ بِآيَاتِنَا فَقُلْ سَلاَمٌ عَلَيْكُمْ كَتَبَ رَبُّكُمْ عَلَى نَفْسِهِ الرَّحْمَةَ أَنَّهُ مَنْ عَمِلَ مِنكُمْ سُوءًا بِجَهَالَةٍ ثُمَّ تَابَ مِن بَعْدِهِ وَأَصْلَحَ فَأَنَّهُ غَفُورٌ رَّحِيمٌ {الأنعام/54}[129]

Therefore, a lot of times a person may be asking constantly an evil outcome with his or her free will and free choice but Allah ﷻ can be delaying the outcome of what the person is asking due to the Infinite Divine Mercy and Fadl. If it is the justice, the person immediately should face the constant insistence of one on evil renderings. It is interesting to note that both verses about Allah ﷻ's Mercy and Fadl are mentioned in the Sûrah An'am which is the chapter of Bounties. In other words, Allah ﷻ's treating the creation with utmost Mercy and Fadl is another bounty from Allah ﷻ. If Allah ﷻ treated creation with what they deserved they would be doomed to punishment and severe deserved recompense. This bounty itself necessitates Hamd, appreciation and recognition by the creation, humans.

On another perspective, as the Rabbul Alamin, Allah ﷻ gives structure, and order to everything. Allah ﷻ controls, interferes, and creates constantly in the full and perfect scales. This can be in the macro scales for humans such as galaxies, stars and universe, or in the micro scale relative to humans such as bacteria, viruses, and other beings. The detailed explanation was in Sûrah Fātiha, about Rabbul Alamin. In this perspective, a human with consciousness, mind, and natural fitrah knows that most of the things the person even within oneself or externally the person does, he or she does not have any say or control over them. Even, within one self, the person does not have any control of his or her heart beats, the processes occurring in the digestive system after eating food, the communications in the parts of the cells etc. So, this is fully and perfectly in control of Rabbul Alamin with the Full

---

128. 6:12 Say: "Unto whom belongs all that is in the heavens and on earth?" Say: "Unto God, who has willed upon Himself the law of grace and mercy." He will assuredly gather you all together on the Day of Resurrection, [the coming of] which is beyond all doubt: yet those who have squandered their own selves—it is they who refuse to believe [in Him],
129. (6:54) And when those who believe in Our messages come unto thee, say: "Peace be upon you. Your Sustainer has willed upon Himself the law of grace and mercy—so that if any of you does a bad deed out of ignorance, and thereafter repents and lives righteously, He shall be [found] much-forgiving, a dispenser of grace."

Divine Power. Then, Allah ﷻ gave a tiny control of free choice or free will. Accordingly, Allah ﷻ creates the results of this person's choice. For example, the person can choose what to eat. The person can choose how to spend one's time. But at this small scale, the person is responsible for his or her choice.

The second category are the people of purposeful negligence oriented kufr, disbelief. This people can know the essence of imān but they can be more in the state of "I don't care. I want to live my life as I am living now." This people may change. The attitude of indifference and not having concern for the purpose and meaning of life may gauge this person until they are hit by an evil looking incident in their life: deadly sicknesses such as cancer, near death syndromes or losing an attached value for example job, husband, wife, or kids.

The third category is the lack of knowledge and lack of ability oriented kufr. This person may not truly know what is right and wrong from the true sciences of religion. He or she may know sometimes but may not have the ability to change their condition because of weakness, laziness or addictions. When lack of knowledge is combined with personal spiritual weakness and laziness, this person can be stuck in this lifestyle for a long time. These people may have a lot of guidance from Allah ﷻ when they increase the true knowledge about Allah ﷻ and about the true religion. With their new life of true knowledge with the Qurān, and the genuine teachings of the Prophet, the person can be uplifted by Allah ﷻ from their weaknesses with the help, Tawfik, of Allah ﷻ and establish a new life style with new positive people on the true path.

The word كَفَرُو[130] is as explained in many classical tafasir with the meaning of covering something. One of the interpretations is that these people covered the ability of loving and appreciating Allah ﷻ. Therefore, they don't love and appreciate the creation truly. The word kufur also may mean, sometimes, if there is something but the person denies it. For example, if a person wears something and looks beautiful or handsome and if someone asks this person, you look so nice and the person says no, I don't look nice to show humbleness. This can imply kufur for some (1) that the person denying something that Allah ﷻ gave to this person. Instead, the person can say "yes, all the true beauty and good is from Allah ﷻ, my Creator, Alhamdulillah, it is not from me or it is not mine."

---

130. Disbelief.

Therefore, if one reviews the Sûrah Duha:

وَالضُّحَى {الضحى/1} وَاللَّيْلِ إِذَا سَجَى {الضحى/2} مَا وَدَّعَكَ رَبُّكَ وَمَا قَلَى {الضحى/3} وَلَلْآخِرَةُ خَيْرٌ لَّكَ مِنَ الْأُولَى {الضحى/4} وَلَسَوْفَ يُعْطِيكَ رَبُّكَ فَتَرْضَى {الضحى/5} أَلَمْ يَجِدْكَ يَتِيمًا فَآوَى {الضحى/6} وَوَجَدَكَ ضَالًّا فَهَدَى {الضحى/7} وَوَجَدَكَ عَائِلًا فَأَغْنَى {الضحى/8} فَأَمَّا الْيَتِيمَ فَلَا تَقْهَرْ {الضحى/9} وَأَمَّا السَّائِلَ فَلَا تَنْهَرْ {الضحى/10} وَأَمَّا بِنِعْمَةِ رَبِّكَ فَحَدِّثْ {الضحى/11}[131]

One can see that Allah ﷻ mentions the blessings and bounties which were given to the Prophet ﷺ specifically. Then, they are given to each individual in their own personal world of life. At the end, وَأَمَّا بِنِعْمَةِ رَبِّكَ فَحَدِّثْ {الضحى/11}, is expected that the person should first recognize it then appreciate those bounties and favors from Allah ﷻ. Not recognizing and not appreciating is kufur, covering it.

Kufur is an attitude in thought, verbal discourse and action. Imān is an attitude in thought, verbal discourse and action. Kufur is knowing but not appreciating. Imān is knowing and appreciating. Kufur is arrogance. Imān is humbleness. Therefore, if a person humiliates or makes a joke about something related with shiar, the building blocks of imān and the respected items ordered by Allah ﷻ, then this person can have the attitude of kufur and then be led to kufur. Even in the thought process, if there is this attitude, this may again lead the person to kufr. Here, a person who doesn't know or wants to genuinely learn is in a different category. Therefore, the Muslim scholars historically try to establish the methodology of tanzih about Allah ﷻ and about the sacred. Tanzih can be simply defined as "to remove from mind and heart what is <u>not</u> about Allah ﷻ." It is because the human mind constructs the relationship with Allah ﷻ with deficiencies therefore the negative constructions or these deficiencies should be constantly removed. It is the false and deficient constructions of humans due to their humanly normal limitations but Allah ﷻ is Perfect with all Divine Attributes and Names.

---

131. 93:1 CONSIDER the bright morning hours, (2) And the night when it grows still and dark.[1] (3) Thy Sustainer has not forsaken thee, nor does He scorn thee: (4) For, indeed, the life to come will be better for thee than this earlier part [of thy life]!
93:5 And, indeed, in time will thy Sustainer grant thee [what thy heart desires], and thou shalt be well-pleased. (6) Has He not found thee an orphan, and given thee shelter? (7) And found thee lost on thy way, and guided thee? (8) And found thee in want, and given thee sufficiency?
93:9 Therefore, the orphan shalt thou never wrong, (10) And him that seeks [thy] help shalt thou never chide, (11) And of thy Sustainer's blessings shalt thou [ever] speak.

Imān is accepting and believing all the structures and details of the true faith, creed or aqāid.

إِنَّ الَّذِينَ يَكْفُرُونَ بِاللَّهِ وَرُسُلِهِ وَيُرِيدُونَ أَن يُفَرِّقُواْ بَيْنَ اللَّهِ وَرُسُلِهِ وَيَقُولُونَ نُؤْمِنُ بِبَعْضٍ
وَنَكْفُرُ بِبَعْضٍ وَيُرِيدُونَ أَن يَتَّخِذُواْ بَيْنَ ذَلِكَ سَبِيلاً 132 {النساء/150} أُوْلَئِكَ هُمُ الْكَافِرُونَ
حَقًّا وَأَعْتَدْنَا لِلْكَافِرِينَ عَذَابًا مُّهِينًا 133 {النساء/151} وَالَّذِينَ آمَنُواْ بِاللَّهِ وَرُسُلِهِ وَلَمْ يُفَرِّقُواْ
بَيْنَ أَحَدٍ مِّنْهُمْ أُوْلَئِكَ سَوْفَ يُؤْتِيهِمْ أُجُورَهُمْ وَكَانَ اللَّهُ غَفُورًا رَّحِيمًا 134 {النساء/152}

The concept of selective belief or acceptance of the teachings of the Qurān and the Prophet is presented as kufr in the above verses as وَيَقُولُونَ نُؤْمِنُ بِبَعْضٍ وَنَكْفُرُ بِبَعْضٍ[135]. This approach is considered as the true kufr as mentioned أُوْلَئِكَ هُمُ الْكَافِرُونَ حَقًّا[136]. On the other hand, the case and attitude of people who have imān presented with وَالَّذِينَ آمَنُواْ بِاللَّهِ وَرُسُلِهِ[137] وَلَمْ يُفَرِّقُواْ بَيْنَ أَحَدٍ مِّنْهُمْ.

Imān and kufur are opposites of each other. Therefore, if one exists the other cannot exist. There is no mixed state or classification of imān and kufur. A person can have the qualities of imān or kufur but one belongs to one group in classification. A person can have imān but when he or she lies then this person has the qualities of kufr. A person can have kufr but when this person is ethical and honest then this person has the qualities of imān. This notion is a fundamental concept separating mutazalites and kharijis from the normative and majority stance of Muslims. Their stance was that with the grave oppressions or sins the person can be having no imān, versus the normative stance is the person can have imān but with fisq, the person is considered as a sinner.

Imān is a perspective and the state of heart and mind. Although, the legal schools, mazhabs, require imān to be verbally pronounced, the real state and essence of imān is at the heart and mind. Therefore, there were a lot of salaf, the prior practicing pious Muslims, who were using this

---

132. Indeed, those who disbelieve in Allah and His messengers and wish to discriminate between Allah and His messengers and say, "We believe in some and disbelieve in others," and wish to adopt a way in between.

133. Those are the disbelievers, truly. And We have prepared for the disbelievers a humiliating punishment.

134. But they who believe in Allah and His messengers and do not discriminate between any of them—to those He is going to give their rewards. And ever is Allah Forgiving and Merciful.

135. And say, "We believe in some and disbelieve in others."

136. Those are the disbelievers, truly.

137. But they who believe in Allah and His messengers and do not discriminate between any of them.

positive uncertainty to increase their relationship with Allah ﷻ till they die. They were genuinely fearful of meeting with Allah ﷻ whether they had genuine imān or not in their heart eventhough they dedicated all their lives in worship and good action. Imān is an attitude, psychology and perspective of the person.

Imān is an attitude. The guidance from Allah ﷻ comes with attitude. In other words, one can also say that guidance from Allah ﷻ comes as a result of this attitude. In that perspective, one can look classical aqāid books of Islam such as Taftazani that he mentions guidance from Allah ﷻ is a Nûr, light, due to this attitude of internal and external critical thinking with experience and open-mindedness (13) with different signs of Allah ﷻ in the nature or in one's consciousness. In another perspective, one can explain this guidance from Allah ﷻ in the field of mysticism as the experiential attitude of open-mindedness, ethical behavior, humbleness, and struggle to practice (7). The guidance in all cases is from Allah ﷻ. Guidance leading to imān is a state of merging this sincere attitude of struggle with the true and correct knowledge about Allah ﷻ and religion. This is the main guidance. After this stage, there can be different levels of guidance through practice and keeping, upholding and refreshing this initial state of imān.

Imān is also the asset of the person. Any possible danger that can challenge the health of imān should be addressed immediately. If not, it can spread in one's spiritual heart and metastasizes in the person's true and genuine relationship with Allah ﷻ.

One of the possible dangers in this relationship are sins. If the effects of the sins are removed with repentance, tawba, then the relationship with Allah ﷻ can grow potentially and positively. Another challenge to uphold a sound imān is unnecessary and useless engagements. Another one is less dhikr and remembrance of Allah ﷻ.

In all cases, one should realize that imān is the biggest lifetime asset of the person, if the person does not give value to it and endanger it with unnecessary and purposeless engagements, then the person can lose it.

Below is a psychological example of kufr and imān:

A person is granted life as a privilege from non-existence to the world of fears and unknowns. As this person is expecting mercy, sicknesses, accidents, fears, anxieties and the evils like an enemy attack this person in everyday life. When the person looks into nature and reasons, this person does not find mercy but darkness. When the person looks at the space, stars, planets and meteors, the possibility of them crashing to earth makes the person tremble and scare more. Finally, the person finds only solution to reflect in silence and meditate, but then this person lively needs scream. Then, his or her conscience become as if it would explode.

In addition, this person looks at his or her needs, and abilities, strength and power, and understands that he or she is weak, poor and very limited. This person knows that no one can truly help her even though she asks for help. She or he starts seeing everything as an enemy on the earth and as an alien. She or he regrets living and curses being in the world.

On the other hand, when the person enters to sirat al mustaqim, when the person's heart, mind and soul are illuminated with imān, then the previous kufur related psychological perspective becomes colorful, delightful and with light.

When the enemies attack this person, such as sickness, accidents, or other evils, this person asks help and protection from Allah ﷻ, the All Powerful. When the person thinks all her or his internal faculties and emotions, they all desire eternity and not dying. Knowing that there is an eternal life after death, then this anxiety cools down and the person becomes calm with longing for God and the afterlife but not scared or fearful as before.

When the person looks at the space stars, moon, and meteors, now he or she understands that they all work together under the control of Allah ﷻ. They see them as all friends and signs from Allah ﷻ instead of seeing them as something scary and fearful as it was before.

Wherever or whatever this person looks now, everything tells this person "please don't be scared and fearful from us, we are all servants of Rabbul Alamin, Allah ﷻ."

When the person compares these two states and perspectives of kufr and imān, this person truly appreciates imān, Islam, and Allah ﷻ and says:

الْحَمْدُ الله على نعمت الايمان والإسلام[138]

---

138. All praise is due to Allah for the blessing of Imān and Islam.

Imān and Itqan

One of the highest levels of imān, the belief is itqan.

The Qurān gives the example of Ibrahim as. [139]وَكَذَلِكَ نُرِي إِبْرَاهِيمَ مَلَكُوتَ السَّمَاوَاتِ وَالْأَرْضِ وَلِيَكُونَ مِنَ الْمُوقِنِينَ

Allah ﷻ opens the door of understanding in its true sense to Ibrahim as. Rasulullah ﷺ's journey of miraj gives the highest itqan among all creation. The case of the Prophet ﷺ with Abu Bakr ra in the cave is another example. Someone may ask why Abu Bakr ra 's imān is heavier than all ummah. Due to itqan, quality of imān, similar to Ibrahim as. For example, Abu Bakr ra, when he was reported about miraj he said that if Rasulullah ﷺ reported it then he said "I believe in miraj." He did not question. This is another example of itqan.

In all above discourses of imān and itqan or kufr, they are all attributes of the heart. In this perspective, humans do not have the skills and authority to truly know and judge if someone has imān, itqan or kufr until the person dies and meets with Allah ﷻ. Because, this is the action and position of the heart. But, there are signs of imān, itqan, kufr, and nifāq. The religious laws are based on external affairs but not the internal affairs in these fields of belief.

In another perspective, everyone is innately given the potential to have imān from birth. But with the person's choice and spending all one's efforts and actions in one's life in a different perspective, a second nature of kufr can establish in the person besides the natural disposition, the fitrah as mentioned in

{ ثُمَّ قَسَتْ قُلُوبُكُم مِّن بَعْدِ ذَلِكَ فَهِيَ كَالْحِجَارَةِ أَوْ أَشَدُّ قَسْوَةً وَإِنَّ مِنَ الْحِجَارَةِ لَمَا يَتَفَجَّرُ مِنْهُ الْأَنْهَارُ وَإِنَّ مِنْهَا لَمَا يَشَّقَّقُ فَيَخْرُجُ مِنْهُ الْمَاء وَإِنَّ مِنْهَا لَمَا يَهْبِطُ مِنْ خَشْيَةِ اللَّهِ وَمَا اللَّهُ بِغَافِلٍ عَمَّا تَعْمَلُونَ [140]{البَقَرة/74} }

The expression ثُمَّ can signify that this is a second fitrah. This is a second nature of kufr, disbelief, unrecognition or unappreciative disposition. As also mentioned similarly that the kufr is a process and it

---

139. And thus did We show Abraham the realm of the heavens and the earth that he would be among the certain [in faith].

140. 2:74 And yet, after all this, your hearts hardened and became like rocks, or even harder: for, behold, there are rocks from which streams gush forth; and, behold, there are some from which, when they are cleft, water issues; and, behold, there are some that fall down for awe of God. And God is not unmindful of what you do!

does not immediately happen. In the verses below, the expressions قَسَتْ[141]
قُلُوبُهُمْ can show that the kufr is a process not an immediate outcome.

وَلَقَدْ أَرْسَلْنَا إِلَى أُمَمٍ مِّن قَبْلِكَ فَأَخَذْنَاهُمْ بِالْبَأْسَاءِ وَالضَّرَّاءِ لَعَلَّهُمْ يَتَضَرَّعُونَ {الأنعام/42}[142]
فَلَوْلَا إِذْ جَاءَهُمْ بَأْسُنَا تَضَرَّعُواْ وَلَكِن قَسَتْ قُلُوبُهُمْ وَزَيَّنَ لَهُمُ الشَّيْطَانُ مَا كَانُواْ يَعْمَلُونَ
{الأنعام/43}[143]

Or

أَلَمْ يَأْنِ لِلَّذِينَ آمَنُوا أَن تَخْشَعَ قُلُوبُهُمْ لِذِكْرِ اللَّهِ وَمَا نَزَلَ مِنَ الْحَقِّ وَلَا يَكُونُوا كَالَّذِينَ أُوتُوا
الْكِتَابَ مِن قَبْلُ فَطَالَ عَلَيْهِمُ الْأَمَدُ فَقَسَتْ قُلُوبُهُمْ وَكَثِيرٌ مِّنْهُمْ فَاسِقُونَ {الحديد/16}[144]

اللَّهم احفظنا من هذا امين[145]

وَخَشِيَ الرَّحْمَنَ بِالْغَيْبِ: *True Imān and Inzar*

One can view the gist of imān, belief is to have taqwa and khashyah of
Allah ﷻ when there is no one around in solitude as mentioned:

وَسَوَاءٌ عَلَيْهِمْ أَأَنذَرْتَهُمْ أَمْ لَمْ تُنذِرْهُمْ لاَ يُؤْمِنُونَ {يس/10}[146] إِنَّمَا تُنذِرُ مَنِ اتَّبَعَ الذِّكْرَ
وَخَشِيَ الرَّحْمَن بِالْغَيْبِ فَبَشِّرْهُ بِمَغْفِرَةٍ وَأَجْرٍ كَرِيمٍ {يس/11}
{[147] مَنْ خَشِيَ الرَّحْمَن بِالْغَيْبِ وَجَاءَ بِقَلْبٍ مُّنِيبٍ {ق/33}[148]

---

141. Their heats hardened.
142. 6:42 And, indeed, We sent Our messages unto people before thy time, [O Prophet,] and
visited them with misfortune and hardship so that they might humble themselves.
143. 6:43) Yet when the misfortune decreed by Us befell them, they did not humble
themselves, but rather their hearts grew hard, for Satan had made all their doings seem
goodly to them.
144. (57:16) IS IT NOT time that the hearts of all who have attained to faith should feel
humble at the remembrance of God and of all the truth that has been bestowed [on them]
from on high, lest they become like those who were granted revelation aforetime, and whose
hearts have hardened with the passing of time so that many of them are [now] depraved?
145. Oh Allah, protect us from this, Amìn.
146. (36:10) thus, it is all one to them whether thou warnest them or dost not warn them:
they will not believe.
147. 36:11 Thou canst [truly] warn only him who is willing to take the reminder to heart,
and who stands in awe of the Most Gracious although He is beyond the reach of human
perception: unto such, then, give the glad tiding of [God's] forgiveness and of a most excellent
reward.
148. (50:33) [everyone] who stood in awe of the Most Gracious although He is beyond the
reach of human perception, and who has come [unto Him] with a heart full of contrition.

The reality of imān and one's relationship with Allah ﷻ reveals one's true disposition when one is alone. If someone wants to spend time in solitude to pray, worship to Allah ﷻ and makes this one's top priority in life and takes the most pleasure to be with Allah ﷻ when the person is alone, then a person can show the signs of being مَنْ خَشِيَ الرَّحْمَنَ بِالْغَيْبِ.[149] A person in this state with the Fadl of Allah ﷻ can be in the steps of وَجَاءَ بِقَلْبٍ مُّنِيبٍ[150]. Here, the word مُنِيب is used instead of سليم compared to other ayahs. This could be that when a person makes a habit of turning to Allah ﷻ constantly, and regularly especially in solitude with بِالْغَيْبِ[151] then, this title of مُنِيب, munib is given to this person, اللهم جعلنا منهم[152] ، امين

وَسَوَاءٌ عَلَيْهِمْ

The expression سَوَاءٌ عَلَيْهِمْ[153] is used instead of سَوَاءٌ عليك. This can imply that the person should still do invitation although it doesn't matter for this people with the expression سَوَاءٌ عَلَيْهِمْ. If there was a discouragement not to invite them عليك سَوَاءٌ can be used which is not the case here. On the other hand, the expression سَوَاءٌ عَلَيْهِمْ can signal the character of these people in an explicit way. In this regards, the people of "I don't care," can fit in this category.

One can think that if there is this expression then, why is inzar or telling people about Allah ﷻ and about true religion important? First, every person is created in a state of pure natural fitrah. Therefore, sometimes, this natural disposition is referred as hanif. In the original state of creation, everyone is in pure, clean and in natural disposition in Islam which can be called as fitrah. The kasb, the acquirement of the person comes later with free choice. It is interesting to note that a person can feel the traces of this fitrah in the early morning hours when a person immediately wakes up. One can call this maybe a pseudo hanif or fitrah state. At this time of the day, the person is not exposed with all the artificial exposure of the thoughts and feelings acquired over the course of the day. Therefore, if one really can look at oneself at those times, the natural fitrah can be gripped and saved against the evil

---

149. [Everyone] who stood in awe of the Most Gracious although He is beyond the reach of human perception.
150. And who has come [unto Him] with a heart full of contrition.
151. Beyond the reach of human perception.
152. Oh Allah, make us from among them.
153. It is the same for them.

encounters of the person's self-thoughts and depression states during the day. Even one can look at this in the morning prayers, duas of the Prophet as " اصبحنا على فطرة الاسلام وعلى كلمة الإخلاص وعلى دين نبينا محمد صلى الله عله وسلم وعلى ملة أبينا إبراهيم حنيفا مسلم وما كان من المشركين [154] " (15). In Sûrah Yâsîn, when people are waken up in their graves, it is mentioned to allude the shocking times when one wakes up to signal the truth and fitrah state of the person, الله اعلم. The ayah is قَالُوا يَا وَيْلَنَا مَن بَعَثَنَا مِن مَّرْقَدِنَا هَذَا مَا وَعَدَ الرَّحْمَنُ وَصَدَقَ الْمُرْسَلُونَ {يس/52}.

Secondly, the prophets, messengers and signs come in one's life to justify the witnesses that Allah ﷻ has sent evidence in one's life. So that, there is no counter logical argument of the person with his or her free choice in front of Allah ﷻ in afterlife. One can review the verses in Sûrah Ahzab 33/45, Sûrah Fatih 48/8 and Sûrah Muzzammil 73/15. In this perspective, the Prophet in his life time asks his followers, this question: "Will you witness me in the afterlife that I gave the message to you?" So, this shows that the messengers also have accountability of fulfilling their mission and they will be also asked this responsibility in the Day of Accountability.

It is interesting to note that the word[155] كَفَرُو comes in the ayah in the past form. This may signify that before all of these external witnesses, self-witnessing in the course of one's life journey is paramount. In other words, it is known that these people made choice for kufr. One can ask the question why أَمْ لَمْ تُنذِرْهُمْ [156] is mentioned? Sometimes, there are types of tabligh or inzar that may prefer silence style instead of verbal or active discourse (1). But, as the remaining part of the ayah mentions as لاَ يُؤْمِنُونَ, even this method may not work out.

The expression of وَسَوَاء عَلَيْهِمْ in Sûrah Baqarah in this ayah also comes in Sûrah Yâsîn as سَوَاء عَلَيْهِمْ أَأَنذَرْتَهُمْ أَمْ لَمْ تُنذِرْهُمْ لاَ يُؤْمِنُونَ {يس/10} [157] إِنَّمَا تُنذِرُ مَنِ اتَّبَعَ الذِّكْرَ وَخَشِيَ الرَّحْمَن بِالْغَيْبِ فَبَشِّرْهُ بِمَغْفِرَةٍ وَأَجْرٍ كَرِيمٍ {يس/11} [158]

---

154. We have become the instinct of Islam, the word of sincerity, the religion of the Prophet Muhammed (ﷺ), and the religion of our father Abraham, a true Muslim, and no polytheists.
155. Disbelieve.
156. Or do not warn them.
157. (36:10) Thus, it is all one to them whether thou warnest them or dost not warn them: they will not believe.
158. 36:11 Thou canst [truly] warn only him who is willing to take the reminder to heart, and who stands in awe of the Most Gracious although He is beyond the reach of human perception: unto such, then, give the glad tiding of [God's] forgiveness and of a most excellent reward

A possible reason can be that it is mainly people's attitude that they don't have وَخَشِيَ الرَّحْمَنَ, fear and respect and appreciation of Allah ﷻ, the Most Merciful, the Most Caring الرَّحْمَن. It is interesting to note that with the word خَشِيَ the name and attribute of Allahالرَّحْمَن ﷻ is present.

In this verse, the expression أَأَنذَرْتَهُمْ أَمْ لَمْ تُنذِرْهُمْ[159], also shows the inzar perspective in order to establish caution for the results of an evil. In a simpler way, it is a warning for them for the evil outcomes. Because, it is at least expected to stop an oppressor by telling them the consequences of their evil by scaring them and make them fearful of the accountability. If this person has still some soundness of mind, then he or she may say "I don't want to continue this evil because I don't want to be in prison."

In the disposition of kufr, this shows that the abd, the person still does not establish fear from the authority and not thinking and appreciating what Allah ﷻ gave to this person. In this case, the person really does not need to be in a group to show this sincere attitude because وَخَشِيَ الرَّحْمَنَ بِالْغَيْبِ[160], shows that this attitude should sincerely present at a solitude بِالْغَيْبِ. In other words, the person without others, being alone, can put his or her true and sincere disposition. If this is not done, a person can be blocking oneself from self-reflection. In other words, some people don't want to be alone and facing their own selves. Because of their attitude, Allah ﷻ creates and enables what they want by:

[7] Translating the Qurān in English

خَتَمَ اللّٰهُ عَلَى قُلُوبِهِمْ وَعَلَى سَمْعِهِمْ وَعَلَى أَبْصَارِهِمْ غِشَاوَةٌ وَلَهُمْ عَذَابٌ عظِيمٌ {البقرة/2}[161]

The English translations of the above ayah have some incorrect renderings. To bring the exegetical meanings to the translation, I think, the above verse should be translated as Allah ﷻ created the means of sealing their hearts due to their desire and persistent kasb, acquirement with their intention, inclination and struggle, الله اعلم[162].

---

159. Whether you warn them or do not warn them.
160. [Everyone) who stood in awe of the Most Gracious although He is beyond the reach of human perception.
161. 2:7 Allah has set a seal upon their hearts and upon their hearing, and over their vision is a veil. And for them is a great punishment.
162. Allah knows best.

One of the problems with translations is the concept and expectation of one word being replaced in another word in the target language. I think that is a full incorrect rendering and assumption, that one may call a myth. Then, another myth occurs when this word by word translations are called "literal" translations. This is another problem. What is literal? Is it word by word translation from source to target language? Is it the immediate meanings in the source language with its all perspectives of context then transferring to target language? I would choose the second case and challenge all this popular discourses in scriptural translations. One should admit that all translations are interpretations. They are not the original.

One of the reasons for the need for this contextual and scholarly translations, especially on this ayah, is that there has been a lot of intellectual war on this verse. With these intellectual wars, different groups and sects were formed: Mutazilah, Qadarriya, Jabriya, and Ahlu Sunnah wal Jamah. Therefore, ignoring all these historical debates, formations and translating to any language can be problematic. For the reader, it is also important to pay attention in these ayahs with perspectives in order to know the reasons and debates about the reasons of separation. The current dominant or normative practice today can be then reflected on the translation.

Without going to the details of these splits, according to the understanding of normative approach of this verse in ahlu sunnah, for everything there are two perspectives: external and internal meanings, reasons and implications. One can call the external as the perspective of "mulk" and the other one, the internal as the "malakut." Both words of mulk and malakut are mentioned in the Qurān. Mulk perspective is immediate and external of what we see and perceive. Malakut is the essence and reasons behind the seen and immediately perceived. The mulk perspective can sometimes look good, ugly or evil. But, the malakut perspective of the same incident is always good and beautiful. In this perspective, there is no absolute evil but there is an absolute good and beauty. The relative evil looking incidents in world of mulk are in their essence are good and beautiful in the world of the malakut. Mulk world is the world and affairs that are visible and observable in the ordinary human realm. Malakut world is the world and affairs that are visible and known to Allah ﷻ and with the permission of Allah ﷻ, it can be visible and known by angels, other beings, and some humans close to Allah ﷻ such as Prophets.

تَبَارَكَ الَّذِي بِيَدِهِ الْمُلْكُ وَ هُوَ عَلَى كُلِّ شَيْءٍ قَدِيرٌ {1/الملك}[163]

So, the above ayah shows that the observable incidents for humans such as death and life are all created by Allah ﷻ. But Allah ﷻ knows and teaches the malakut perspective by

الَّذِي خَلَقَ الْمَوْتَ وَالْحَيَاةَ لِيَبْلُوَكُمْ أَيُّكُمْ أَحْسَنُ عَمَلًا وَ هُوَ الْعَزِيزُ الْغَفُورُ {2/الملك}[164]

Then, another perspective can be

الَّذِي خَلَقَ سَبْعَ سَمَاوَاتٍ طِبَاقًا مَّا تَرَى فِي خَلْقِ الرَّحْمَنِ مِن تَفَاوُتٍ فَارْجِعِ الْبَصَرَ هَلْ تَرَى مِن فُطُورٍ {3/الملك}[165]

that there are seven layers. Once the person knows the realities, maybe their names, then the malakut perspectives is shown by Allah ﷻ such as in the case of Ibrahim as, الله اعلم. All this discussion has connection with the concepts of destiny, qadar, evil, good, qada, kasb in this ayah as some explanations will follow (1).

One should differentiate that there is a fine line between the concept of the action of Allah ﷻ creating and the person's intention, inclination and fulfilling the means to achieve that action. For example, if a person had an intention to hurt someone with a gun, and takes the gun to shoot someone, the effect of this shooting on the other individual, for example death is created by Allah ﷻ. The person has the free will to do good or bad with free choice but there is an accountability for this person in the world and in the afterlife. In this case of shooting, the person is blamed who performed this evil. If Allah ﷻ did not create the effects of the means and reasons, then there would not be the concept of free will or free choice in good or bad. The people will not get or achieve what they desire to achieve.

---

163. 67:1 HALLOWED be He in whose hand all dominion rests, since He has the power to will anything.

164. 67:2 [He] who created death and life to test you [as to] which of you is best in deed—and He is the Exalted in Might, the Forgiving.

165. (3) [Hallowed be] He who has created seven heavens in full harmony with one another: 2 No fault will thou see in the creation of the Most Gracious. And turn thy vision [upon it] once more: canst thou see any flaw?

On the other hand, Allah ﷻ limits the extend of evils that humans potentially deserve and intend due to Allah's ﷻ mercy and fadl. These ways of Allah ﷻ can be mystical, unknown for most people but not mystical for a few elect people close to Allah ﷻ. In this reality, if a person achieves doing good or protected from evil engagements in one's life, it is truly due to the fadl and mercy of Allah ﷻ but a tiny portion of this effort, maybe as an intention or inclination (kasb) can be credited to the person. Oppositely, if an evil touches the person, the person should in reality look one's free choice or free will in desiring the occurrence of this evil. In some cases, the evil looking incidents can hit the person without their control. This may have another perspective to elevate one's level in one's relation to Allah ﷻ. In other words, it could be a recall message to go back to Allah ﷻ and establish positive relationship with the Creator.

In another perspective, there is the Full Will Power of Allah ﷻ. Then, Allah ﷻ created humans with a microscopic will power due to their free will and free choice in their short span of lives. Humans' will power is so small that there are discussions in the Islamic scholarship if it should be called intention, or inclination of the person rather than willpower. In this perspective, when the person intents and inclines towards an action, then Allah ﷻ makes and creates the intended action for the free choice of the human being. In this sense, the Creator of this action is Allah ﷻ but the one who made the choice is the person. So, the person cannot blame anyone but oneself in dealing with a bad outcome of an action.

In addition, the action emerges in the world of ours, when the Infinite Will Power coincides with the tiny will power of humans. Because, most of the time Allah ﷻ does not allow the evil to emerge due to the Divine Mercy and Fadl. But, the person keeps asking and struggling for the outcome of this evil. Then, at this time, due to this person's free will and choice, Allah ﷻ creates this action. On the other hand, Allah ﷻ gives the Mercy and Fadl without the person deserving it. For example, creation from nothing, seeing, hearing, eating, tasting, imān and guidance are all due and from the Fadl and Mercy of Allah ﷻ.

Another important methodology in the aqāidah is that knowing something, i'lm follows the knowledge, malum. In other words, when someone knows something, it is a discovery of a reality that is already there. If the person does not know or does know discover, the reality, the existing knowledge, and the science, i'lm, are still there. Therefore, the title of this book is al-istinbatu meaning knowing, and discovering what is already there. The authors and the people's discovery does not make a change to the reality of the ocean of the Qurān. Similarly, in the essence of creation, Allah ﷻ created humans so that they can discover and do istinbāt, synthesis and analysis from what is already there. So that, the person can reveal this fact to oneself and others. In short, there is no invention but discovery.

Therefore, asma is used in the Qurān that Allah ﷻ taught to Adam as. Name of something as mentioned as asma does not add a value to that reality, and science. Humans' knowledge does not add anything but the effort of discovery. In this effort, all synthetizes, critical thinking and discovery can all happen. We can call this science today. If there is the conservation of energy in physics, we did not make it. It is there existing. Allah ﷻ made it. We discovered it. We are using it in different applications of engineering. Then, we can call this theoretical science, knowing the conservation of energy. Applying this discovery, on an appliance such as refrigerator can be called applied science. We are using and synthesizing what is already there.

Finally, knowing Allah ﷻ truly can be related with one of the statements believed to be Hadis Qudsi although not cited in authentic hadith books, about the Kanz can possibly support this notion (16), الله اعلم [166]. Allah ﷻ is always there, Present, Al-Hayy and Al-Kayyum. Humans' true knowledge Allah ﷻ is the purpose of creation. The positive sciences are the steps to serve this ultimate goal of knowing the Creator, the One, Allah ﷻ. If a person does not know Allah ﷻ truly then it does not change anything from the reality but a miserable and incorrect rendering of the meanings and purpose in life and afterlife. If a person knows Allah ﷻ it does change everything but a happy, falāh, and true renderings of the meanings and purpose in this life and afterlife.

In another perspective, the infinite knowledge of Allah ﷻ can be also referred as qadar, destiny or the Divine Determination. Knowing the

---

166. Allah knows best.

outcome does not make the person avoid their responsibility of free will and free choice.

The interpretations of this verse generally focus on the concept and belief of destiny, qadar. Besides these main discussions on destiny, one can look different perspectives on this ayah as well. As the similar ayah is present in Sûrah Yâsîn as [167] وَجَعَلْنَا مِن بَيْنِ أَيْدِيهِمْ سَدًّا وَمِنْ خَلْفِهِمْ سَدًّا فَأَغْشَيْنَاهُمْ فَهُمْ لاَ يُبْصِرُونَ {يس/9}

The ones attitude towards not appreciation and appreciating Allah ﷻ is expressed with their perspective of not seeing [168] وَعَلَى أَبْصَارِهِمْ غِشَاوَةٌ in Sûrah Baqarah above. A similar expression is present in Sûrah Yâsîn as فَأَغْشَيْنَاهُمْ فَهُمْ لاَ يُبْصِرُونَ {يس/9}.

If one corresponds two ayahs respectively a possible interpretation can reveal. The expression خَتَمَ اللهُ عَلَى قُلُوبِهِمْ وَعَلَى سَمْعِهِمْ in Sûrah Baqarah can correspond to وَجَعَلْنَا مِن بَيْنِ أَيْدِيهِمْ سَدًّا وَمِنْ خَلْفِهِمْ سَدًّا in Sûrah Yâsîn. One can view basirah is the final perspective that is gained through qalb and sam. In other perspective, a person can see with two eyes بَيْنِ أَيْدِيهِمْ سَدًّا through his qalb. The same person can hear and learn وَمِنْ خَلْفِهِمْ سَدًّا from all the directions with his ear and listening and being humble, [169] الله اعلم.

Here, the qulub does not refer to the biological heart. The sam' is hearing but it is not the biological ear organ which has another name as uzun. The basar is not biological eye, which is a'yn. In that perspective, these people can still have biological hearts, ears and eyes. But they are not used properly. The words, qulub and absar are plural and sam is singular. In other words, one singular is presented among two plurals. This can signify that there can be many internal ways to reach to Allah ﷻ through heart. Similarly, there can be many external ways to Allah ﷻ through eyes and seeing. But, the wahy or revelation is one and from Allah ﷻ. Allah ﷻ is one and the Prophet is one. If the person hears the one with one sam then with the guidance of Allah ﷻ and with the free choice of the person the person can be guided, الله اعلم.

Also, Qalb can endure different thoughts, feelings, states, and inspirations. Similarly, when a person looks there can be a lot of objects

---

167. (36:9) and We have set a barrier before them and a barrier behind them, and We have enshrouded them in veils so that they cannot see.
168. And over their vision is a veil.
169. Allah knows best.

in one's eye view. On the other hand, a person can only focus and analyze on one sound with a meaning, الله اعلم. If there are more than one sound there is a the state of confusion. Therefore, in sound systems, one considers everything as noise other than the desired sound for meaning, الله اعلم as mentioned:Except for our own voices, which reach us primarily through the bony structures in our heads, most sounds reach us through the air. We say they are airborne.

Noise is produced when an object or surface rapidly enough to generate a pressure wave or disturbance in the surrounding air (17).

It is interesting to note that the word خَتَمَ[170] is used for[172], قُلُوبِهِمْ[171] سَمْعِهِمْ qulub and sam' but not for basar. There is غِشَاوَةٌ[173]for basar. The person can use one's eyes at one direction. At that point, the person has the choice and free will to form one's perspective. Therefore, there is curtain on their eyes that they form their own perspectives or curtains with their free will. They don't see the meanings of things beyond and behind. So, it is continuous act on this person's part till they die.

Also, عَلَى أَبْصَارِهِمْ غِشَاوَةٌ[174] is a jumla ismiyyah to reflect this continuity of the person's choice as a free will of not appreciating, believing and recognizing God. Therefore, with this person's continuous choice, then Allah ﷻ creates what they want with خَتَمَ أللّٰه عَلَى قُلُوبِهِمْ وَعَلَى سَمْعِهِم[175]. This is Jumla fiiliyah. It is done due to the desire of their jumla ismiyyah of their free choice.

Then, عَلَى قُلُوبِهِمْ وَعَلَى سَمْعِهِم[176] is used. Hearing and internalizing the meanings can come with wrong meanings. In other words, when the person looks external with basar with arrogance and not humbleness, then they internalize the meanings all over the place not through one direction with the word خَتَمَ, as their kasb, of their initial choice. Kasb can be translated into English with the word of acquirement. In other words, the person makes intention and inclination to acquire an action. The seed of acquirement is inclination and intention.

---

170. Seal.
171. On their hearts.
172. On their vision.
173. A veil.
174. Over their vision is a veil.
175. Allah has set a seal upon their hearts and upon their hearing.
176. Upon their hearts and upon their hearing.

In another perspective, one can also consider checking one's inclinations towards injustice or justice or fairness. Because, as stated

وَلاَ تَرْكَنُوا إِلَى الَّذِينَ ظَلَمُوا فَتَمَسَّكُمُ النَّارُ وَمَا لَكُم مِّن دُونِ اللَّهِ مِنْ أَوْلِيَاء ثُمَّ لاَ تُنصَرُونَ {هود/311}[177]

in the above ayah, the inclinations can transform into acquirement. One can see this approach of inclination in the phrase وَلاَ تَرْكَنُوا[178] that one should check one's heart and mind when there is an oppression where the person stands or feels towards.

The process of disbelief, (kufr)

كَلَّا بَلْ رَانَ عَلَى قُلُوبِهِم مَّا كَانُوا يَكْسِبُونَ[179] {المطففين/14}

The above ayah can signify the disconnection from imān. The isolation from the imān due to sins is a process not a one day or instant event. If a person can think the scientific process of رَانَ, rusting, it needs time for chemical reaction to happen. Allah ﷻ mentions this exactly as the process of rusting on the hearts with the expression رَانَ عَلَى قُلُوبِهِم[180]. This is exactly a literal translation of this expression. This rusting and detachment occur as a process due to the choices and actions of the person as the word يَكْسِبُونَ[181] can imply. In this regard, the word kasb is the person's acquirement and no one can blame, astaghfirullah and na'uzu billah Allah ﷻ that the choice of disbelief or misguidance, kufr, was a force or compulsion, اللَّه اعلم[182]. It is interesting to note that one of the ways to prevent rusting is painting. If the sins are like rust and painting can be the istighfār then, refreshment of imān will occur through tawba, i'lm, knowledge and ibadah, worship.

---

177. (11:113) And do not incline towards, nor rely upon, those who are bent on evildoing lest the fire [of the hereafter] touch you: for [then] you would have none to protect you from God, nor would you ever be succoured [by Him].
178. Do not incline.
179. No! Rather, the stain has covered their hearts of that which they were earning.
180. The stain has covered their hearts.
181. They were earning.
182. Allah knows best.

Therefore, one of the terms also mentioned in the Qurān is sibgah, صبغت[183], as the painting or anointed. The one who is painted or anointed by Allah ﷻ is protected against these rusting:

قُولُواْ آمَنَّا بِاللّهِ وَمَا أُنزِلَ إِلَيْنَا وَمَا أُنزِلَ إِلَى إِبْرَاهِيمَ وَإِسْمَاعِيلَ وَإِسْحَقَ وَيَعْقُوبَ وَالأَسْبَاطِ وَمَا أُوتِيَ مُوسَى وَعِيسَى وَمَا أُوتِيَ النَّبِيُّونَ مِن رَّبِّهِمْ لاَ نُفَرِّقُ بَيْنَ أَحَدٍ مِّنْهُمْ وَنَحْنُ لَهُ مُسْلِمُونَ {البقرة/136}[184] فَإِنْ آمَنُواْ بِمِثْلِ مَا آمَنتُم بِهِ فَقَدِ اهْتَدَواْ وَّإِن تَوَلَّوْاْ فَإِنَّمَا هُمْ فِي شِقَاقٍ فَسَيَكْفِيكَهُمُ اللّهُ وَهُوَ السَّمِيعُ الْعَلِيمُ {البقرة/137}[185] صِبْغَةَ اللّهِ وَمَنْ أَحْسَنُ مِنَ اللّهِ صِبْغَةً وَنَحْنُ لَهُ عَابِدونَ {البقرة/138}[186]

These are first the Prophets of Allah ﷻ. In Christianity the term, the anointed one is used for the Prophet Isa, Jesus as.

When the person sins then makes istighfār, the person may still feel remorse or regret in his or her heart although the person made istighfār. This is a good sign because the abilities of differentiating right or wrong is still present in the person. If the person does not make any istighfār the person can lose this ability over time. The sign of is that this person may not know or differentiate right or wrong.

It is important to look at the arguments and disagreements of the ideas about this ayah between groups of mutazilah, jabrriya, and ahlu Sunnah wal jamah. As one of the groups does give full power to the person in choice while the other does not give any power in choice of the person. Ahlu Sunnah stays in the middle way but not being in one end. One can review these discussions. When the kasb, the person's choice, coincide with the Divine Choice, then the action of something is required and happens immediately. In this perspective, Allah ﷻ does not make evil, a'zubillah and astagfirullah, or prevents people from belief. Oppositely, Allah ﷻ gives mahl, time to the person and does not create the evil action what the person has been constantly asking. But,

---

183. The religion.
184. 2:136 Say: "We believe in God, and in that which has been bestowed from on high upon us, and that which has been bestowed upon Abraham and Ishmael and Isaac and Jacob and their descendants, 111 and that which has been vouchsafed to Moses and Jesus; and that which has been vouchsafed to all the [other] prophets by their Sustainer: we make no distinction between any of them.112 And it is unto Him that we surrender ourselves."
185. 2:137 And if [others] come to believe in the way you believe, they will indeed find themselves on the right path; and if they turn away, it is but they who will be deeply in the wrong, and God will protect thee from them: for He alone is all-hearing, all-knowing.
186. 2:138 [Say: "Our life takes its] hue from God! And who could give a better hue [to life] than God, if we but truly worship Him?"

the person continues asks and asks, then fulfills all the means for the formation of this evil. After, Allah ☬creates what this person wants as this person demands it with free choice.

On the other hand, for the good again this person desires it to happen. Then, Allah ☬helps and gives blessings and barakah in this person's renderings in this world and afterlife. Even if the person may not achieve what he or she wanted Allah ☬ still rewards this person according his or her intention.

The expression خَتَمَ أللهُ [187] can classify some people in another category. The negative influence of one to another at the level of imãn can be possibly prevented by recognizing who the people of kãfir, munãfiq and who the wali are. These classification can be knowing them and letting oneself to affect their influence in one's core of imãn or not.

In other words, the imãn is the core, pure and genuine asset of the person. In these perspective, the harmful effects are closed and sealed in order not to affect others. This can be another interpretation for خَتَمَ أللّهُ. In other words, when the person does not recognize Allah ☬, there are some harmful radiation that can come from the heart of the person which can be deadly for others. Allah ☬ seal this invisibly in order to protect others, 1, (أللهُ اعلم[188]).

The word خَتَمَ is also used by the Prophet ﷺ in one of the hadith (18) (932) in a positive context for the word امين, amin. When one person finishes prayer, the person can say "Amìn" as a stamp and a seal as similar to a person mailing an important package with express mail which the person expects the delivery with certainty and insurance. In this hadith, as the word خَتَمَ alludes to the last action in a process, similarly the expression خَتَمَ أللّهُ can allude to the fact that a person in his or her all life was in the state and struggle of kufr, therefore due to this kasb possibly before or by death this person's heart is sealed and stamped and sent to the next world after death, [189] أللهُ اعلم أللهم احفظنا من هذا امين

The expression وَلَهُمْ عَذَابٌ عظيم[190] signifies that due to this kasb لَهُمْ[191] is used. In other words, instead of عليهم the word لَهُمْ is used to possibly underline their kasb, acquirement. After the accountability of each

---

187. Allah has veiled.
188. Allah knows everything.
189. Oh Allah, protect us from this.
190. And they have a great punishment.
191. They have.

person in the Day of Judgement, they are due to punishment not given for any reason but due to their acquirement as underlined with the expression and harf lam in لَهُمْ as the case of the specificity.

اللّهم احفظنا من هذا امين

The word عَذَابٌ have the similar letters of عذب, a'zbun which means sweet water. In this perspective, similar combination of letters of punishment alluding to sweetness can increase the feelings of regret and remorse for a person that this person had the potential to be in the state of sweetness and pleasure in paradise, Jannah but now due to his or her free choice and constant struggle in this choice, this person resides in an opposite venue.

اللّهم احفظنا من هذا امين

In another perspective, the expression وَلَهُمْ عَذَابٌ عَظِيمٌ[192] can signify the state of spiritual punishment with fear, stress and anxiety in this world. In other words, there is the precious and diamond like valuable imān, but they preferred the opposite position with their choice. Now, they are in the spiritual distress although they may look confident and happy. The more devastating part will be in the afterlife. In this person's life, the burden and fear of death can already be imposing these uneasy moments.

اللّهم احفظنا من هذا امين

In the expression وَعَلَى سَمْعِهِمْ[193], a person can use one's hearing skills in order to get meaning. These meanings can change heart, mind, and spiritual state of the person. The utmost positive change of the heart and mind can be through the type of hearings. These can be related with increasing or decreasing one's imān. The Quranic recitation, sounds of dhikr, hadith, prayers with their meanings as well as the sounds in the nature, birds, animals, sounds of leaves, a gushing water or sounds in the space can be some of the examples. These sounds or hearings can

---

192. And they have a great punishment.
193. And on their hearing.

put the person to the utmost positive spiritual change of heart and mind if the person connects all this with Allah ﷻ.

On the other hand, if the person hears these sounds but does not get any meaning and does not connect with Allah ﷻ. These sounds can possibly lead the spiritual state of the person to melancholy, sadness, stress, anxiety, fear and uneasiness. For example in one room, in one space or a garden, two people can share the same space. One can enjoy everything with the nour of imān and the other can feel fearful and uneasy with the darkness of kufr.

اللّٰهم احفظنا من هذا امين

Similarly, if one looks at the expression وَعَلَى أَبْصَارِهِمْ[194], one can use the ability of seeing, the eyesight, either to get a meaning and pleasure or to get a pain or torture. For a person with imān, the person can connect everything with Rabbul Alamin and get a meaning and pleasure. On the other hand, if the person looks everything with randomness, with no structure, order or purpose, the eye sight, watching, looking and seeing can be a source of torture and pain.

In this ayah, Allah ﷻ sealed their hearts as a result of their choice. In other words, they chose not to believe in the previous ayahs as mentioned إِنَّ الَّذِينَ كَفَرُواْ سَوَاءٌ عَلَيْهِمْ أَأَنذَرْتَهُمْ أَمْ لَمْ تُنذِرْهُمْ لاَ {البقرة/66}[195]. Then, as a result of this خَتَمَ اللّٰهُ عَلَى قُلُوبِهِمْ وَعَلَى سَمْعِهِمْ وَعَلَى أَبْصَارِهِمْ غِشَاوَةٌ وَلَهُمْ عَذَابٌ عظِيمٌ {البقرة/7}[196] followed (1).

One can also view the light of imān, belief as an opportunity. In other words, when the signs, guidance and the Nûr of imān comes to the heart constantly and continuously, if the person is in uncaring attitude then, because of this attitude Allah ﷻ can seal the person's heart. Therefore, constant reflection, muraqaba about all the external and internal sciences are very critical in order one's heart not to be sealed or locked. The attitude of getting into the meaning of signs is very important. Here, I am not saying that one should leave all the clear guidelines of the Qurān and the Prophet and go behind these signs. No, in its actually all the clear guidelines from these clear two sources are in

---

194. And on their sight.
195. 2:6 BEHOLD, as for those who are bent on denying the truth—it is all one to them whether thou warnest them or dost not warn them: they will not believe.
196. (2:7) God; has sealed their hearts and their hearing, and over their eyes is a veil; and awesome suffering awaits them.

harmony if one knows or puts the effort of understanding them but not ignoring them.

اللهم اجعلنا ممن يستمعون القول ويتبعون احسنه [197]، آمين

On another note, in the expression خَتَمَ أللّٰه عَلَى [198] the word خَتَمَ is muteaddi verb and could have been used without the harf jar عَلَى but it is used with the harf jar عَلَى. This usage may signify that the sealing of the heart is not on the physical but spiritual heart, (1) (اللّٰه اعلم).

The expression خَتَمَ أللّٰه عَلَى قُلُوبِهِمْ [199] can also literally allude to a type of seal that cannot be known by humans but maybe possibly by angels, (1) (اللّٰه اعلم).

As one can see in this ayah خَتَمَ اللّٰه عَلَى قُلُوبِهِمْ وَعَلَى سَمْعِهِمْ وَعَلَى أَبْصَارِهِمْ, the heart comes before the ear and eyes. The possible reason for this can be that the place of imān is at the heart. The one who searchs, desires and needs the Creator is one's heart and conscience (1) . When heart thinks about life, it feels that it is weak and it has a lot of needs and immediately seeks something or someone to rely on. When heart thinks about its desires and goals to fulfill, it seeks something or someone for expectations and help. All these can be fulfilled with imān. Therefore, heart precedes others in the ayah.

In this perspective, qalb or heart has a critical sense for the person. The proper functioning of the physical heart as a piece of flesh is so critical for the body. Similarly, in this ayah, the spiritual heart or qalb has its critical importance to make decision for the person in the affairs of imān. When the physical heart stops the person dies. When the spiritual heart stops, then there is no imān. The person becomes not more than a moving body similar to a moving sculpture or statue.

It is interesting to note that in the ayah with the expression خَتَمَ [200] اللّٰه عَلَى قُلُوبِهِمْ وَعَلَى سَمْعِهِمْ وَعَلَى أَبْصَارِهِمْ, there are three times عَلَى is used instead of one. This can allude to different types of khatm or seal for each case of heart, hearing and seeing, اللّٰه اعلم.

Another phrase that comes in the Qurān is لَهُمْ عَذَابٌ عَظِيمٌ[201]. In this expression لَهُمْ is used with لـ instead of عَلَى. This can be their punishment

---

197. Oh Allah, make us from those who listen to the saying, and follow the best.
198. Allah has sealed upon.
199. Allah has sealed upon their hearts.
200. Allah has sealed upon their hearts, and their hearing, and over their vision.
201. And they have a great punishment.

is due to their kasb or what they deserve with this lam, الله اعلم. Therefore, in the upcoming ayahs this kasb is explained more as وَلَهُم عَذَابٌ أَلِيمٌ بِمَا كَانُوا يَكْذِبُونَ} 10/البقرة}[202]. In that sense, there is no zulm or oppression to them but the person gets what they deserve, الله اعلم.

اللّهم احفظنا من هذا امين

The expression وَعَلَى أَبْصَارِهِمْ غِشَاوَةٌ[203] is jumla ismiyyah. This may show that the objects that one views with one's eyes can be constant and not changing. When compared to the expression خَتَمَ اللهُ عَلَى قُلُوبِهِمْ[204] وَعَلَى سَمْعِهِمْ with jumla fiiliyah can signal changing ideas, thoughts and engagements of listening, الله اعلم.

In another perspective, the expression وَعَلَى أَبْصَارِهِمْ غِشَاوَةٌ[205] as jumla ismiyyah can signify that this is their kasb. Therefore, خَتَمَ اللهُ عَلَى قُلُوبِهِمْ وَعَلَى سَمْعِهِمْ, that Allah ﷻ sealed their hearts and uzun.

In the expression عَلَى أَبْصَارِهِمْ غِشَاوَةٌ, the word غِشَاوَة[206] is in nakrah but not in marifah. So, this spiritual cover, غِشَاوَة, is not definite and is not explicit. However, it is something that cannot be seen with normal eyes to everyone, الله اعلم.

In the expression عَذَابٌ عَظِيمٌ, the word عظيم can be used also for positive things. However, the usage of this word with punishment can also signal a type of humiliation for the people, الله اعلم. One can also reflect on the relationship of heart, hearing, uzun and seeing, basar in the ayah:

أَفَلَمْ يَسِيرُوا فِي الْأَرْضِ فَتَكُونَ لَهُمْ قُلُوبٌ يَعْقِلُونَ بِهَا أَوْ آذَانٌ يَسْمَعُونَ بِهَا فَإِنَّهَا لَا تَعْمَى الْأَبْصَارُ وَلَكِن تَعْمَى الْقُلُوبُ الَّتِي فِي الصُّدُورِ} 46/الحج}[207]

So, qalb is the essence and it has a special relationship both with uzun and basar. Seeing with heart is an expression that is used in the language. In other words, a person first sees an object, then the meanings

202. (2:10) In their hearts is disease, and so God lets their disease increase; and grievous suffering awaits them because of their persistent lying.
203. And over their vision a veil.
204. Allah has set a seal upon their hearts and upon their hearing.
205. And over their vision is a veil.
206. A veil.
207. 22:46 Have they, then, never journeyed about the earth, letting their hearts gain wisdom, and causing their ears to hear? Yet, verily, it is not their eyes that have become blind—but blind have become the hearts that are in their breasts!

and emotions related with it are processed in the mind and heart. Then, a person forms an opinion and emotion in the heart. In other words, hearts in this case process the data and puts a disposition. Therefore, as one can see with both expressions of وَلَكِن تَعْمَى الْقُلُوبُ الَّتِي فِي الصُّدُورِ[208] and خَتَمَ أللهُ عَلَى قُلُوبِهِمْ[209] the heart has a critical stance of being blind or sealed as the responsible agent of what to do in one's life, الله اعلم.

One can ask why is the hikmah of the expression وَلَهُمْ عَذَابٌ عظِيمٌ[210]? As people are different why they choose to do something or not, there are a lot of people they tend to do evil or harm others but they don't do it due to their fear of imprisonment. Similarly, there are people in the discourses of religion who will follow the guidelines of Allah ﷻ because it is logical, and peaceful and they want to do it because they want to be grateful and appreciative to Allah ﷻ. Oppositely, there are people who would do it because they would be scared of imprisonment similar to the law enforcement in the world, الله اعلم.

In addition, extinction is an absolute evil. Even though a person is in punishment or in prison, he or she still would prefer to live instead of extinction or non-existence. In this perspective, the accountability on one angle reflects justice as mentioned in the above paragraph. On another angle, it is still the Rahmah of Allah ﷻ that even in accountability and punishment there is no extinction or non-existence, الله اعلم.

[8]

وَمِنَ النَّاسِ مَن يَقُولُ آمَنَّا بِاللهِ وَبِالْيَوْمِ الآخِرِ وَمَا هُم بِمُؤْمِنِينَ {البَقَرة/8} يُخَادِعُونَ اللهَ وَالَّذِينَ آمَنُوا وَمَا يَخْدَعُونَ إِلاَّ أَنفُسَهُم وَمَا يَشْعُرُونَ {البَقَرة/9} فِي قُلُوبِهِم مَّرَضٌ فَزَادَهُمُ اللهُ مَرَضاً وَلَهُم عَذَابٌ أَلِيمٌ بِمَا كَانُوا يَكْذِبُونَ {البَقَرة/10}[211]

There are 13 ayahs that follows the description of the munafiqûn immediately after the descriptions of the people of kufr and believers. As one can see the style of munafiqûn is itnab that the Qurān explains their situation in detail. When there is harm from outside one can take

---

208. But their hearts in their chest are blinded.
209. Allah has set a seal upon their hearts
210. And they have a great punishment.
211. 2:8 And there are people who say, "We do believe in God and the Last Day," the while they do not [really] believe. (2:9) They would deceive God and those who have attained to faith—the while they deceive none but themselves, and perceive it not. (2:10) In their hearts is disease, and so God lets their disease increase; and grievous suffering awaits them because of their persistent lying

precaution and prevention to increase one's immune and defense system. However, when one damage is happening inside and it is very difficult to detect then, it can harm the person more than outside harms. This can be similar to cancer cells that it is very difficult detect because they look normal but there is a disease which can be very difficult to its spread. Therefore, a lot of research needs to be done with separate hospitals to detect this type of disease. On the other hand, if it is a visible scar even one can treat it at home or at a clinic as an outpatient.

On the other hand, the matters related with internal matters of family such as between the children, spouses, between the parents and children or the cases of divorce can be more destructive for the person psychologically. Because, a person lives with another person and loves this person with high opinion and expectations. Then, when a problem occurs and continues with a chronicle case of no solution, then the end result becomes more destructive and devastating for the person. One can then rationalize and normalize the cases and warnings against the family matters in the Qurān in different Surahs such as Sūrah Yūsuf and other ayahs as for example:

وَاعْلَمُواْ أَنَّمَا أَمْوَالُكُمْ وَأَوْلَادُكُمْ فِتْنَةٌ وَأَنَّ اللَّهَ عِنْدَهُ أَجْرٌ عَظِيمٌ {الأنفال/28} يَا أَيُّهَا الَّذِينَ آمَنُواْ إِن تَتَّقُواْ اللَّهَ يَجْعَل لَّكُمْ فُرْقَاناً وَيُكَفِّرْ عَنكُمْ سَيِّئَاتِكُمْ وَيَغْفِرْ لَكُمْ وَاللَّهُ ذُو الْفَضْلِ الْعَظِيمِ {الأنفال/29} وَإِذْ يَمْكُرُ بِكَ الَّذِينَ كَفَرُواْ لِيُثْبِتُوكَ أَوْ يَقْتُلُوكَ أَوْ يُخْرِجُوكَ وَيَمْكُرُونَ {الأنفال/30} وَيَمْكُرُ اللَّهُ وَاللَّهُ خَيْرُ الْمَاكِرِينَ Allah ﷻ mentions the solution to be safe from these family trials as فُرْقَاناً وَيُكَفِّرْ عَنكُمْ سَيِّئَاتِكُمْ وَيَغْفِرْ لَكُمْ وَاللَّهُ ذُو الْفَضْلِ الْعَظِيمِ {الأنفال/29} which emphasizes the taqwa of Allah ﷻ. In this case if people internal or external still have plans, games, or plots as mentioned وَإِذْ يَمْكُرُ بِكَ الَّذِينَ كَفَرُواْ لِيُثْبِتُوكَ أَوْ يَقْتُلُوكَ أَوْ يُخْرِجُوكَ وَيَمْكُرُونَ وَيَمْكُرُ اللَّهُ وَاللَّهُ خَيْرُ الْمَاكِرِينَ {الأنفال/30}, then the person should not be worried when Allah ﷻ is on the side of this person, الله اعلم. One can review other ayahs of the Qurān in this context such as:

يَا أَيُّهَا الَّذِينَ آمَنُوا إِنَّ مِنْ أَزْوَاجِكُمْ وَأَوْلَادِكُمْ عَدُوًّا لَّكُمْ فَاحْذَرُوهُمْ وَإِن تَعْفُوا وَتَصْفَحُوا وَتَغْفِرُوا فَإِنَّ اللَّهَ غَفُورٌ رَّحِيمٌ {التغابن/14} إِنَّمَا أَمْوَالُكُمْ وَأَوْلَادُكُمْ فِتْنَةٌ وَاللَّهُ عِندَهُ أَجْرٌ عَظِيمٌ {التغابن/15}[212]

---

212. 64:14 O YOU who have attained to faith! Behold, some of your spouses and your children are enemies unto you: so beware of them! But if you pardon [their faults] and forbear, and forgive—then, behold, God will be much-forgiving, a dispenser of grace. (64:15) Your worldly goods and your children are but a trial and a temptation, whereas with God there is a tremendous reward.

On a side note, the case of children or family, wealth can be still trial and test but at a different perspective as

{ وَاسْتَفْزِزْ مَنِ اسْتَطَعْتَ مِنْهُم بِصَوْتِكَ وَأَجْلِبْ عَلَيْهِم بِخَيْلِكَ وَرَجِلِكَ وَشَارِكْهُمْ فِي الأَمْوَالِ وَالأَوْلَادِ وَعِدْهُمْ وَمَا يَعِدُهُمُ الشَّيْطَانُ إِلاَّ غُرُورًا }الإسراء/64[213]

وَقَالُوا نَحْنُ أَكْثَرُ أَمْوَالاً وَأَوْلَادًا وَمَا نَحْنُ بِمُعَذَّبِينَ {سبأ/35} قُلْ إِنَّ رَبِّي يَبْسُطُ الرِّزْقَ لِمَن يَشَاء وَيَقْدِرُ وَلَكِنَّ أَكْثَرَ النَّاسِ لَا يَعْلَمُونَ {سبأ/36} وَمَا أَمْوَالُكُمْ وَلَا أَوْلَادُكُم بِالَّتِي تُقَرِّبُكُمْ عِندَنَا زُلْفَى إِلَّا مَنْ آمَنَ وَعَمِلَ صَالِحًا فَأُوْلَئِكَ لَهُمْ جَزَاء الضِّعْفِ بِمَا عَمِلُوا وَهُمْ فِي الْغُرُفَاتِ آمِنُونَ {سبأ/37}[214]

Finally, in this discussion of nifāq, the internal affairs of fitnah, one should realize that whatever happens the end result which is the dhikr of Allah ﷻ and the relationship with Allah ﷻ should not be affected as mentioned:

يَا أَيُّهَا الَّذِينَ آمَنُوا لَا تُلْهِكُمْ أَمْوَالُكُمْ وَلَا أَوْلَادُكُمْ عَن ذِكْرِ اللَّهِ وَمَن يَفْعَلْ ذَلِكَ فَأُوْلَئِكَ هُمُ الْخَاسِرُونَ {المنافقون/9}[215]. It is interesting to note that the case of family affairs is mentioned in Sûrah munafiqûn , الله اعلم.

In another verse, Allah ﷻ mentions that

وَلَوْ نَشَاء لَأَرَيْنَاكَهُمْ فَلَعَرَفْتَهُم بِسِيمَاهُمْ وَلَتَعْرِفَنَّهُمْ فِي لَحْنِ الْقَوْلِ وَاللَّهُ يَعْلَمُ أَعْمَالَكُمْ {محمد/30}[216]

---

213. (17:64) Entice, then, with thy voice such of them as thou canst, and bear upon them with all thy horses and all thy men, and be their partner in [all sins relating to] worldly goods and children, and hold out [all manner of] promises to them: and [they will not know that] whatever Satan promises them is but meant to delude the mind.

214. (34:35) And they would add, "Richer [than you] are we in wealth and in children, and [so] we are not going to be made to suffer!" 34:36 (36) Say: "Behold, my Sustainer grants abundant sustenance, or gives it in scant measure, unto whomever He wills: but most men do not understand [God's ways]." (34:37) For, it is neither your riches nor your children that can bring you nearer to Us: only he who attains to faith and does what is right and just [comes near unto Us]; and it is [such as] these whom multiple recompense awaits for all that they have done; and it is they who shall dwell secure in the mansions [of paradise]

215. O you who have believed, let not your wealth and your children divert you from the remembrance of Allah. And whoever does that—then those are the losers.

216. And if We willed, We could show them to you, and you would know them by their mark; but you will surely know them by the tone of [their] speech. And Allah knows your deeds.

The above and below ayahs can show that Allah ﷻ did not inform about all the munāfiqs to the Prophet ﷺ. Allah ﷻ informed about some of them, maybe their leaders, but not all of them.

وَمِمَّنْ حَوْلَكُم مِّنَ الأَعْرَابِ مُنَافِقُونَ وَمِنْ أَهْلِ الْمَدِينَةِ مَرَدُواْ عَلَى النِّفَاقِ لاَ تَعْلَمُهُمْ نَحْنُ نَعْلَمُهُمْ سَنُعَذِّبُهُم مَّرَّتَيْنِ ثُمَّ يُرَدُّونَ إِلَى عَذَابٍ عَظِيمٍ [217]{التوبة/101}

The above ayah and in many others the expression الْمَدِينَةِ interestingly used generally for the potential social conflicts and problems, and fitnah in social engagements. In this perspective, our social interactions can build and encourage this type of hypocrisy built in these verses for the nifāq. In other words, our human civilizations necessitate that we become social beings with our houses next to each other, working together in the companies, schools or other institutions, and buying together. This is an advancement of our humanity perspective that we can tolerate, learn and be together although we are all different.

At the same time, these social advancements will generate people with ingenuine characters, traits, and intentions, defined as the hypocrisy. This can be similar to a nice garden of different flowers but there are flower looking poisonous plants. We don't know them. Everything looks the same from outside. So, in this perspective, to normalize the existing of hypocrisy in all cases of genuine people similar to weeds. In this perspective, Satan was not known but known to be the pious and being with angels. No one knew but Allah ﷻ knew. This is the part that one should strive throughout the life to remove from oneself from the remnants of spiritual diseases of hypocrisy, nifāq. Therefore, one can witness that friends of Allah ﷻ always had the fear till they die if they had the possible traits of hypocrisy. Allah ﷻ knows the reality of each person.

اللهم احفظنا من النفاق امين[218]

As we look at the classification in وَمِنَ النَّاسِ مَن يَقُولُ آمَنَّا بِاللَّهِ وَبِالْيَوْمِ الآخِرِ } {البقرة/8} the expression مِنَ النَّاسِ has a different wording and classification for munafiqūn compared the expression for the believers:

---

217. And among those around you of the bedouins are hypocrites, and [also] from the people of Madinah. They have become accustomed to hypocrisy. You, [O Muhammad], do not know them, [but] We know them. We will punish them twice [in this world]; then they will be returned to a great punishment.
218. Oh Allah, protect us from hypocrisy.

الَّذِينَ يُؤْمِنُونَ بِالْغَيْبِ وَيُقِيمُونَ الصَّلاةَ وَمِمَّا رَزَقْنَاهُمْ يُنفِقُونَ 219{البقرة/3}

وَالَّذِينَ يُؤْمِنُونَ بِمَا أُنزِلَ إِلَيْكَ وَمَا أُنزِلَ مِن قَبْلِكَ وَبِالآخِرَةِ هُمْ يُوقِنُونَ 220{البقرة/4}

The expression for kãfir has

إِنَّ الَّذِينَ كَفَرُواْ سَوَاءٌ عَلَيْهِمْ أَأَنذَرْتَهُمْ أَمْ لَمْ تُنذِرْهُمْ لاَ يُؤْمِنُونَ 221{البقرة/6}

In both cases of believers and kafirs, الَّذِينَ[222] is used compared to munafiqûn where مِنَ النَّاسِ[223] is used. This could be identifiable characters of both believers and kafirs with the sila of الَّذِينَ compared to the munafiqûn who are not easily identifiable, الله اعلم. Since munafiqûn are going back and forth between the believers, and kãfir, they are addressed with their humaneness attribute, with the word النَّاسِ[224]. In this case, this type of referral can send a message to this group of people that at the minimum level we are all humans and share values. We are expected to not to deceive, cause chaos, lie, and pretend. اللّهم احفظنا من هذا امين[225]

Another perspective can be that the real spiritual state of these people are unknown to humans. Allah ﷻ is not exposing them with the expression مِنَ النَّاسِ. One of the names of Allah ﷻ is al-Sattar, the Concealer of the mistakes and sins.

The word النَّاسِ can be the plural of الانسان[226]. This word can have the possibility of derived from the word انس , uns, which can mean a being of sociable. Or, it can be from the word نسيان, nisyan, a being who can forget. In this context, it can be this being who can forget the favors, especially the favors of Allah ﷻ and have tendency not to recognize and appreciate them.

---

219. Who believe in the unseen, establish prayer, and spend out of what We have provided for them.
220. And who believe in what has been revealed to you, [O Muhammad], and what was revealed before you, and of the Hereafter they are certain [in faith].
221. Indeed, those who disbelieve—it is all the same for them whether you warn them or do not warn them—they will not believe.
222. Those who.
223. From the people.
224. The people.
225. Oh Allah, protect us from this.
226. Mankind.

The expression يَقُولُ آمَنَّا[227] in the above ayah is interesting. Although يَقُولُ[228] is in singular form, the word آمَنَّا is in the plural. It is as if they have the group psychology of talking for other members. Or, people can lie better when they hide themselves in a group that we see a lot today this type of language of plural versions of public speech in political discourses.

In another perspective, if a person has a genuine problem with something, this person can express this in the first pronoun as "I have a problem about this because...etc." Once the person can tackle the problem then the perspective can change because there can be a genuine intention to learn. Oppositely, in a plural pronoun with آمَنَّا, the problem is not clear and who has the problem is not clear. So, one can always look at either the genuine effort of learning and changing or it is only for argument purposes.

The expression وَمَا هُم بِمُؤْمِنِينَ[229] comes in the form of jumla ismiyyah instead of jumla fiiliyah. This expression in this form can signify that they did not believe in the past although they may have seemed to believe but they did not. And, they will not believe in the future. In this perspective, there is a continuous position of these people towards the genuine religion and teachings although externally they may call themselves as Muslims, الله اعلم.

One can look at the relationship between وَمَا هُم بِمُؤْمِنِينَ[230] and وَمَا[231] يَشْعُرُونَ. So, what is the relationship between belief and knowing, or belief and understanding? In one perspective, one can say they did not believe because they did not know or understand. They did not understand because they did not pay attention to understand the importance of belief compared to the temporary engagements of the world. This is a preference or choice of not putting the effort to understand. This was possibly not due to having a sound heart but the sick heart as will be mentioned in the next ayah.

In the expression مَن يَقُولُ آمَنَّا[232], the word آمَنَّ is in the past, mādi, form which can imply the implicit mockery of these people by saying "before you we were already believers." Especially, depending on the context

---

227. They say they believe.
228. They say.
229. And they do not believe.
230. And they will not believe.
231. And perceive [it] not.
232. Who say: "we believe."

of these people, they used to spend time with the people of the book. But, in its real sense, if they truly and humbly believed the previous scriptures, they would have also accepted and believed in the Qurān and the teachings of the Prophet.

The expression مَن يَقُولُ آمَنَّا بِاللهِ وَبِالْيَوْمِ الآخِرِ[233] can also signify the demagogy of these people. In other words, one can tell others what they want to hear although they may not believe in what they say.

Here, the main two concepts mentioned about imān are belief in Allah ﷻ and the akhirah. They especially emphasize these two points. In group or identity relations the entrance and exit points is the belief in the mission. Similarly, in Islam, the entrance or exit points is the creed. In this case, in order to enter, these people proclaim the main creed. Therefore, the Prophet does not take stance against them. Because the religious creed affairs among humans are based on external proclamations but not on internal intentions. The real case with intention is judged only by Allah ﷻ. Humans and religious laws are based on external as this is one of the usuals, methodologies in Islamic jurisprudence.

Another perspective for the expression آمَنَّا بِاللهِ وَبِالْيَوْمِ الآخِرِ can be that these people do not want to take the people of the book against themselves as well by mentioning that they believe in God and afterlife.

It is also interesting to note that in the expression آمَنَّا بِاللهِ وَبِالْيَوْمِ الآخِرِ that they do not mention clearly that they believe in the Qurān and the Prophet. This can be another type of discourse to hide their real belief identity, الله اعلم.

In the expression فِي قُلُوبِهِم مَّرَضٌ فَزَادَهُمُ اللهُ مَرَضاً[234] when فَزَادَهُم[235] is mentioned there is the harf ف. This harf can signify the sababiyah, causality that due to their kasb, their sickness increased, الله اعلم.

On another perspective, when Allah ﷻ mentions فِي قُلُوبِهِم مَّرَضٌ[236], then it means that there is an existing sickness. If a person looks at different means or medicines to cure one's sickness, if it is a wrong medicine then, it can increase the complications and aggravate the sickness itself as mentioned فَزَادَهُمُ اللهُ مَرَضاً[237], الله اعلم.

---

233. Who say, "We believe in Allah and the Last Day,"
234. In their hearts is disease, so Allah has increased their disease.
235. Increase.
236. In their hearts is disease.
237. So Allah has increased their disease.

As mentioned before in the ayah وَمِنَ النَّاسِ مَن يَقُولُ آمَنَّا بِاللَّهِ وَبِالْيَوْمِ [238] الآخِرِ وَمَا هُم بِمُؤْمِنِينَ, the expression وَمِنَ النَّاسِ [239] can signify the high and respectful status of a human. Yet, if a human is respectful and high, the disposition of مَن يَقُولُ آمَنَّا بِاللَّهِ وَبِالْيَوْمِ الآخِرِ وَمَا هُم بِمُؤْمِنِينَ [240] does not really fit to a proper human being.

As mentioned before, the expression وَمِنَ النَّاسِ leaves an ambiguity of not specifiying the munāfiqs. If they were identified there could have been some harms. One can be for the existing Muslims. Muslims would have some type of waswasa if they would not understand the realities of each person why they were identified as munāfiqs. In this perspective, this could have led them to have waswasa with their own belief or imān. Also, if they knew the names and individuals clearly they would also have the fear of being identified due to certain traits. This type of fear can also lead some to have some traits in order to not to be identified as munāfiqs. If this is not done sincerely for God then this may lead to showing off and lead and form another group of munāfiqs, الله اعلم. Therefore, in similar cases identifying and publicizing these people can have different complications and problems.

Sometimes when a person's evil is not publicized there is a possibility that the person can stop this evil in the natural discourse of correcting oneself. Oppositely, when it is publicized there is the possibility of aggravation and increase of this evil in this person due to hate and anger of knowing that now, everyone publicly knows this person's evil.

In the address of وَمِنَ النَّاسِ, the discourses of general human values are present. If nifāq is against to general human values, then it should be already against to specific human values. In other words, a true imān is a trait that one can find in some groups. A person who has imān is expected to have all the general human values already. A person of true imān is not expected to have nifāq as a trait, الله اعلم At the same time وَمِنَ النَّاسِ [241] can also allude that every human can have some remnants of nifāq as mentioned with the word النَّاسِ.

On another perspective, with the expression of وَمِنَ النَّاسِ, there is an address to all humanity that the problem of nifāq is all human's

---

238. And of the people are some who say, "We believe in Allah and the Last Day," but they are not believers.

239. And of the people.

240. Who say, "We believe in Allah and the Last Day," but they are not believers.

241. And of the people.

common problems. In other words, humans come together and solve this problem together. In this person, one can understand the efforts the efforts in middle and high public schools in the West the courses of character education and the courses of ethics and morality at colleges with all the policies of academic integrity can allude to this effort of humans collectively to remove the bad the traits of nifāq on humans. As discussed before, lying, deception, and all unethical behaviors are in nifāq, the curriculum of these courses take this as human phenomena rather as a religious matter.

In the ayah وَمِنَ النَّاسِ مَن يَقُولُ آمَنَّا بِاللَّهِ وَبِالْيَوْمِ الآخِرِ وَمَا هُم بِمُؤْمِنِينَ[242], the expression يَقُولُ can signify that they just say it but they don't believe in it. In other words, it is just a claim but nothing more.

In the expression مَن يَقُولُ[243] shows something that these people constantly say as it comes in mudari form. In this sense, it is not sincere but perhaps to show off and to only please people.

In another perspective, to support their argument, they use the plural form in the expression آمَنَّا بِاللَّهِ وَبِالْيَوْمِ الآخِرِ[244] as آمَنَّا. In one meaning, they want to support their weak claim when they just say يَقُولُ[245] as only in the form of words. In another meaning, as narrated at the early times for the sabab nazul of this ayah, if these people were from ahlu-kitāb they would imply that they were already believers of Allah ﷻ and afterlife before Islam, الله اعلم.

When they mention آمَنَّا بِاللَّهِ وَبِالْيَوْمِ الآخِرِ[246], they try to emphasize that they believe in the most critical two pillars of the belief. On another perspective, it can be the opposite that when Allah ﷻ mentions this, they possibly do not genuinely and truly believe the most critical two pillars of the imān, الله اعلم.

If one reviews the expression آمَنَّا بِاللَّهِ وَبِالْيَوْمِ الآخِرِ, the harf, ba, ب, is repeated. This may signify that they really don't believe but they claim or utter the words of belief. In other words, belief in Allah ﷻ means to believe the existence and oneness of Allah ﷻ. Belief in akhirah means to believe that there is a day that there will be an accountability for all life

---

242. And of the people are some who say, "We believe in Allah and the Last Day," but they are not believers.
243. Those who say.
244. "We believe in Allah and the Last Day."
245. Who say.
246. We believe in Allah and the Last Day."

engagements. If their actions do not match what they say, then there is a question of if they really believe or not, الله اعلم.

The expression وَمَا هُم بِمُؤْمِنِينَ[247] in jumla ismiyyah signifies the continuity of their disbelief. This is also an answer to their claim of آمَنَّا بِاللَّهِ وَبِالْيَوْمِ الآخِر. This claim may include a possibility of belief. The structure in jumla ismiyyah is a strong answer to refute this claim, الله اعلم.

In addition, one can focus on the letter ba, ب, in the expression وَمَا هُم بِمُؤْمِنِينَ with its possible reason in the expression instead of و ما هم مؤمنون without ب. In this case, this may signify that although they claim to be believers, mumins, but in reality they are not from the group of believers. So, the letter ب signifies the true group identity of people where they belong to, الله اعلم.

When one reviews the ayahs وَمِنَ النَّاسِ مَن يَقُولُ آمَنَّا بِاللَّهِ وَبِالْيَوْمِ الآخِرِ وَمَا هُم بِمُؤْمِنِينَ {البقرة/8} يُخَادِعُونَ اللَّهَ وَالَّذِينَ آمَنُوا وَمَا يَخْدَعُونَ إِلاَّ أَنفُسَهُم وَمَا يَشْعُرُونَ {البقرة/9} they فِي قُلُوبِهِم مَّرَضٌ فَزَادَهُمُ اللَّهُ مَرَضاً وَلَهُم عَذَابٌ أَلِيمٌ بِمَا كَانُوا يَكْذِبُونَ {البقرة/10}[248] mention بِمُؤْمِنِينَ يَقُولُ آمَنَّا بِاللَّهِ وَبِالْيَوْمِ الآخِرِ وَمَا هُم بِمُؤْمِنِينَ. In the following ayahs, their belingerent claim is explained with يُخَادِعُونَ اللَّهَ وَالَّذِينَ آمَنُوا وَمَا يَخْدَعُونَ إِلاَّ[249] أَنفُسَهُم وَمَا يَشْعُرُونَ {البقرة/9} فِي قُلُوبِهِم مَّرَضٌ[250]. The key words here are khud from the word يُخَادِعُونَ and marad from the word مَّرَضٌ.

In the above set of ayahs and others, one can ask what is the hikmah of explaining them in detail with itnab? One reason is that possibly they may stop their evil similar to the case that a person gives a long advice to a trouble maker. After, that if the person still continues what he or she is doing then that is their fault. If especially this is a case that may affect the harmony and unity of the families, friendships, communities and societies, then this needs to be publicized. Therefore, a itnab style is observed to publicize their possible evil renderings.

---

247. But they are not believers.
248. 2:8 And there are people who say, "We do believe in God and the Last Day," the while they do not [really] believe. (2:9) They would deceive God and those who have attained to faith—the while they deceive none but themselves, and perceive it not. (2:10) In their hearts is disease, and so God lets their disease increase; and grievous suffering awaits them because of their persistent lying.
249. They would deceive God and those who have attained to faith—the while they deceive none but themselves, and perceive it not.
250. In their hearts is disease.

[9]

{ يُخَادِعُونَ اللَّهَ وَالَّذِينَ آمَنُوا وَمَا يَخْدَعُونَ إلاَّ أَنفُسَهُم وَمَا يَشْعُرُونَ 251 {البقرة/9}

The expression يُخَادِعُونَ اللَّه[252] has the lafzu Mubarak, اللَّه but not other Attributes or Names of Allah ﷻ. This shows these people's idiocy and senselessness trying to rationalize their deception against Allahﷻ[253] اللهم. احفظنا من النفاق، امين.

The word يُخَادِعُونَ[254] is used in the form of mudari, the present and future tense, to allude the fact that these people of this trait will exist and continue until the End of Days. There will be this type of people at all times. Another reason of mudari form can allude to the dynamically changing deceptions of these people according to the time and place. They change their deception techniques according to time, people, place, and conditions.

One of the notions in aqaid is the insistence of a person on a sin or evil. This can be worst than the sin itself because of the attitude of insisting. In this case the form of mudari in يُخَادِعُونَ[255] can allude to this notion of insistence. So, this attitude can make it worse than the act itself. The attitude of insisting makes it more worse when someone is doing in one's relationship with Allah ﷻ as mentioned يُخَادِعُونَ اللَّه[256]. Since, a person cannot do to deception to Rabbul Alamin, Allah ﷻ therefore. وَمَا يَخْدَعُونَ إلاَّ أَنفُسَهُم[257] follows. It can be similar to a case a person shooting a bullet to harm another but the bullet comes and makes U turn and hits back the shooter.

The phrase وَالَّذِينَ آمَنُو[258] can normalize the idiocy of this psychology for the believers if a person or group has already an attitude of Hûd or deception against Allah ﷻ. Then, it is normal to have it to humans, believers. In other words, it can mean that the believers can normalize for their position so that they don't need worry because this person

---

251. They would deceive God and those who have attained to faith—the while they deceive none but themselves, and perceive it not.
252. They [think to] deceive Allah.
253. Oh Allah, protect us from hypocrisy.
254. They [think to] deceive Allah.
255. Deceive.
256. They [think to] deceive Allah.
257. But they deceive not except themselves.
258. And those who believe.

or people have a higher senselessness of attempt to the Creator of all existence.

In another note, the ayahs also mention that their deceptions or evil planning will be in vain in the long run although it may seem to work immediately, اعلم الله.

Another perspective of this ayah shows that when a person tries to show this type of idiocy and senselessness that they can deceive someone that they cannot in reality then the expression وَمَا يَخْدَعُونَ إِلاَّ أَنفُسَهُم وَمَا [259] يَشْعُرُونَ comes in. This means that in reality they are really deceiving themselves and they even don't know this basic fact as mentioned with the word shu'ur in يَشْعُرُونَ[260]. A person in this category is not aware of this and cannot rationalize fully the notion that the One, Allah ﷻ, knows all the inner dynamically changing feelings of a person in the heart, continuous showering thoughts in the mind, constant forming inclinations, and actions in secret and public. Therefore, they really deceive themselves by not realizing who Allah ﷻ is.

The word يَشْعُرُونَ[261] is the first step of knowing something. In other words, it is the first encounter of mind before going through critical thinking and analysis. For example, a person touching a hot object and knowing that it is hot can be expressed with this word, shuur in Arabic. So, it is the first encounter. After, if the person uses this first encounter analyzes, synthesis and perform critical thinking then, this is called mind. The person goes beyond the first encounter of knowing but now involving one's intellectual faculties through mind. The synthesis and progress of all the sciences are achieved through mind, by actively using the intellectual faculties but not through a raw and immediate response with shuur.

In other words, mind uses the ingredients that is first discovered by shuur. Or, in another description, if shuur and mind are two people, shuur finds and presents things to mind, then mind makes decision. Depending on the critical analysis of mind, this knowledge can be called science, i'lm. Not all the ingredients hunted by shuur and analyzed by mind can be called i'lm, science. For example, if a person looks at the sun and the earth, the person can say with the observation of shuur and analysis of mind that earth is not moving stationary and sun is moving

---

259. But they deceive not except themselves and perceive [it] not.
260. Perceive [it].
261. Perceive [it].

because there is the change of night and day. This was the understanding in the past but now with technological advancements, it is known that that was wrong. Both are moving. So, science or i'lm is defined as the last stage of mind with critical analysis and technological advancements within the faculties of causality. Therefore, a person cannot build the scientific methodology on hypothesis or assumptions (1) .

So, in this perspective, these group of people even fail to recognize something very basic that a natural tendency, fitrah can give a correct response through shuur but they cannot understand and implement this basic and simple notion. For example, when a person is walking on the street, she or he passes next to a beggar and do not help the beggar. After a while, a disturbing feeling and state can occur in the person that the person may not realize the reason. In this case the fitrah is responding naturally to help but the person does not understand through shuur, then a conflict occurs. This disturbing feelings are the good responses for an alive fitrah. If the fitrah is dead this natural tendency, fitrah responses may not be there. In terminology, one can also call this the true response of conscience to sins, the unpleasant immoral and unethical dispositions. If the person's fitrah decrease the response rate against immoral, unethical or sins, and one day become responseless or dead, then one can say the true fitrah is covered with a secondary one as mentioned in the above verses with the word khatm or seal.

Shuur also leaves some marks on the nafs, or ego. These marks can be called memories. These marks left by shuur can be sometimes stored in the memory with strong and weak magnitudes. Life shocking experiences can be those strong memories. An incident that may make the person disturbed or happy but the person may not know the reason of this disturbance or happiness can be related with the weak memories that the person cannot fully recall and name and identify it.

In another perspective, the first reaction of the mind, aqil, of knowing can be called shuur. At another level, the first reaction of nafs, of true knowing can be called intuition or conscience, wijdan in ajam languages but not in Arabic. This first knowing of nafs as wijdan can be called shuur of wijdan. In this case, although the person can be alive but the faculties of wijdan, the true intuition or conscience can be dead. Therefore, this first true knowing of wijdan is always right and correct if it is still alive and active. In the case of munafiqûn , if the wijdan is dead they cannot use this faculty to know and to implement. Ultimately, all knowledge through mind, wijdan and also experience through practices should triangulate to the same result.

The below diagram shows the interpretations of feelings and knowledge through external and internal faculties.

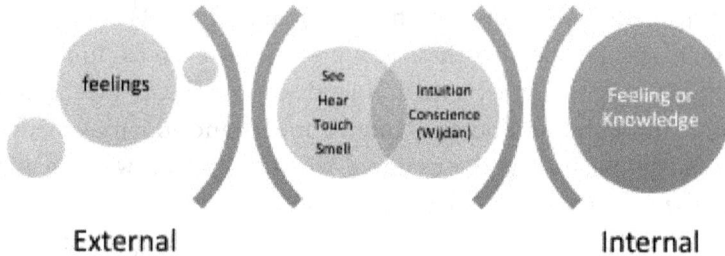

External   Internal

Ideally, in a natural fitrah, both external and internal should be complementary and harmonizing and confirming each other in their results.

One can ask if there are people who are smart in a worldly sense and they have the above attitude, how can one reconcile the intelligence with not understanding basic premises of the true religion? A possible explanation is that when people genuinely specialize in one field the person can also shut off oneself to other perspectives of life. In other words, a person specialized in the materialistic teachings of the seen world can very well have a minute or no clue about the teachings of the real spiritual life and the life after death. So, this can be a disadvantage of specialization. A person who is specialized in one field still needs to have some idea and knowledge in others. An example of this Albert Einstein that it was reported that he did not have much clue about the incidents of the world (19).When a person does khud with Allah ﷻ as mentioned يُخَادِعُونَ أَللَّهَ[262], this state can really show a mental disorder. Especially, today's popular book titles and concepts such as "challenging God" etc. show really inanity, absurdity and idiocy of some of the humans' spiritual state. Is this done to only gain a cheap wordily fame? Is it worth in this short life while the person will face Allah ﷻ very soon? One can identify and cognize a person with a weak will-power being involved with some actions which are displeasing to Allah ﷻ. Yet, a sane and smart person would return back to Allah ﷻ and ask apology and

---

262. They [think to] deceive Allah.

forgiveness from Allah ﷻ like Adam as did. So, this concept of khud and its representations at our time really show ridiculousness, and absurdity of some of the humans' spiritual state that even Shaytan did know his limits when he showed arrogance in his relationship with Allah ﷻ and begged for permission from Allah ﷻ until the Day of Qiyamah. May Allah ﷻ protect us from even any minor type of explicit or implicit khud in our relationships with Allah ﷻ! Amìn.

One can assume that when a person does khud it is expected that there is a benefit in return for the person. In this case, the attempt of making khud with Allah ﷻ does not make any sense. There is no benefit but harm to the person. This shows the lack of their understanding and critical thinking. In other words, if a person cannot differentiate between benefit and harm then there can be some problems either due to lack of knowledge or due to ignorance. For example, a child can touch the fire. If the child knows touching fire burns the person, then he or she wouldn't do it. Similarly, not able to understand something simple such as khud with Allah ﷻ can be similar to burning one's ownself in the fire, الله اعلم. Allah ﷻ, the Exalted is beyond from all the human renderings, سُبْحَانَهُ وَتَعَالَى عَمَّا يَصِفُونَ [263].

One can ask in the expression يُخَادِعُونَ اَللّٰہ [264] how that is possible? khud to Allah ﷻ? Khud to Rasulullah ﷺ can be considered khud to Allah ﷻ.

In addition, in the expression يُخَادِعُونَ اَللّٰہَ وَالَّذِينَ آمَنُوا وَمَا يَخْدَعُونَ إلا أَنْفُسَهُم [265], when a person does khud, the person can expect a benefit but in reality he or she harms oneself as mentioned in the expression يَخْدَعُونَ [266] إِلا أَنْفُسَهُم. Every khud can start with at least one disease of the heart such as jealousy and anger or others. If we take the case for example the case of jealousy, the Prophet ﷺ mentions the jealousy eats the person him or herself before its harm reaches to others (20). In this perspective, by having this disease in one's heart, the person can go through so uncomfortable, self-rendering depressive dialogues that this person's energy is wasted and becomes a self-destructive poison. With this disease, the person constantly plans, thinks and involves in different

---

263. Glory be to Him and Exalted is He.
264. They [think to] deceive Allah.
265. They [think to] deceive Allah and those who believe, but they deceive not except themselves.
266. They deceive not except themselves.

multiple version of khud. Yet, at the end the person's own self is harmed. Still, the person does not understand all this as the expression mentions وَمَا يَشْعُرُونَ[267], اللہ اعلم[268].

May Allah ﷺ protect us from all types of khud, amin.

In this sick state as mentioned فِي قُلُوبِهِم مَّرَضٌ[269], they want to execute decisions and actions, since the person is in sickness such as in jealousy, anger or others, the decisions made in this state can worsen the case. For example, when a person is in the state of anger then with anger, he or she may do things which may make the situation worse as mentioned [270] فَزَادَهُمُ in the following verses.

In the expression يُخَادِعُونَ اللہ وَالَّذِينَ آمَنُو[271], instead of the name of the Prophet ﷺ is present and instead of المومينون[272] there is وَالَّذِينَ آمَنُو[273]. Both imply the continuity. In other words, the continuous attitude of khud until the End of Day. In addition, the type of the verb form in its sigah of يُخَادِعُونَ can imply that there is recompense against their khud which makes nullifies their khud and turns it against themselves, اللہ اعلم.

It is interesting to note that the sifah or attribute of imān is mentioned in the expression وَالَّذِينَ آمَنُو. In other words, when they do khud they can be using or pretending to have the same sifah of imān like the real believers.

It is futile to make khud with Allah ﷺ as mentioned in the discussion of the phrase يُخَادِعُونَ اللہ وَالَّذِينَ آمَنُو[274]. Similarly, due to the link and sila to Allah ﷺ through imān as mentioned in الَّذِينَ آمَنُو, it is also useless to make khud to the believers, to the people of imān. In other words, a person of imān can understand people's khud towards them with the light, Nûr, of imān.

It is interesting to note that in the expression وَمَا يَخْدَعُونَ إِلاَّ أَنفُسَهُم[275] the word يَخْدَعُونَ is preferred instead of يضرون[277] أَنفُسَهُمُ إِلاَّ[276] or يظلمون[278].

---

267. And perceive [it] not.
268. Allah knows best.
269. In their hearts is disease.
270. Increased.
271. They [think to] deceive Allah and those who believe.
272. The believers.
273. And those who believe.
274. They [think to] deceive Allah and those who believe.
275. But they deceive not except themselves.
276. Except themselves.
277. They hurt.
278. They oppressed.

Because in zulm or dharar, a person may still have a mind and give some harm to oneself. However, the word يُخْدَعُونَ[279] showing deceiving or tricking one's own self can be a sign of again the lack of basic recognition, assessment and reason which is then expressed with the immediate following expression وَمَا يَشْعُرُونَ[280].

The word أَنْفُسَهُم[281] can show that they are in these discourses of khud due to benefitting their own nafs. In other words, their own nafs is so sweet and lovely for them that they can do anything to please it. However, it becomes so devastating that this lovely nafs would not be able to taste the sweetness or taste with the khud renderings of the person but perhaps the opposite, a taste of poison affect bitterness and may be more in this dunya and after. This is due to inclinations to make khud with Allah ﷻ, may Allah ﷻ protects us from our internal and external, implicit and explicit, known and unknown khuds, amin.

The word وَمَا يَشْعُرُونَ shows that they don't understand that they are harming their own selves. Here, instead of يعقلون[282] the word يَشْعُرُونَ is used. As mentioned aqil comes before shuur. Aqil can be the critical thinking and shuur can be the basic recognition of harms and benefits. In this perspective, animals can have shuur that they can understand the basic harms and benefits of things. So, their level in this case can be lower than the animals as mentioned: وَلَقَدْ ذَرَأْنَا لِجَهَنَّمَ كَثِيرًا مِّنَ الْجِنِّ وَالْإِنسِ لَهُمْ قُلُوبٌ لاَّ يَفْقَهُونَ بِهَا وَلَهُمْ أَعْيُنٌ لاَّ يُبْصِرُونَ بِهَا وَلَهُمْ آذَانٌ لاَّ يَسْمَعُونَ بِهَا أُوْلَئِكَ كَالْأَنْعَامِ بَلْ هُمْ أَضَلُّ أُوْلَئِكَ هُمُ الْغَافِلُونَ [283]{الأعراف/179} أَمْ تَحْسَبُ أَنَّ أَكْثَرَهُمْ يَسْمَعُونَ أَوْ يَعْقِلُونَ إِنْ هُمْ إِلَّا كَالْأَنْعَامِ بَلْ هُمْ أَضَلُّ سَبِيلًا [284]{الفرقان/44}

---

279. They deceive.
280. And perceive [it] not.
281. Themselves.
282. They know.
283. And We have certainly created for Hell many of the jinn and mankind. They have hearts with which they do not understand, they have eyes with which they do not see, and they have ears with which they do not hear. Those are like livestock; rather, they are more astray. It is they who are the heedless.
284. Or do you think that most of them hear or reason? They are not except like livestock. Rather, they are [even] more astray in [their] way.

[10]

فِي قُلُوبِهِم مَّرَضٌ فَزَادَهُمُ اللَّهُ مَرَضاً وَلَهُم عَذَابٌ أَلِيمٌ بِمَا كَانُوا يَكْذِبُونَ 285 {10/البقرة}

One should realize the subtle translation of this verse. The meanings can be that these people had spiritual sickness because of their circular character in this sickness, their existence sickness were amplified and increased because they wanted to aggravate it but not treat it. Accordingly, in our world of causality, the results of these people's engagements were created by Allah ﷻ In other words, Allah ﷻ created the means for what they wanted and desired constantly. It is the flow of evil. Once the person is in the evil and wants more and more, then the result and effects are created or enabled by Allah ﷻ. At least, if they had a little bit remorse of repentance before it was too late then, the things could have been different.

Expectations, Disappointments and Formation of Physiological or Psychological Sickness

Here, one can try to identify the process of a sickness. The existing stage, it is development and metastasis until one dies. One can ask how can the worsening of a sickness can occur.

When one declares a position against the teachings of Allah ﷻ, or in such an extent in some cases that if a person declares a war against Allah ﷻ as mentioned in the Qurãn, then it is important to analyze and understand psychology of this person(s). In one possible case of humanly engagement, if a person expects a lot from another person but cannot get what he or she desires to receive, then the person can get upset. Overtime, with this agitation, the person who he or she seem to love a lot can get disappointed and question the relationship with this person. Over time with agitation, and disappointment, the person can lead to the next stage of an unimaginable anger. With this increasing anger, the next stage can start with hate.

When a person is in the disposition of anger and hate, it is very difficult to expect reason, logic, and rationale. Now, at this position, the

---

285. In their hearts is disease, so Allah has increased their disease; and for them is a painful punishment because they [habitually] used to lie.

person becomes spiritually and mentally sick as mentioned مرض[286] in the Qurān. Then, a person in this position can even question Allah ﷻ, astaghfirullah, a'zubillah.

This psychology can be in non-Muslims as well as in some Muslims occasionally. Among the Muslims, this disposition can reveal itself especially at the times of loss, trials and tests. Then, the person can become upset with Allah ﷻ, astaghfirullah, a'zubillah, and ruin one's relationship with the One who the person constantly needs to appreciate all the bounties.

In this ayah, one can see that the disease of lying became as part of their fitrah and character. They lie so much that lying becomes part of their traits. They lie but they don't consider lying as a lie or evil. Furthermore, they consider lying, deceiving, and related engagements with marketing or politics as a positive and virtuous trait to achieve their goals (21). They lie in political life to deceive people. They lie in executive manners to force clerks to follow their instructions. They lie in social affairs to manipulate massive crowds and nations.

It is also interesting to see that since this people lie, they think that others lie too. This is a sickness. When the Prophet ﷺ presented the message, they had the same position towards the Prophet. They demonstrate highest level of skepticism and distrust due to their position of continuous lying. With this psychology, they constantly think that people constantly plot against them as mentioned in يَحْسَبُونَ كُلَّ صَيْحَةٍ[287] عَلَيْهِمْ هُمُ الْعَدُوُّ فَاحْذَرْهُمْ قَاتَلَهُمُ اللَّهُ أَنَّى يُؤْفَكُونَ {المنافقون/4}.

It is also interesting to see that as the highest evil or sin, lying is presented in كَانُوا يَكْذِبُونَ[288]. In this perspective one can see their lying is against Allah ﷻ as mentioned in وَمِنَ النَّاسِ مَن يَقُولُ آمَنَّا بِاللَّهِ وَبِالْيَوْمِ الْآخِرِ وَمَا هُم بِمُؤْمِنِينَ[289] {البقرة/8}.

If one analyzes the expression وَلَهُم عَذَابٌ أَلِيمٌ بِمَا كَانُوا يَكْذِبُونَ[290], one can see that the consequence of punishment comes due to lying as

---

286. Disease.
287. 63:4 Now when thou seest them, their outward appearance may please thee; and when they speak, thou art inclined to lend ear to what they say. [But though they may seem as sure of themselves] as if they were timbers [firmly] propped up, they think that every shout is [directed] against them. They are the [real] enemies [of all faith], so beware of them. [They deserve the imprecation,] "May God destroy them!" How perverted are their minds!
288. And they would lie.
289. And of the people are some who say, "We believe in Allah and the Last Day," but they are not believers.
290. And for them is a painful punishment because they [habitually] used to lie.

mentioned بِمَا كَانُوا يَكْذِبُونَ[291]. If one looks at the opposite poles in this regard, shaytan has a nick name and title as "al-kazzab", the liar and the Prophet Muhammad ﷺ has a nick name and title of "as-Sadiq and al-Amìn." اللهم جعلنا من الصادقين وجعلنا من التبع محمد الصادق وعد الامين[292]

According to some scholars, lying is interchangeable with kufur. In other words, lying is another name of kufur. When a person starts lying then it becomes a very difficult path to come back. Therefore, the Prophet mentions that lying leads to fujur and fujur leads to Jahannam and oppositely, the truth, sidq leads to good action and disposition and this leads to Jannah, (9) (12). One can always reflect on the trait of lying both in personal affairs and social and political affairs. In the sociological phenomena of group dynamics lying can be painted with the notions of achieving something good. However, Islam with the main teachings of the Qurãn and the Prophet ﷺ does not approve achieving a high goal with the means of unethical and immoral paths. One should also remember that the affairs that are based on lies can possibly engulf the liars one day with different social and personal dynamics and incidents due to the Perfect Wisdom of Allah ﷻ. The expression for this cyclical justice of Allah ﷻ can be referred as sunnatullah in terminology.

One can also analyze the social effects of lying and truthfulness in the societies in relation with their decline or advancement of their civilizations. One can examine the societies where lying and all related social discourses is dominant and how the societies can be poor, backwards and unhappy. Conversely, one can also examine societies where lying is not much prevalent as others how this disposition affects help the advancement of civilizations and prosperity in these societies, الله اعلم.

The Qurãn relates all these traits of a person with the expression فِي قُلُوبِهِم مَّرَضٌ[293], as the disease of the heart. As lying is a major disease of the heart another disease mentioned here is the negative group identities or identity politics with the expressions in the following ayahs

---

291. Because they [habitually] used to lie.
292. Oh Allah, make us from the truthful and make us from among the followers of Muhammad Al-Sadiqul Wa'dul Amin.
293. In their hearts is disease.

وَإِذَا لَقُوا الَّذِينَ آمَنُوا قَالُوا آمَنَّا وَإِذَا خَلَوا إِلَى شَيَاطِينِهِمْ قَالُوا إِنَّا مَعَكُمْ إِنَّمَا نَحْنُ مُسْتَهْزِؤُونَ as
{البقرة 14/4}. [294]

One can ask what is the hikmah of detailing the characters of munafiqûn in the Qurãn? First, in the encounters of life, a person will encounter people with different backgrounds, motifs and intentions. One of the difficult ones to understand is munãfiqs. When they externally proclaim to be with you but in reality when they are not, a naïve person can be confused with this type of stance.

The second hikmah can be to normalize existing of these people and not to be frustrated in their engagements. Most of the time when humans cannot categorize or identify the reasons they may get frustrated and hopeless. Therefore, the explanations in the Qurãn can help the person to normalize the existence of such a group of people, الله اعلم.

Both the expression خَتَمَ اللهُ عَلَى قُلُوبِهِمْ [295] in the seventh ayah of this Sûrah and the expression[296] فِي قُلُوبِهِم مَّرَضٌ in this ayah focus on the heart. The first case can be related with the kãfir and the second case of the heart is related with the munãfiq. In this perspective, both have some problems in their hearts, الله اعلم[297].

Also, the word مَّرَضٌ[298] can be translated as disease. If one looks at the definition of the word "disease" in Oxford dictionary, it is "a disorder of structure or function in a human, a particular quality, habit, or disposition regarded as adversely affecting a person or group of people." (21) In this perspective, a person with this trait cannot differentiate between the right and wrong, or authentic and false. Although this disease can be solidified in munãfiqs and kãfir, it can have also affects and traits among Muslims. As the Prophet underlines this fact of the person having the qualities of a munãfiq if he or she lies, breaks one's promise and do not fulfill one's commitments (9) (hadith #33) (3) (hadith #59).

According to Tabiin such as Katadah (rh), Ikrimah (rh) and Dahhak (rh), this disease is the doubt and skepticism about the belief in Allah ﷻ that they did not have a robust imãn, belief (8). Another disease can be assuming others in the same category as theirs in this type of disease.

---

294. 2:14 And when they meet those who have attained to faith, they assert, "We believe [as you believe]"; but when they find themselves alone with their evil impulses, they say, "Verily, we are with you; we were only mocking!"
295. Allah has set a seal upon their hearts.
296. In their hearts is disease.
297. Allah knows best.
298. Disease.

At a perspective of sabab nuzûl, one can analyze the formation of munãfiqs in Madinah. There were people who were expecting a prophet of God. There were people who were expecting to be leaders in their community. When the Prophet came, some people who were expecting a messenger from God did not follow the Prophet truly because the Prophet was not from their group or class. The others did not follow the Prophet because they lost the possibility of being leaders. In both cases, these people first tried to openly show their stance. Later, when there was an increasing appeal to Islam with the increase in the number of people and expansion of land, these people were not able to afford to challenge Muslims openly. They turned into their own cliques to challenge by having a Muslim identity externally but not internally. This was the early formation of the group of munãfiqs.

In the expression مَّرَضٌ قُلُوبِهِم فِي[299], the harfi jar فِي[300], can allude to interior of something literally. In this sense, these diseases can be inside depths of their hearts that it can be very difficult to identify, reveal and treat, الله اعلم.

In addition, a person is born with a natural healthy state of heart and mind as called "fitrah" in terminology. If Allah ☙created everyone on a sound heart or a natural fitrah, then this means that in their hearts, there is a type of disease that damages the health of natural fitrah, or sound heart. Then, one can ponder on the expression مَّرَضٌ قُلُوبِهِم فِي that this state is earned and acquired state with one's disposition, tendency and free-choice in life. So, no one can blame any person except him or herself in this regard. One can review the previous discussions about the concepts of person's acquirement referred as kasb in terminology, الله اعلم, Allah ☙knows everything's true meanings.

In the expression مَّرَضٌ قُلُوبِهِم فِي[301], the word مَّرَضٌ[302] comes as tanwin, as indefinite article. This can signify that it is difficult to define or diagnose this sickness or disease. It can be difficult for the person who has the disease to know and diagnose it. It can also be difficult for others to understand when they interact with this person that this person has a disease, الله اعلم.

---

299. In their hearts is disease.
300. In.
301. In their hearts is disease.
302. Disease.

On another perspective, one can interpret the root of this disease to be at the heart as mentioned فِي قُلُوبِهِم مَّرَضٌ. Then, it metastases to other parts of the body such as mind, eyes or ears. Therefore, the ayah خَتَمَ اللهُ عَلَى قُلُوبِهِمْ وَعَلَى سَمْعِهِمْ وَعَلَى أَبْصَارِهِمْ غِشَاوَةٌ وَلَهُمْ عَذَابٌ عظِيمٌ [303]{البقرة/7} presents itself with heart as the source of the tumor or cancer cells as in medical terms then metastasis occurs to other parts. To support this interpretation, أَفَلَمْ يَسِيرُوا فِي الْأَرْضِ فَتَكُونَ لَهُمْ قُلُوبٌ يَعْقِلُونَ بِهَا أَوْ آذَانٌ يَسْمَعُونَ بِهَا فَإِنَّهَا لَا تَعْمَى الْأَبْصَارُ وَلَكِن تَعْمَى الْقُلُوبُ الَّتِي فِي الصُّدُورِ {الحج/46}[304]. This ayah show that main disease is at the heart then other parts are affected, الله اعلم.

In the expression فِي قُلُوبِهِم مَّرَضٌ, one can understand that a physical sickness is a blessing for mu'min, believer as mentioned by the Prophet (9) (chapter of al-birr, 51). A sickness, tribulation or difficulty can be a means for a believer to come close to Allah ﷻ. In this perspective, one can argue that the sickness that the munafiqûn had, was not a physical sickness but a spiritual one because they were not real mu'min, believers, الله اعلم. One can see the similar perspective for the Qurãn that وَنُنَزِّلُ مِنَ الْقُرْآنِ مَا هُوَ شِفَاء وَرَحْمَةٌ لِّلْمُؤْمِنِينَ وَلاَ يَزِيدُ الظَّالِمِينَ إَلاَّ خَسَارًا {الإسراء/82}[305] as, mentioned for some people it is a blessing but some it is the opposite, اللهم جعلنا من الذين يتبعون الحق[306]

فِي قُلُوبِهِم مَّرَضٌ فَزَادَهُمُ اللّهُ مَرَضاً[307] One can also review the expression with the ayah mentioned as وَأَمَّا الَّذِينَ فِي قُلُوبِهِم مَّرَضٌ فَزَادَتْهُمْ رِجْسًا إِلَى رِجْسِهِمْ وَمَاتُواْ وَهُمْ كَافِرُونَ {التوبة/125}[308]. In this perspective, their رِجْسًا[309] attracted more رِجْسٌ. Or, their مَّرَضٌ[310] attracted more مَّرَضٌ.

When one reviews the ayah وَلَهُم عَذَابٌ أَلِيمٌ بِمَا كَانُوا يَكْذِبُونَ[311], the punishment or azab reveals itself due to mainly the sickness of lying.

---

303. Allah has set a seal upon their hearts and upon their hearing, and over their vision is a veil. And for them is a great punishment.
304. 22:47 And [so, O Muhammad,] they challenge thee to hasten the coming upon them of [God's] chastisement but God never fails to fulfil His promise—and, behold, in thy Sustainer's sight a day is like a thousand years of your reckoning.
305. 17:82 THUS, step by step, We bestow from on high through this Qur'an all that gives health [to the spirit] and is a grace unto those who believe [in Us], the while it only adds to the ruin of evildoers:
306. Oh Allah, make us among those who follow the truth.
307. In their hearts is disease, so Allah has increased their disease.
308. 9:125 But as for those in whose hearts is disease, it has [only] increased them in evil [in addition] to their evil. And they will have died while they are disbelievers.
309. Evil.
310. Disease.
311. And for them is a painful punishment because they [habitually] used to lie.

Lying, the opposite of siddiq, is such a bad trait that it hurts the person immediately if the person still has some portions of a sound and healthy heart and conscience. These feelings can make the person constantly doubtful, uneasy, stressful and anxious. This itself is an immediate azab, let alone the expected azab in the afterlife. Oppositely, if a person is on siddiq, truthfulness and honesty, this makes the person very firm, clear and peaceful. There are not complications of mismatch of verbal utterances with the internal heart and conscience related renderings. They both math with each other. In the case of a liar, there is always the complicated process of normalizations of outward affairs of words and actions with the inward affairs of intentions, and feelings.

One should remember that health is the default state of a person. Sickness is an exception. In a normal healthy sound heart and mind, a person puts an effort to maintain this given healthy state by Allah ﷻ. In spiritual discourses, this can be called fitrah, natural correct traits given by Allah ﷻ. Sometimes, a virus can make the person sick. If the person does not care for this virus, then it can grow and spread. Something trivial can become major and kill the person. Similarly, a virus of doubt can come to the person with the matters of the religion. In this sense, if a person does not take care of this virus immediately, this trivial virus can grow and spread in such a way that the person can become munāfiq فِي قُلُوبِهِم مَّرَضٌ فَزَادَهُمُ اللّهُ مَرَضاً وَلَهُم عَذَابٌ أَلِيمٌ بِمَا كَانُوا يَكْذِبُونَ[312] {البقرة/10}. In this sense, increase of sickness is due to the person's fault but as Allah ﷻ creates everything in the world of causality, this also happens as well. At the end, the person should blame him or herself, may Allah protect us, amin.

When one compares the expressions وَلَهُمْ عَذَابٌ عظِيمٌ[313] as mentioned in the previous ayahs and وَلَهُم عَذَابٌ أَلِيمٌ in this ayah, the first one is a general for especially for the kāfir. The first word عظِيمٌ[314] alludes to the quantity of the punishment. The latter one is especially for the munafiqûn . The latter one with the word أَلِيمٌ[315] alludes to the quality of the punishment. If one looks the word أَلِيمٌ as a quality of the punishment for the munafiqûn, this can be very devastating. Because, due to their sickness of their heart

---

312. In their hearts is disease, so Allah has increased their disease; and for them is a painful punishment because they [habitually] used to lie.
313. And for them is a painful punishment.
314. Painful.
315. Painful.

they will already be in different types of عَذَابٌ in this world before the one after life. Their psychological, conscience or human trait related internal conversations can kick in sometimes and disturb them if not totally lost. So, in reality, there is no respite for the munāfiq truly both in this world and afterlife. Oppositely, the kāfir may have some but not full respite due to not knowing the truth, الله اعلم.

The expression بِمَا كَانُوا يَكْذِبُونَ[316] underlines the concept of kizb. One should realize that there could be different levels of kizb, lie in each person's life. The important part here is to regret and ask forgiveness from Allah ﷻ in each possible case of kizb, lie rendeings. A true believer is expected to do constant muraqaba in one's relationship with Allah ﷻ. In other words, he or she always see himself or herself as the oppressor, making zulm to oneself. Because, one cannot truly appreciate Allah ﷻ until he or she understands that he or she is an oppressor. In other words, appreciating or being grateful to Allah ﷻ requires embodying and personalizing that one cannot truly do thanking to Allah ﷻ. Therefore, one of the duas mentioned in the Qurān is[317] لا اله الا انت سبحانك اني كنت من الظالمين. This is does not mean that someone did something but embodying and personalizing this attitude as a trait is the main step on the true path of Allah ﷻ. There is a statement attributed to Adam as that when he understood and embodied that being grateful to Allah ﷻ requires another thanking to Allah ﷻ that Allah ﷻ gave this understanding to this person. Then, Allah ﷻ told him that if he really understood this then he is at the real state of hamd, or gratitude. The similar is embodied by the Prophet when he ﷺ was asked why he was praying so much. He said "should not I be grateful to Allah ﷻ??". In all these discussions, the people who are in the group of بِمَا كَانُوا يَكْذِبُونَ[318] are in the opposite pole. They are not even aware of the bounties of Allah ﷻ and they are not aware of their own selves.

Any type of disease related with the heart is considered dangerous. Because heart is a critical organ for the body. In this sense, the expression فِي قُلُوبِهِم مَّرَضٌ[319] has the harf-jar فِي. This can allude to the fact and notion that this disease is extremely serious, hidden and deeply inside the layers but not something easy to recognize, understand, and handle, الله اعلم.

---

316. Because they [habitually] used to lie.
317. There is no deity except You; exalted are You. Indeed, I have been of the wrongdoers."
318. Because they [habitually] used to lie.
319. In their hearts is disease.

Also, instead of فِي قُلُوبِهِم مَّرَضٌ[320], the expression is فِي قُلُوبِهِم مَّرَضٌ can show the hasr and emphasis that their sickness is in their hearts but not in other parts. Therefore, heart precedes the sickness in the structure, الله اعلم.

One can analyze the expression فِي قُلُوبِهِم مَّرَضٌ from its as well . A healthy heart will require a sound imān. In this perspective, the Qurān first and foremost reveals the importance of the main disease in the heart. If the essence is sound and healthy then one can focus on the details such as the health of the body. A heart with sound imān will have a positive effect on the health of the body. However, if the spiritual heart of the person is sick then, it is going to have effect on the physical heart. Then, all the body, mind and the person will suffer due to this. In this perspective, the word[321] فَزَادَهُم can refer to the technical term of metastasis, the spread of the disease from its core to other places in the body.

The above can be explained with a case of a person who has regular connection with Allah. A person constantly prays and takes refuge in Allah for all the fears, needs and depressions removes all the burden from oneself. In this perspective, the body can have better immune system to be healthy.

The natural state of a human is both physically and spiritually to be healthy. Sickness is not the essence but is an auxiliary state. Similarly, fasad and destruction is an auxiliary sickness. No one claim to have this state permanently. Therefore, claims of munāfiqs to be in this state permanently is solely their fault but no one else's. Allah created everyone including them in a healthy state of sound heart, mind and body.

In the expression of فِي قُلُوبِهِم مَّرَضٌ فَزَادَهُمُ[322], one can think ف as harf of sababiyah. Therefore, in many translations as mentioned before this is presented as "there was sickness therefore there was an increase..." I think it is important to possibly add the side note or in the meaning to show that "there was a sickness they did not take care of it and ignore it. Therefore, with the causality rule of Allah, it increased."

---

320. A disease in their hearts.
321. Has increased.
322. In their hearts is disease, so Allah has increased [their disease].

[11]

وَإِذَا قِيلَ لَهُمْ لاَ تُفْسِدُواْ فِي الأَرْضِ قَالُواْ إِنَّمَا نَحْنُ مُصْلِحُونَ [323]{البقرة/11}

The words تُفْسِدُ[324] and مُصْلِحُونَ[325] are almost opposite to each other. It is interesting to see that a person can be in a totally opposite situation when what he or she thinks. When one reviews the historical events of fasad, no one claimed that they were doing fasad. In all of their engagements, all of them asserted that they were doing sulh and they were the muslih. This ayah alludes to this fact as well.

At a personal level, identifying oneself as إِنَّمَا نَحْنُ مُصْلِحُونَ[326] although the reality can be opposite, can show the change in fitrah, natural traits of a person overtime. In this perspective, one cannot differentiate the wrong from right and the lie from the truth. This shows the change of fitrah as mentioned in the previous ayahs with the discussions of diseases and kasb, acquirements of person in one's life.

At a social or community level, this perspective can be very dangerous. A decision can be executed to claim that the purpose is to bring sulh as مُصْلِحُونَ[327]. However, in reality this can be fasad leading to polarizations in a society, killings, and mischief. In this regard, this confusion of perspectives can be very dangerous. One can review all the incidents happened in the past due these iniquitous valuations. One can view all the emerge of liberalism, capitalism and communism in this dilemma of مُصْلِحُونَ versus مفسدون[328] at our recent social history.

There are people even among Muslims when they are involved in a fitnah or in a social, group, or family related matters and disputes, they may see themselves as muslih, peacemakers or arbitrators. In this case, they can be surprised or shocked when people try to give them advice about their problematic approach to solve the arguments. They may not see their position as a possible source of evil, adding more fuel to the fire. Even, they may get upset when hearing some advice from others for self-reflection. In this regard, the statement of إِنَّمَا نَحْنُ مُصْلِحُونَ

---

323. And when it is said to them, "Do not cause corruption on the earth," they say, "We are but reformers."
324. Cause corruption.
325. Reformers.
326. We are but reformers.
327. Reformers.
328. The corrupters.

in the ayah وَإِذَا قِيلَ لَهُمْ لاَ تُفْسِدُواْ فِي الأَرْضِ قَالُواْ إِنَّمَا نَحْنُ مُصْلِحُونَ[329] states this shocking attitude of their position possibly, الله اعلم With this approach, sometimes a person may look a problematic approach in oneself or at a social level. By using a wrong medicine or approach the problem could be aggravated. In this regards, فِي قُلُوبِهِم مَّرَضٌ فَزَادَهُمُ اللّهُ مَرَضاً[330] can be also related with the discourse of مُصْلِحُونَ versus مفسدون, الله اعلم.

The expression وَإِذَا قِيلَ لَهُم[331] can show that when people are involved with some evil renderings it is important to advise and warn them about their engagement. In this perspective, nahyu anil munkar is a key concept. The ummah of Rasulullah ﷺ is praised in the Qurān for this trait. The methodology of how to communicate the message has been always the key and the most daunting task historically. Many times, due to incorrect methodology, a lot of grave mistakes has been done and the content of the message is wasted.

In addition, in the expression وَإِذَا قِيلَ لَهُم[332] since majhul, passive voice is used as a sentence structure then one can deduce that the obligation of "nahyu anil munkar" is farz-kifayah. When some Muslims fulfill this obligation then the others are not obliged to do it.

The expression لاَ تُفْسِدُو[333] in the form of mudari can allude to the fact that there is continuous and recurring fasad, mischief, الله اعلم. It can also refer to changing and new types of fasad, depending on the context and time. For example, the types of fasad today and one hundred years ago can have similarities and also differences depending on the problems of that time and place. Therefore, the revivers of religion, mujaddid are present to encounter these different types of fasad at their different times with different styles and formats, الله اعلم.

The expression فِي الأَرْضِ[334] can denote that everyone is sharing the same space. In this case, if a person makes fasad then everyone will be affected from it. So, one should not be deceived with the vastness of the earth that if there is a fasad then it has only local effects. Nevertheless,

---

329. And when it is said to them, "Do not cause corruption on the earth," they say, "We are but reformers."
330. In their hearts is disease, so Allah has increased their disease.
331. And when it is said to them.
332. And when it is said to them.
333. Do not cause corruption.
334. On the earth.

when there is fasad everything, even non-humans, are affected as mentioned in the ayah:

ظَهَرَ الْفَسَادُ فِي الْبَرِّ وَالْبَحْرِ بِمَا كَسَبَتْ أَيْدِي النَّاسِ لِيُذِيقَهُم بَعْضَ الَّذِي عَمِلُوا لَعَلَّهُمْ يَرْجِعُونَ {الروم 41/}[335]

In physics, this current phenomenon is known as butterfly effect described as "the phenomenon whereby a minute localized change in a complex system can have large effects elsewhere," (21). Similar incident in mathematics is known as the chaos theory to allude to this fact that a minute chaos or fasad can have big effects defined as "the branch of mathematics that deals with complex systems whose behavior is highly sensitive to slight changes in conditions, so that small alterations can give rise to strikingly great consequences," (21).

The expression فِي الْأَرْضِ[336] can allude that the people share the earth like a home with other fellow humans. In this sense making fasad, for their same brothers and sisters does not qualify with the human traits of solidarity, mercy and care.

The expression قَالُو[337] can show that they are not really in the position of listening and getting some advice and suggestions. However, they try to normalize and produce somewhat demagogical discourses, الله اعلم. It is interesting to note the definition of demagogue as a person who "seeks support by appealing to popular desires and prejudices rather than by using rational argument" (21).

In the expression قَالُواْ إِنَّمَا نَحْنُ مُصْلِحُونَ[338], the word إِنَّمَا[339] can be used as a takid for something that is obvious and clear. In this perspective, when they use this word for something that is not really clear, can display hints for their real disposition. In other words, when people see that what they are doing an they know that their renderings are completely

---

335. 30:40 IT IS GOD who has created you, and then has provided you with sustenance, and then will cause you to die, and then will bring you to life again. Can any of those beings or powers to whom you ascribe a share in His divinity do any of these things? Limitless is He in His glory, and sublimely exalted above anything to which men may ascribe a share in His divinity!
336. On the earth.
337. They said.
338. They say, "We are but reformers."
339. We are but.

wrong, then but still pointing out an emphasis and takid with إِنَّمَا make them really disgraced in front of the people of mind and heart.

Also, people evaluate the things according to their judgment values. A person can tell them for example "if you avoid the evil and do good then Allah ﷻ can reward you in Heaven." Then, they may respond as "we have a good house with a big backyard like heaven so this is my heaven." The person can try to take them out of their boundaries of values but it can be difficult or impossible until they are hit with something evil-seeming incident.

In the expression قَالُواْ إِنَّمَا نَحْنُ مُصْلِحُونَ, the word مُصْلِحُونَ[340] is a ismi-fail. This can mean that muslih, establishing peace or peace making is their trait, sifah because it is in the form of ismi-fail. This is interesting. For something to become the trait of a person, then it should be clearly observed and agreed upon by almost everyone. When something is obvious but if some people are claiming otherwise then one party should be not saying the truth. For example, when there are firefighters, they try to extinguish fire constantly then everyone knows their position and duty as a trait. They go and stop and extinguish the fire. If someone comes says "you are not extinguishing the fire but you are always increasing the fire and therefore, you should not be called firefighter." Then, one party should not be saying the truth. Similarly, in this case, putting themselves as a position of having the trait of مُصْلِحُونَ[341], can also be a sign that they are not saying the truth. To have this trait, almost everyone should agree upon this trait about them. However, when one analyzes the cases of munafiqûn at the early times with the Prophet صلى الله عليه وسلم, they were always involved with a type of fitnah and they were often at the position of advocating and defending themselves. Early Muslims, sahabah, had the idea of who were doing the fasād[342] and nifāq[343], and they almost agreed on who these individuals were (22). Yet, the Prophet ﷺ did not want to challenge them openly in order not to cause more disunity.

In addition, in the expression قَالُواْ إِنَّمَا نَحْنُ مُصْلِحُونَ[344], one can realize and feel an attitude of promotion about their disposition. In other

340. Reformers.
341. Reformers.
342. Corruption.
343. Hypocrisy.
344. They say, "We are but reformers."

words, they encourage others to join them in whatever their disposition is, الله اعلم.

To summarize, it is very difficult find people who accept any blame or true advice. Similarly, the above categorized may have similar attitude. Alternatively, as mentioned before, that since their true fitrah was disabled for its genuine capacity to differentiate between right and wrong, they can have this setback to see fasād as falāh.

[12]

أَلا إِنَّهُمْ هُمُ الْمُفْسِدُونَ وَلَكِن لاَّ يَشْعُرُونَ {البقرة/12}345

The expression أَلا إِنَّهُمْ هُمُ الْمُفْسِدُونَ[346] has a lot of takid, emphasis, and strong disposition. First, the word أَلا has the meanings of caution, warning and paying attention. It has the meanings of waking up and realizing the reality. So, this أَلا has a strong emphasis as the starting point of the ayah. Then, the word إِنَّهُمْ[347] is combined of two words ان(inna) +هم. The word inna itself is emphasis. Then, it gets stronger with when it is combined with هم. Then, another هم is added to make it stronger. The word المفسدون[348] is ismi-fail that can also add emphasis for the message, الله اعلم.

The people who do fasad in the previous ayah mentions their stance with إِنَّمَا نَحْنُ[349] to emphasize their disposition. This ayah with all the above analysis of أَلا إِنَّهُمْ هُمُ الْمُفْسِدُونَ[350] destroys their emphasis. Also, in the previous ayah قَالُواْ إِنَّمَا نَحْنُ مُصْلِحُونَ[351], the word مُصْلِحُونَ does not have marifah, definite article which shows more blurriness, ambiguity, vagueness and fuzziness about their stance. When Allah mentions in أَلا إِنَّهُمْ هُمُ الْمُفْسِدُونَ with the word الْمُفْسِدُونَ which is the opposite and counter word of مُصْلِحُونَ[352], the word الْمُفْسِدُونَ has marifah and definiteness without ambiguity but with certainty. So, one can here witness this literal war and the destruction of fasad makers by Allah in this literal analysis before the physical and spiritual destructions in this life and after death. The reason for all this was their implicit or explicit disposition of يُخَادِعُونَ

---

345. (2:12) Oh, verily, it is they, they who are spreading corruption—but they perceive it not?
346. Oh, verily, it is they, they who are spreading corruption.
347. Verily they are.
348. The ones who are spreading corruption.
349. We are but.
350. Unquestionably, it is they who are the corrupters.
351. They say, "We are but reformers."
352. Reformers.

{البقرة/9} 353 ﴿يُخَادِعُونَ اللَّهَ وَالَّذِينَ آمَنُوا وَمَا يَخْدَعُونَ إِلَّا أَنفُسَهُم وَمَا يَشْعُرُونَ﴾ that they declared position against Allah and believers, الله اعلم.

The default state of a Muslim is expected to have husnu-zann, good opinion for everyone. However, it is important not to be harmed by others as the Prophet mentions that a believer is not to be bitten twice from the same hole (3). This means that if someone is harmed from a person than it is not wise not to recognize it and protect oneself from a second possibility of harm. It does not mean harming others but protecting oneself from potential future harms. Similarly, this ayah أَلَا ﴿إِنَّهُمْ هُمُ الْمُفْسِدُونَ وَلَكِن لَّا يَشْعُرُونَ﴾ 354 {البقرة/12} can be a suggestion to protect oneself from potential harms by educating oneself. This group of people have very complex character traits that can be very difficult to decipher. Therefore, the Qurān explains in detail the inner psychological dialogues in order to allude to this educational process, الله اعلم.

In this education process, the purpose is to recognize and know people with each person's own critical thinking and assessment but not with the assessment of others delivered to the person. Especially, one can see the valid reason of this today with the massive media influence on people informing them what and how to think about others. In this practice, often, there is the implicit notion of blocking and belittling everyone's own ability of critical judgement and thinking.

The word يَشْعُرُونَ 355 is mentioned first in يُخَادِعُونَ اللَّهَ وَالَّذِينَ آمَنُوا وَمَا ﴿لَا يَخْدَعُونَ إِلَّا أَنفُسَهُم وَمَا يَشْعُرُونَ﴾ 356 {البقرة/9} then repeated in here إِنَّهُمْ هُمُ الْمُفْسِدُونَ وَلَكِن لَّا يَشْعُرُونَ﴾ 357 {البقرة/12}

One can see the that the word ﴿وَمَا يَشْعُرُونَ﴾ 358 shows that they don't understand that they are harming their own selves. Here, instead of يعقلون 359 the word يَشْعُرُونَ is used. As mentioned aqil comes before shuur. Aqil can be the critical thinking and shuur can be the basic recognition of harms and benefits. In this perspective, animals can have shuur that they can understand the basic harms and benefits of things. So it is not

---

353. They [think to] deceive Allah and those who believe, but they deceive not except themselves and perceive [it] not.
354. Unquestionably, it is they who are the corrupters, but they perceive [it] not.
355. They perceive.
356. They [think to] deceive Allah and those who believe, but they deceive not except themselves and perceive [it] not.
357. The corrupters, but they perceive [it] not.
358. And perceive [it] not.
359. They know.

wise to expect benefit from the people who can't have the basic cognition skills of differentiating harmful from the beneficial.

The word اَلاَ[360] and other types of ta'kid in this ayah can show that it may be easy to be misled from their look and their eloquence in their speech. As mentioned in the ayahs:

وَإِذَا رَأَيْتَهُمْ تُعْجِبُكَ أَجْسَامُهُمْ وَإِن يَقُولُوا تَسْمَعْ لِقَوْلِهِمْ كَأَنَّهُمْ خُشُبٌ مُسَنَّدَةٌ يَحْسَبُونَ كُلَّ صَيْحَةٍ عَلَيْهِمْ هُمُ الْعَدُوُّ فَاحْذَرْهُمْ قَاتَلَهُمُ اللّٰهُ أَنَّى يُؤْفَكُونَ [361] {المنافقون/4}

Yet, Allah ﷻ gives importance to the traits and characters, the disposition of the heart and mind but not the looks (9) as mentioned by the Prophet ﷺ. Therefore, the word اَلاَ and other types of ta'kid in this ayah emphasizes that one's value system of others should not be based on their externalities, والله اعلم.

One can view that the expression إِنَّمَا نَحْنُ مُصْلِحُونَ[362] in the previous ayah has a lot of takid and emphasis that they are the peace makers. Oppositely, this ayah أَلا إِنَّهُمْ هُمُ الْمُفْسِدُونَ وَلَكِن لاَّ يَشْعُرُونَ[363] {البقرة/12} emphasizes by including more ta'kid elements in its expressions that they are not the peace makers but fasad makers. We discussed these elements of emphasis above for this ayah.

As it was mentioned before the word لاَّ يَشْعُرُونَ[364], shuur, can be the ability of person for simple differentiation and knowledge of things through senses. Therefore, animals can have shuur of this basic ability of knowing the harms and benefits of things for their life. When a person makes obvious fasad and claims to be a mufsih, peacemaker then it can be said that they don't have shuur. Or, if a person kills another person for their belief, for their saintly disposition, or for their invitation to Allah ﷻ such as the prophets then, it can be said that they don't have shuur as mentioned in لاَّ يَشْعُرُونَ.

One can see that that when a person kills another because of their belief that is against the basic animal and human recognition of

---

360. Verily.
361. And when you see them, their forms please you, and if they speak, you listen to their speech. [They are] as if they were pieces of wood propped up—they think that every shout is against them. They are the enemy, so beware of them. May Allah destroy them; how are they deluded?
362. "We are but reformers."
363. Oh, verily, it is they, they who are spreading corruption but they perceive [it] not.
364. And perceive [it] not.

differentiating beneficial from harmful. In this case, one can see the similar appeal when the person, al-mumin, defends Musa as against Firawn, he appeals to their human basics as "are you going to kill someone because he believes and invites to Allah ﷺ?":

وَقَالَ رَجُلٌ مُّؤْمِنٌ مِّنْ آلِ فِرْعَوْنَ يَكْتُمُ إِيمَانَهُ أَتَقْتُلُونَ رَجُلاً أَن يَقُولَ رَبِّيَ اللّهُ وَقَدْ جَاءكُم بِالْبَيِّنَاتِ مِن رَّبِّكُمْ وَإِن يَكُ كَاذِباً فَعَلَيْهِ كَذِبُهُ وَإِن يَكُ صَادِقاً يُصِبْكُم بَعْضُ الَّذِي يَعِدُكُمْ إِنَّ اللّهَ لَا يَهْدِي مَنْ هُوَ مُسْرِفٌ كَذَّابٌ {غافر/28} [365]

One can see similar discourse with magicians' appeal to Firawn as well:

وَمَا تَنقِمُ مِنَّا إِلاَّ أَنْ آمَنَّا بِآيَاتِ رَبِّنَا لَمَّا جَاءتْنَا رَبَّنَا أَفْرِغْ عَلَيْنَا صَبْراً وَتَوَفَّنَا مُسْلِمِينَ {الأعراف/126} [366]

The expression هُمُ الْمُفْسِدُونَ can allude to the fact that it is not difficult to point out who these people can be. In other words, with the pronoun of هُم, one can see that they are identifiable. When one looks at the cases of Badr, Uhud, Tabuk or other cases, these people (munāfiqs) stance was to confuse people among sahabah and try to make the Prophet be left alone in these endeavors (8).

One can see in the above ayahs that nifāq and fasad are such elements to destroy the peace and harmony a society. Therefore, one can see details with strong emphasis and strong words to allude to this fact. At the same time, it is also difficult to point out and to decipher the elements of nifāq and fasad due to its complexity. Another Quranic verse alludes to this complexity as

[367] {مُذَبْذَبِينَ بَيْنَ ذَلِكَ لَا إِلَى هَؤُلَاء وَلَا إِلَى هَؤُلَاء وَمَن يُضْلِلِ أللہ فَلَن تَجِدَ لَهُ سَبِيلًا النساء/143}

---

365. (40:28) At that, a believing man of Pharaoh's family, who [until then] had concealed his faith, exclaimed: "Would you slay a man because he says, 'God is my Sustainer'—seeing, withal, that he has brought you all evidence of this truth from your Sustainer? Now if he be a liar, his lie will fall back on him; but if he is a man of truth, something [of the punishment] whereof he warns you is bound to befall you: for, verily, God would not grace with His guidance one who has wasted his own self by lying [about Him].

366. (7:126) for thou takest vengeance on us only because we have come to believe in our Sustainer's messages as soon as they came to us. O our Sustainer! Shower us with patience in adversity, and make us die as men who have surrendered themselves unto Thee!"

367. (4:143) wavering between this and that, [true] neither to these nor those. But for him whom God lets go astray thou canst never find any way.

One can view above ayah as an identity crisis at one angle. This can reflect itself as a complex personal spiritual disease at the heart and mind in their experiential and cognition process. Then, when the group of people with similar and different spiritual diseases come together they can cause immense damage at a social level.

In the expression أَلَا إِنَّهُمْ هُمُ الْمُفْسِدُونَ[368] and others, the trait of fasad generally attributed to munāfiqs. In other words, when there is action or attitude of fasad, either the person is munāfiq or have traits of munāfiq, (الله اعلم).

When one reviews the above ayahs, one can realize the reality of human's heart and intention is only truly known by Allah. In this perspective, although it is important establish law enforcements measures to prevent mischief and disorders as mentioned with the word الْمُفْسِدُونَ, the real prevention and enforcement can prevail itself when the fear and accountability in front of Allah is truly instilled in the hearts and minds of people (23).

[13]

وَإِذَا قِيلَ لَهُمْ آمِنُواْ كَمَا آمَنَ النَّاسُ قَالُواْ أَنُؤْمِنُ كَمَا آمَنَ السُّفَهَاءُ أَلَا إِنَّهُمْ هُمُ السُّفَهَاء
وَلَكِن لاَّ يَعْلَمُونَ {البقرة/13}[369]

In the above discussions, it is very interesting to see that the munāfiqs converse with the Prophet. Yet, they know that the Prophet constantly gets revelation about the seen and unseen. Still, they think and assume that they can deceive the Prophet. This shows another huge gap in their mental reasoning along with other illogical engagements of theirs.

In the above ayah, one can see their approach of identifying, classifying, and grouping people. In this process of identity formation, the highest and noblest group comes with wealth, power and position. In other words, they don't want to be identified and belong to the individuals, groups or identities that do not have wealth, power and

---

368. Oh, verily, it is they, they who are spreading corruption.
369. 2:13 And when they are told, "Believe as other people believe," they answer, "Shall we believe as the weak-minded believe?" Oh, verily, it is they, they who are weak-minded—but they know it not!

position as mentioned in the word السُّفَهَاء[370]. To relate with the previous ayahs, the definition of مُصْلِحُونَ[371] is ensuring wealth, power and position.

For a believer and mu'min, the core of wealth is believing in Allah ﷻ, the Prophet ﷺ and believing in the akhirah. The rest such as the physical wealth is considered as a detail or auxiliary besides this core.

In the analysis of this ayah, one sees that there is a dialogue and interaction between the muminun and munāfiqs. The essence of this dialogue is about amr-bil ma'ruf and nahy-I a'nil munkar. In this perspective, it seems that the belivers, al-muminun, first giving them nasiha as وَإِذَا قِيلَ لَهُمْ آمِنُواْ كَمَا آمَنَ النَّاسُ[372]. Then they respond, reject the advice and re-direct the dialogue to another platform by saying قَالُوٓاْ[373] أَنُؤْمِنُ كَمَا آمَنَ السُّفَهَاء. Then, between these two groups, Allah ﷻ mentions and reveal the real disposition of the second group, the munāfiqs as أَلَا[374] إِنَّهُمْ هُمُ السُّفَهَاء وَلَكِن لاَّ يَعْلَمُونَ.

In this ayah, as mentioned above, amr-bil ma'ruf and nahy-I a'nil munkar is done which is considered farz kifayah in Islamic rulings (24). In other words, it is required to invite people to Islam. This requirement can be fulfilled by some or many Muslims. There are for this is not generalized but mentioned in وَإِذَا قِيلَ لَهُمْ آمِنُواْ كَمَا آمَنَ النَّاسُ[375] with the form قِيلَ[376], majhul, passive voice that if some does it then this responsibility would be fulfilled, الله اعلم.

Especially, in non-Muslim countries, since the Muslims are minority, there are not many Muslims. Then, this ruling can be farz-ayn, absolute requirement, for Muslims in the West, الله اعلم . In this obligation, one can do the call for everyone without any discrimination

therefore, كَمَا آمَنَ النَّاسُ[377] can allude to this generalizability. Yet, at the same time, it can also allude to the auxiliary stance of the munafiqin as marginal groups. Then, their response alludes that they try to rationalize their stance with knowledge but it is not the case as referred لاَّ يَعْلَمُونَ[378]. So, their disposition is not I'lm but jahalah.

---

370. The Foolish.
371. Reformers.
372. And when it is said to them, "Believe as the people have believed."
373. They say, "Should we believe as the foolish have believed?"
374. Unquestionably, it is they who are the foolish, but they know [it] not.
375. And when it is said to them, "Believe as the people have believed."
376. Said to them.
377. As the people have believed."
378. They do not know.

Also, in this expression, لاَ يَعْلَمُونَ is used instead of مَا يَعْلَمُونَ. If it was
مَا يَعْلَمُونَ[379], then it can indicate that they don't know now with I'lm but
they may know later. Yet, لاَ يَعْلَمُونَ is used to allude the quality of munāfiq
is same and does not change with time, present or future, الله اعلم. Yet,
still one can assume their disposition but still invite them and teach
them about the true Islam as mentioned with إِذ. In Arabic, اِن can allude
to a possibility that calling or inviting them can be optional but إِذ has
certainty but does not have any meaning of possibility of a choice in
inviting them or not as mentioned in the ayah, الله اعلم.

When one reviews the ayah وَإِذَا قِيلَ لَهُمْ آمِنُواْ كَمَا آمَنَ النَّاسُ قَالُواْ أَنُؤْمِنُ كَمَا[380]
آمَنَ السُّفَهَاء, one can realize the attitude of arrogance when they mention
وَإِذَا قِيلَ لَهُمْ آمِنُواْ كَمَا آمَنَ النَّاسُ[381]. One's verbal response often embody their
disposition of hearts. There is a disease in their heart as mentioned
above, thus their hearts entail arrogance. Then, this arrogance can lead
to making fasad, mischief on earth and everywhere.

One of the proofs of their arrogance is not following what is agreed
as reasonable by other people. The word النَّاسُ[382] in the expression آمِنُواْ[383]
كَمَا آمَنَ النَّاسُ can indicate this sound stance of normal people. There are
always ones who want to be extraordinary, different, and singular due to
the disease of arrogance and riya, showing off. Therefore, they expect an
exclusive treatment from the Prophet and others (8). The word السُّفَهَاء[384]
and their phrase قَالُواْ أَنُؤْمِنُ كَمَا آمَنَ السُّفَهَاء[385] can suggest this very explicitly.
So, this attitude of singularity due the disease of arrogance and riya is
not new but the source of the disease demonstrated with Shaytan:

{ فَإِذَا سَوَّيْتُهُ وَنَفَخْتُ فِيهِ مِن رُّوحِي فَقَعُواْ لَهُ سَاجِدِينَ {الحجر/29}[386]

---

379. They will never know.
380. And when it is said to them, "Believe as the people have believed," they say, "Should we
believe as the foolish have believed?"
381. And when it is said to them, "Believe as the people have believed."
382. The people.
383. Believe as the people have believed.
384. The foolish.
385. They say, "Should we believe as the foolish have believed?"
386. (15:29) And when I have proportioned him and breathed into him of My [created] soul,
then fall down to him in prostration."

فَسَجَدَ الْمَلَائِكَةُ كُلُّهُمْ أَجْمَعُونَ {الحجر/30} إلاَّ إِبْلِيسَ أَبَى أن يَكُونَ مَعَ السَّاجِدِينَ {الحجر/31}387

قَالَ يَا إِبْلِيسُ مَا لَكَ أَلاَّ تَكُونَ مَعَ السَّاجِدِينَ {الحجر/32} قَالَ لَمْ أَكُن لِّأَسْجُدَ لِبَشَرٍ خَلَقْتَهُ مِن صَلْصَالٍ مِّنْ حَمَإٍ مَّسْنُونٍ {الحجر/33}

All the angels submitted and surrendered to Allah except shaytan which is similar to the submission of Muslims to Allah with the guidance of the Qurān and the Prophet except munafiqūn . One can see very similar equivalents between قَالُواْ أَنُؤْمِنُ كَمَا آمَنَ السُّفَهَاء388 and قَالَ لَمْ أَكُن لِّأَسْجُدَ لِبَشَرٍ خَلَقْتَهُ مِن صَلْصَالٍ مِّنْ حَمَإٍ مَّسْنُونٍ {الحجر/33}389. One can see here that munāfiqs clearly follow shaytan instead of the guidance of Allah represented with the Qurān and the Prophet.

The scholars of heart, mutasawwifun or a'rifun have different ways to handle this attitude or disease of expecting an exceptional treatment. They try to emphasize the notion of being with people among them but being with God at the same time. They suggest to perform some lowly duties in public among people to break this disposition and to treat this sickness. They constantly teach being humble as abd of Allah similar to all creation. This disposition in reality elevates the person but not other titles or qualities, الله اعلم.

In addition, the word النَّاسُ390 in the expression وَإِذَا قِيلَ لَهُمْ آمِنُواْ كَمَا391 آمَنَ النَّاسُ can indicate that to be a real human being, one should have imān. The word النَّاسُ is also mentioned previously وَمِنَ النَّاسِ مَن يَقُولُ آمَنَّا بِاللّهِ وَبِالْيَوْمِ الآخِرِ وَمَا هُم بِمُؤْمِنِينَ {البقرة/8}392. The meaning of this ayah can allude to the bewilderment or astonishment that among humans there are ones who do not act like humans.

In other words, the real title of human, insān, as the khalifah of Allah is present when the person has imān, الله اعلم.

---

387. (15:30)So the angels prostrated—all of them entirely,
(15:31)Except Iblees, he refused to be with those who prostrated.
388. They say, "Should we believe as the foolish have believed?"
389. (15:33) He said, "Never would I prostrate to a human whom You created out of clay from an altered black mud."
390. The people.
391. And when it is said to them, "Believe as the people have believed."
392. And of the people are some who say, "We believe in Allah and the Last Day," but they are not believers.

Yet, they have a position among humans. This can be similar to the case as

وَإِذْ قُلْنَا لِلْمَلَائِكَةِ اسْجُدُوا لِآدَمَ فَسَجَدُوا إِلَّا إِبْلِيسَ كَانَ مِنَ الْجِنِّ فَفَسَقَ عَنْ أَمْرِ رَبِّهِ أَفَتَتَّخِذُونَهُ وَذُرِّيَّتَهُ أَوْلِيَاء مِن دُونِي وَهُمْ لَكُمْ عَدُوٌّ بِئْسَ لِلظَّالِمِينَ بَدَلًا {الكهف/50}393.

Shaytan was among angels but not an angel. The similar order was for shaytan too since shaytan was among them. Similarly, among humans, there may be shaytans like munāfiqs but they are not humans in reality, الله اعلم.

Another view point can be that when they had a spiritual disease in their heart and it increased as mentioned in فِي قُلُوبِهِم مَّرَضٌ فَزَادَهُمُ اللّهُ مَرَضاً 394{البقرة/10}وَلَهُم عَذَابٌ أَلِيمٌ بِمَا كَانُوا يَكْذِبُونَ. Then, they lost the essentials of being a human. Therefore, as a friendly and kindly approach, there is an advice to treat this increasing disease with the statement وَإِذَا قِيلَ 395 لَهُمْ آمِنُواْ كَمَا آمَنَ النَّاسُ. In other words, when a person genuinely has imān and puts the effort to practice and ask forgiveness from Allah ﷻ, then, this aggravating disease that is terminating the life of the person can be cured, insAllah, الله اعلم.

Alternatively, the word النَّاسُ396 can allude to the believers because this word has marifah with alif and lam so they are specific group of people. In this case, the word النَّاسُ can allude to the early Muslims who would be the sahabah around the Prophet ﷺ. So, sahabah are the role model humans as the word النَّاسُ alludes. They were role models for their time as well the times after them until day of qiyamah, الله اعلم. In this perspective, when one reviews the rules of tashbih, similitude, as used with كَ in the expression كَمَا آمَنَ النَّاسُ397, the thing that is resembled to is not exactly the same as the original. In other words, if the word النَّاسُ represent the sahabah as the sabab-I nuzûl of ayahs indicate, the believers

---

393. 18:50 AND [remember that] when We told the angels, "Prostrate yourselves before Adam," they all prostrated themselves, except Iblis: he [too] was one of those invisible beings, but then he turned away from his Sustainer's command. Will you, then, take him and his cohorts for (your), masters instead of Me, although they are your foe? How vile an exchange on the evildoers' part!

394. In their hearts is disease, so Allah has increased their disease; and for them is a painful punishment because they [habitually] used to lie.

395. And when it is said to them, "Believe as the people have believed."

396. The people.

397. As the people have believed.

will take the sahabah as role models but they will not be exactly at the same level like them. They will not reach to their level, الله اعلم.

In another perspective, there will be always group of people in each time period who would be called لنَّاس, as they would be the role models living a life similar to sahabah, الله اعلم.

The word لنَّاس can also indicate that before Islam they were all together. As others believe and accept this reasonable offer and teachings of Islam, then they should accept it with them too in order not to make disharmony in their community or society. One can have disagreements and criticism as the person have mind and they think. Yet, if they already accept these reasonable teachings of Islam then, they should move on but not cause fitnah and discord by going back and forth with some of the unreasonable old customs and attitudes of unethical, immoral and unjust discourses and engagements الله اعلم .

One can review the expression قَالُوٓا۟ أَنُؤْمِنُ كَمَآ ءَامَنَ ٱلسُّفَهَآءُ أَلَآ إِنَّهُمْ هُمُ ٱلسُّفَهَآءُ[398], that when people blame others with a quality, they actually get this blame on themselves due to the adl, Justice of Allah ﷻ. In this case when they blame the believers as ٱلسُّفَهَآءُ[399] they in reality actualize this quality in their lives as mentioned هُمُ ٱلسُّفَهَآءُ[400], الله اعلم.

The word قَالُو in the above expression can allude to the type of people when you tell them something they immediately defend themselves. Instead of benefitting what the other person is saying about them and perhaps doing some self-reflection, they immediately try to justify their position. One can know this attitude from the children. Yet, if the adults do it they lose their trusted and reliable positions among people, الله اعلم.

One of the important viewpoints in the expression وَلَٰكِن لَّا يَعْلَمُونَ[401] is that people who realize their own problems and glitches about their nafs can benefit advises of others. In other words, if a person gives an advice to someone but if the person does not think or agree that the point of advice is not related with him or her then, this person cannot benefit from this advice, الله اعلم.

The word ءَامِنُو in the expression وَإِذَا قِيلَ لَهُمْ ءَامِنُو[402] can indicate that the Muslims are asking to these people to accept the belief with its all

---

398. They say, "Should we believe as the foolish have believed?"
399. The foolish.
400. They are the foolish.
401. But they know [it] not.
402. When it is said to them, "Believe."

articles but not pick and choose, . اعلم الله Allah ﷺ mentions that the real believers know and are aware of the actual situation of munāfiqs that they don't have the true imān. Instead of the word آمَنُو in the ayah, the expression could have been with the word اخلصوا so that they should have ikhlas in their belief. However, this shows that imān cannot be called a true imān if it has defects in its proper articles. If the heart of a person has diseases, then other diseases can be auxiliary and secondary. Similarly, having true imān is the heart of the religious teachings. Other religious duties are secondary and auxiliary compared to the issues of imān. Once the heart, the core, the imān of a person is sound at least with the minimums than others can follow. Once this minimum is there then there should be always the struggle and the goal in one's life to perfect it as mentioned:

يَا أَيُّهَا الَّذِينَ آمَنُواْ آمِنُواْ بِاللّهِ وَرَسُولِهِ وَالْكِتَابِ الَّذِي نَزَّلَ عَلَى رَسُولِهِ وَالْكِتَابِ الَّذِيَ أَنزَلَ مِن قَبْلُ وَمَن يَكْفُرْ بِاللّهِ وَمَلاَئِكَتِهِ وَكُتُبِهِ وَرُسُلِهِ وَالْيَوْمِ الآخِرِ فَقَدْ ضَلَّ ضَلاَلاً بَعِيدًا {النساء/136}403.

In the expression يَا أَيُّهَا الَّذِينَ آمَنُواْ آمِنُواْ404, the word آمِنُواْ is repeated. This can mean that the word آمِنُواْ is used for the ones who have the minimums of imān but the struggle of perfection is advised with آمِنُواْ again. This perfection, the struggle and goal should be to increase one's imān as mentioned with the key word فَزَادَتْهُمْ إِيمَانًا as in the ayah:

وَإِذَا مَا أُنزِلَتْ سُورَةٌ فَمِنْهُم مَّن يَقُولُ أَيُّكُمْ زَادَتْهُ هَذِهِ إِيمَانًا فَأَمَّا الَّذِينَ آمَنُواْ فَزَادَتْهُمْ إِيمَانًا وَهُمْ يَسْتَبْشِرُونَ {التوبة/124}405

In the expression قَالُواْ أَنُؤْمِنُ406, the word أَنُؤْمِن can indicate an attitude of belittling type of questioning. In English, one of the common expressions can be "are you kidding me?" In other words, they belittle

---

403. 4:136 O you who have attained to faith! Hold fast unto your belief in God and His Apostle, and in the divine writ which He has bestowed from on high upon His Apostle, step by step, as well as in the revelation which He sent down aforetime: for he who denies God, and His angels, and His revelations, and His apostles, and the Last Day, has indeed gone far astray.
404. O you who believe.
405. 9:124 YET WHENEVER a Sûrah [of this divine writ] is bestowed from on high, some of the deniers of the truth are prone to ask, "Which of you has this [message] strengthened in his faith?" Now as for those who have attained to faith, it does strengthen them in their faith, and they rejoice in the glad tiding [which God has given them].
406. They say, "Should we believe.

the person for the content of their discourse. The word أَنُؤْمِنُ can also imply to their arrogance and their fasad, الله اعلم.

When the munāfiqs were invited for imān there were three stages. First, they tried to understand what was said or advised. Then, they went to their friends and discussed the issue as mentioned in وَإِذَا خَلَوْاْ إِلَى شَيَاطِينِهِمْ قَالُواْ إِنَّا مَعَكُمْ إِنَّمَا نَحْنُ مُسْتَهْزِؤُونَ {البقرة 14/5}[407]. Lastly, they expressed verbally their disposition as mentioned in قَالُواْ أَنُؤْمِنُ كَمَا آمَنَ السُّفَهَاء[408]. One can realize that their verbal statement is emerging as a result of a process but not something said randomly.

The expressions وَإِذَا قِيلَ لَهُمْ آمِنُواْ كَمَا آمَنَ النَّاسُ[409] and their response as قَالُواْ أَنُؤْمِنُ كَمَا آمَنَ السُّفَهَاء can also suggest a type of imān that these people had. Yet, this type of belief was not accepted by Allah ﷻ. Therefore, آمِنُواْ كَمَا آمَنَ النَّاسُ was suggested to them, الله اعلم. Due to the problems in their imān, they were opposed to the imān of the Muslims and they designated their imān as the belief of the lowly class as mentioned قَالُواْ أَنُؤْمِنُ كَمَا آمَنَ السُّفَهَاء. This is again an interesting identity formation in regards to the attachment and taxonomy of belief according to the social class. In other words, they implied that each class in the society should carry different types of belief according to their social status, الله اعلم. One can further analyze this notion when different groups, religious or non-religious grant themselves with the notions as "we are selected or chosen people by God," or "we are the descendent of this holy person." I think, the Qurān encourages positive group formations to achieve good, gratitude, ethical and moral but discourages negative class formations to form discrimination, ungratefulness, racism, or religious superiority to one's identity, الله اعلم. In this regards, the word Muslim is a group name who have the qualities attitude with gratitude of positive since the beginning of creation from Adam as, Ibrahim as, Musa as, Isa as, Muhammad ﷺ and others. The word kufr is a group name who have the qualities of attitude of negative with ingratitude since the beginning of creation from shaytan until the end of world, الله اعلم.

---

407. 2:14 And when they meet those who have attained to faith, they assert, "We believe [as you believe]"; but when they find themselves alone with their evil impulses, they say, "Verily, we are with you; we were only mocking!"
408. They say, "Should we believe as the foolish have believed?"
409. And when it is said to them, "Believe as the people have believed,"

In the expression قَالُواْ أَنُؤْمِنُ كَمَا آمَنَ السُّفَهَاء, the word السُّفَهَاء[410] can indicate that Islam is the place of refuge, shelter and protection for the weak, poor, humiliated in the society, discriminated and as well as intellectuals. One can realize that the teachings of Islam is for everyone and for all humanity but not for an elect group of people, الله اعلم.

On another perspective, the word السُّفَهَاء can also allude to implicit social class understandings at our times among different people with different college, graduate or post-graduate degrees. In other words, the trend of peering with the same educational level or higher but viewing others as السُّفَهَاء can be some of the renderings of this ayah in our current time, الله اعلم.

One can ask why there are too much emphasis and warning against nifāq, fasad and mischief in the Qurān? The answer is very simple. One can look at today the history of Islam and realize the immense damage received continuously through the discourses of nifāq, fasad and mischief executed by people. Yet, in spite of existence of these serious warnings and emphasis in the Qurān, the historical outcome shows that Muslims had difficulty executing these Quranic teaching in practical life, الله اعلم.

There are different opinions in the tafasir when they say قَالُواْ أَنُؤْمِنُ[411] كَمَا آمَنَ السُّفَهَاء if it is directly in conversation to the Muslims or if it is a conversation in their own groups. Imān Ali ibn Ahmad Al-Wahidi rh (25) mentions that it was when they were in their own groups because they did not have the valor to explicitly express it to the believers. Yet, when one reviews and analyses the siyāq and sibāq, the context of the verses and the characters of munāfiqs, it is highly possible that they bluntly uttered those words directly to the faces of Muslims as well, الله اعلم.

Their utterance of أَنُؤْمِنُ كَمَا آمَنَ السُّفَهَاء can also allude their psychological state of anger, irritation, hostility, and frustration. The reason people have this state can be due to various reasons. Some of them can be due to not receiving recognition, position, wealth, and leadership.

The expression of أَنُؤْمِنُ كَمَا آمَنَ السُّفَهَاء can also indicate two meanings. In other words, they state purposefully a statement that may have two meanings. One meaning is positive and affirmative. This can mean that

---

410. The foolish.
411. They say, "Should we believe as the foolish have believed?"

"for sure, we believe, how can we not believe! If we don't believe in the genuine teachings, then we would be السُّفَهَاء[412]." The other meaning is that "we don't believe like السُّفَهَاء. If we believe, then we would be ",السُّفَهَاء. الله اعلم.

In the expression أَلَا إِنَّهُمْ هُمُ السُّفَهَاء, the word أَلَا is also publicizing agent of their realities. In other words, the word أَلَا exposes their inner and secret realities to public. This can be also taki'd, emphasis that one takid follows it with إِنَّهُمْ. Then, another taki'd, emphasis follow with another word with هُمْ. This can show that a person or group of people preferring this short worldly life with their deceptions to an eternal afterlife, in reality, has lack of logic and reasoning as mentioned with the word السُّفَهَاء, الله اعلم.

In the expression أَلَا إِنَّهُمْ هُمُ السُّفَهَاء[413], the word السُّفَهَاء is marifah. This is another point of ta'kid that it has alif and lam. In other words, these group of people are known by others. Everyone knows that they are السُّفَهَاء. They represent the most recent and popular version of being السُّفَهَاء, الله اعلم.

In the expression وَلَكِنْ لَا يَعْلَمُونَ[414], the word يَعْلَمُونَ alludes to the notion that to differentiate between the truth, facts and falsehood, haqq and batil, one needs knowledge, i'lm. As mentioned in أَلَا إِنَّهُمْ هُمُ الْمُفْسِدُونَ وَلَكِن لَا يَشْعُرُونَ[415]{البقرة/12}, the word يَشْعُرُونَ[416] is the basic skill of recognition with shuur that il'm, knowledge and critical analysis come later. The order of the ayahs is in this consecutive sequence as: لَا يَشْعُرُونَ {البقرة/13}, الله اعلم[417] and لَا يَعْلَمُونَ. If these people don't have the basic skills of realization and then differentiation right from wrong as mentioned in لَا يَشْعُرُونَ {البقرة/12} and لَا يَعْلَمُونَ[418]{البقرة/13}, then it would not be wise to trust and depend on them, الله اعلم.

In this perspective, one can also ask the question how can one make a right choice with free-will? There can be the process of recognition, raw thinking, thinking with focus and acquiring the perspective. This acquired perspective can be also called as nazar in terminology.

---

412. The foolish.
413. Unquestionably, it is they who are the foolish.
414. But they perceive [it] not.
415. The corrupters, but they perceive [it] not.
416. Perceive [it].
417. They perceive [it] not.
418. They know [it] not.

One can realize in this ayah as mentioned above that these group of people had some type of imān. Yet, one should recognize that when there is a clear book, the Qurān and a clear messenger and a prophet, the Prophet ﷺ sent by Allah ﷻ, then all the implicit renderings of religion through experience and mind should submit themselves to these clear teachings from Rabbul Alamin. In other words, when and if there are times as called times of fatrah, that there is no clear book and a messenger from Allah ﷻ, then the renderings of mind and experience can somehow acceptable with some mistakes possibly, الله اعلم. But, when there is clear book and messenger, then the person is expected to follow and submit oneself to these teachings. In this perspective, the position of ahlu kitap, Christians and others are similar. The Qurān underlines the clear, authentic and original stance of the teachings of the Qurān and the Prophet that submission is expected.

In other words, the true core principles of the imān does not change according to different people how they understand and interpret. It has only one way, one color and one understanding. In this perspective, إِنَّ الدِّينَ عِندَ اللَّهِ الإِسْلاَمُ وَمَا اخْتَلَفَ الَّذِينَ أُوتُوا الْكِتَابَ إِلاَّ مِن بَعْدِ مَا جَاءهُمُ الْعِلْمُ بَغْيًا بَيْنَهُمْ وَمَن يَكْفُرْ بِآيَاتِ اللَّهِ فَإِنَّ اللَّهِ سَرِيعُ الْحِسَابِ {آل عمران/19}[419]. The ayah can allude with the critical word الإِسْلاَم that the core principles of imān does not change.

This is what is accepted by Allah ﷻ. If the rest are outside the boundaries of the core principles of الإِسْلاَم then, people, groups or religions are not following an authentic path. This notion is mentioned as {آل عمران/85}[420] وَمَن يَبْتَغِ غَيْرَ الإِسْلاَمِ دِينًا فَلَن يُقْبَلَ مِنْهُ وَهُوَ فِي الآخِرَةِ مِنَ الْخَاسِرِينَ.

Is Islam a group identity?

One can ask then what is الإِسْلاَم Islam as mentioned in the above ayahs? Is it a group identity? How does the word Muslim, مُسْلِم, comes as an identifier in the Qurān? If we first review a few occurrences in the Qurān for the word Muslim, it is interesting that this word comes in many places immediately in the beginning chapters of the Qurān as below:

---

419. 3:19 Behold, the only [true] religion in the sight of God is [man's] self-surrender unto Him; and those who were vouchsafed revelation aforetime took, out of mutual jealousy, to divergent views [on this point] only after knowledge [thereof] had come unto them. But as for him who denies the truth of God's messages—behold, God is swift in reckoning!
420. 3:85 For, if one goes in search of a religion other than self-surrender unto God, it will never be accepted from him, and in the life to come he shall be among the lost.

رَبَّنَا وَاجْعَلْنَا مُسْلِمَيْنِ لَكَ وَمِن ذُرِّيَّتِنَا أُمَّةً مُسْلِمَةً لَّكَ وَأَرِنَا مَنَاسِكَنَا وَتُبْ عَلَيْنَا إِنَّكَ أَنتَ التَّوَّابُ الرَّحِيمُ {البقرة/128}421

وَوَصَّى بِهَا إِبْرَاهِيمُ بَنِيهِ وَيَعْقُوبُ يَا بَنِيَّ إِنَّ اللّهَ اصْطَفَى لَكُمُ الدِّينَ فَلاَ تَمُوتُنَّ إَلاَّ وَأَنتُم مُّسْلِمُونَ {البقرة/132}422 أَمْ كُنتُمْ شُهَدَاء إِذْ حَضَرَ يَعْقُوبَ الْمَوْتُ إِذْ قَالَ لِبَنِيهِ مَا تَعْبُدُونَ مِن بَعْدِي قَالُواْ نَعْبُدُ إِلَهَكَ وَإِلَهَ آبَائِكَ إِبْرَاهِيمَ وَإِسْمَاعِيلَ وَإِسْحَقَ إِلَهًا وَاحِدًا وَنَحْنُ لَهُ مُسْلِمُونَ {البقرة/133}423

وَقَالُواْ كُونُواْ هُودًا أَوْ نَصَارَى تَهْتَدُواْ قُلْ بَلْ مِلَّةَ إِبْرَاهِيمَ حَنِيفًا وَمَا كَانَ مِنَ الْمُشْرِكِينَ {البقرة/135}424

} قُولُواْ آمَنَّا بِاللّهِ وَمَا أُنزِلَ إِلَيْنَا وَمَا أُنزِلَ إِلَى إِبْرَاهِيمَ وَإِسْمَاعِيلَ وَإِسْحَقَ وَيَعْقُوبَ وَالأسْبَاطِ وَمَا أُوتِيَ مُوسَى وَعِيسَى وَمَا أُوتِيَ النَّبِيُّونَ مِن رَّبِّهِمْ لاَ نُفَرِّقُ بَيْنَ أَحَدٍ مِّنْهُمْ وَنَحْنُ لَهُ مُسْلِمُونَ {البقرة/136}425

فَلَمَّا أَحَسَّ عِيسَى مِنْهُمُ الْكُفْرَ قَالَ مَنْ أَنصَارِي إِلَى اللّهِ قَالَ الْحَوَارِيُّونَ نَحْنُ أَنصَارُ اللّهِ آمَنَّا بِاللّهِ وَاشْهَدْ بِأَنَّا مُسْلِمُونَ {آل عمران/52}426

---

421. 2:182 If, however, one has reason to fear that the testator has committed a mistake or a [deliberate] wrong, and thereupon brings about a settlement between the heirs, he will incur no sin [thereby]. Verily, God is much-forgiving, a dispenser of grace.

422. 2:132 And this very thing did Abraham bequeath unto his children, and [so did] Jacob: "O my children! Behold, God has granted you the purest faith; so do not allow death to overtake you ere you have surrendered yourselves unto Him."

423. 2:133 Nay, but you [yourselves, O children of Israel,] bear witness that when death was approaching Jacob, he said unto his sons: "Whom will you worship after I am gone?" They answered: "We will worship thy God, the God of thy forefathers Abraham and Ishmael and Isaac, the One God; and unto Him will we surrender ourselves."

424. 2:135 AND THEY say, "Be Jews"—or, "Christians"—"and you shall be on the right path." Say: "Nay, but [ours is] the creed of Abraham, who turned away from all that is false, and was not of those who ascribe divinity to aught beside God."

425. 2:136 Say: "We believe in God, and in that which has been bestowed from on high upon us, and that which has been bestowed upon Abraham and Ishmael and Isaac and Jacob and their descendants,111 and that which has been vouchsafed to Moses and Jesus; and that which has been vouchsafed to all the [other] prophets by their Sustainer: we make no distinction between any of them.112 And it is unto Him that we surrender ourselves."

426. 3:52 And when Jesus became aware of their refusal to acknowledge the truth,41 he asked: "Who will be my helpers in God's cause?" The white-garbed ones replied: "We shall be [thy] helpers [in the cause] of God! We believe in God: and bear thou witness that we have surrendered ourselves unto Him!

قُلْ يَا أَهْلَ الْكِتَابِ تَعَالَوْاْ إِلَى كَلَمَةٍ سَوَاء بَيْنَنَا وَبَيْنَكُمْ أَلاَّ نَعْبُدَ إِلاَّ اللّهَ وَلاَ نُشْرِكَ بِهِ شَيْئًا وَلاَ يَتَّخِذَ بَعْضُنَا بَعْضاً أَرْبَابًا مِّن دُونِ اللّهِ فَإِن تَوَلَّوْاْ فَقُولُواْ اشْهَدُواْ بِأَنَّا مُسْلِمُونَ

{آل عمران/64}[427]

مَا كَانَ إِبْرَاهِيمُ يَهُودِيًّا وَلاَ نَصْرَانِيًّا وَلَكِن كَانَ حَنِيفًا مُّسْلِمًا وَمَا كَانَ مِنَ الْمُشْرِكِينَ

{آل عمران/67}[428]

مُوسَى وَعِيسَى وَالنَّبِيُّونَ مِن رَّبِّهِمْ لاَ نُفَرِّقُ بَيْنَ أَحَدٍ مِّنْهُمْ وَنَحْنُ لَهُ مُسْلِمُونَ

{آل عمران/84}[429]

The above ayahs show that the word Muslim is not a group identity of today but it has the identity of people who truly believe in Allah ﷻ with the true core principles of imān. In other words, the true core principles of the imān does not change according to different people how they understand and interpret. It has only one way, one color and one understanding. In that perspective Ibrahim as, Musa as, Isa as and their true followers were Muslims.

In this perspective, if one focuses on the ayah

قُلْ يَا أَهْلَ الْكِتَابِ تَعَالَوْاْ إِلَى كَلَمَةٍ سَوَاء بَيْنَنَا وَبَيْنَكُمْ أَلاَّ نَعْبُدَ إِلاَّ اللّهَ وَلاَ نُشْرِكَ بِهِ شَيْئًا وَلاَ يَتَّخِذَ بَعْضُنَا بَعْضاً أَرْبَابًا مِّن دُونِ اللّهِ فَإِن تَوَلَّوْاْ فَقُولُواْ اشْهَدُواْ بِأَنَّا مُسْلِمُونَ

{آل عمران/64}

then, this quality and attitude of who is really a Muslim is defined. In other words, the ayah can allude to Christianas and Jews that you are originally Muslim as well. Muslim is not a mere group identity but But, [430].أَلاَّ نَعْبُدَ إِلاَّ اللّهَ وَلاَ نُشْرِكَ بِهِ شَيْئًا وَلاَ يَتَّخِذَ بَعْضُنَا بَعْضاً أَرْبَابًا مِّن دُونِ اللّهِ

427. 3:64 Say: "O followers of earlier revelation! Come unto that tenet which we and you hold in ommon:[49] that we shall worship none but God, and that we shall not ascribe divinity to aught beside Him, and that we shall not take human beings for our lords beside God." And if they turn away, then say: "Bear witness that it is we who have surrendered ourselves unto Him."

428. (3:67) Abraham was neither a "Jew" nor a "Christian", but was one who turned away from all that is false, having surrendered himself unto God; and he was not of those who ascribe divinity to aught beside Him.

429. 3:84 Say: "We believe in God, and in that which has been bestowed from on high upon us, and that which has been bestowed upon Abraham and Ishmael and Isaac and Jacob and their descendants, and that which has been vouchsafed by their Sustainer unto Moses and Jesus and all the [other] prophets: we make no distinction between any of them. And unto Him do we surrender ourselves."

430. That we shall worship none but God, and that we shall not ascribe divinity to aught beside Him, and that we shall not take human beings for our lords beside God."

it is the person or group of people who have the genuine teachings of belief, imān. After this, if they don't want to come back to their original genuine and authentic belief then, we would still be the ones holding thsese authentic core teachings, الله اعلم.

If we analyze the words in the Qurān in their context with the word الإِسْلَامُ:

} إِنَّ الدِّينَ عِندَ اللهِ الإِسْلَامُ وَمَا اخْتَلَفَ الَّذِينَ أُوتُواْ الْكِتَابَ إِلاَّ مِن بَعْدِ مَا جَاءهُمُ الْعِلْمُ بَغْيًا بَيْنَهُمْ وَمَن يَكْفُرْ بِآيَاتِ اللهِ فَإِنَّ اللهَ سَرِيعُ الْحِسَابِ [431] {آل عمران/19}

مَن يَبْتَغِ غَيْرَ الإِسْلَامِ دِينًا فَلَن يُقْبَلَ مِنْهُ وَهُوَ فِي الآخِرَةِ مِنَ الْخَاسِرِينَ [432] . {آل عمران/85}

حُرِّمَتْ عَلَيْكُمُ الْمَيْتَةُ وَالْدَّمُ وَلَحْمُ الْخِنزِيرِ وَمَا أُهِلَّ لِغَيْرِ اللهِ بِهِ وَالْمُنْخَنِقَةُ وَالْمَوْقُوذَةُ وَالْمُتَرَدِّيَةُ وَالنَّطِيحَةُ وَمَا أَكَلَ السَّبُعُ إِلاَّ مَا ذَكَّيْتُمْ وَمَا ذُبِحَ عَلَى النُّصُبِ وَأَن تَسْتَقْسِمُواْ بِالأَزْلاَمِ ذَلِكُمْ فِسْقٌ الْيَوْمَ يَئِسَ الَّذِينَ كَفَرُواْ مِن دِينِكُمْ فَلاَ تَخْشَوْهُمْ وَاخْشَوْنِ الْيَوْمَ أَكْمَلْتُ لَكُمْ دِينَكُمْ وَأَتْمَمْتُ عَلَيْكُمْ نِعْمَتِي وَرَضِيتُ لَكُمُ الإِسْلاَمَ دِينًا فَمَنِ اضْطُرَّ فِي مَخْمَصَةٍ غَيْرَ مُتَجَانِفٍ لِّإِثْمٍ فَإِنَّ اللهَ غَفُورٌ رَّحِيمٌ [433] {المائدة/3}

فَمَن يُرِدِ اللهُ أَن يَهْدِيَهُ يَشْرَحْ صَدْرَهُ لِلإِسْلاَمِ وَمَن يُرِدْ أَن يُضِلَّهُ يَجْعَلْ صَدْرَهُ ضَيِّقًا حَرَجًا كَأَنَّمَا يَصَّعَّدُ فِي السَّمَاءِ كَذَلِكَ يَجْعَلُ اللهُ الرِّجْسَ عَلَى الَّذِينَ لاَ يُؤْمِنُونَ {الأنعام/125} [434]

---

431. Behold, the only [true] religion in the sight of God is [man's] self-surrender unto Him; and those who were vouchsafed revelation aforetime took, out of mutual jealousy, to divergent views [on this point] only after knowledge [thereof] had come unto them. But as for him who denies the truth of God's messages—behold, God is swift in reckoning!

432. For, if one goes in search of a religion other than self-surrender unto God, it will never be accepted from him, and in the life to come he shall be among the lost.

433. Prohibited to you are dead animals, blood, the flesh of swine, and that which has been dedicated to other than Allah, and [those animals] killed by strangling or by a violent blow or by a head-long fall or by the goring of horns, and those from which a wild animal has eaten, except what you [are able to] slaughter [before its death], and those which are sacrificed on stone altars, and [prohibited is] that you seek decision through divining arrows. That is grave disobedience. This day those who disbelieve have despaired of [defeating] your religion; so fear them not, but fear Me. This day I have perfected for you your religion and completed My favor upon you and have approved for you Islam as religion. But whoever is forced by severe hunger with no inclination to sin—then indeed, Allah is Forgiving and Merciful.

434. 6:25 And there are among them such as [seem to] listen to thee [O Prophet]: but over their hearts We have laid veils which prevent them from grasping the truth, and into their ears, deafness.[18] And were they to see every sign [of the truth], they would still not believe in it—so much so that when they come unto thee to contend with thee, those who are bent on denying the truth say, "This is nothing but fables of ancient times!"

يَحْلِفُونَ بِاللهِ مَا قَالُواْ وَلَقَدْ قَالُواْ كَلِمَةَ الْكُفْرِ وَكَفَرُواْ بَعْدَ إِسْلامِهِمْ وَهَمُّواْ بِمَا لَمْ يَنَالُواْ وَمَا نَقَمُواْ إِلاَّ أَنْ أَغْنَاهُمُ اللهُ وَرَسُولُهُ مِن فَضْلِهِ فَإِن يَتُوبُواْ يَكُ خَيْرًا لَّهُمْ وَإِن يَتَوَلَّوْا يُعَذِّبْهُمُ اللهُ عَذَابًا أَلِيمًا فِي الدُّنْيَا وَالآخِرَةِ وَمَا لَهُمْ فِي الأَرْضِ مِن وَلِيٍّ وَلاَ نَصِيرٍ {التوبة/74}435

أَفَمَن شَرَحَ اللهُ صَدْرَهُ لِلإِسْلامِ فَهُوَ عَلَى نُورٍ مِّن رَّبِّهِ فَوَيْلٌ لِّلْقَاسِيَةِ قُلُوبُهُم مِّن ذِكْرِ اللهِ أُوْلَئِكَ فِي ضَلالٍ مُبِينٍ {الزمر/22}436

يَمُنُّونَ عَلَيْكَ أَنْ أَسْلَمُوا قُل لَّا تَمُنُّوا عَلَيَّ إِسْلامَكُم بَلِ اللهُ يَمُنُّ عَلَيْكُمْ أَنْ هَدَاكُمْ لِلإِيمَانِ إِن كُنتُمْ صَادِقِينَ {الحجرات/17}437

وَمَنْ أَظْلَمُ مِمَّنِ افْتَرَى عَلَى اللهِ الْكَذِبَ وَهُوَ يُدْعَى إِلَى الإِسْلامِ وَاللهُ لَا يَهْدِي الْقَوْمَ الظَّالِمِينَ {الصف/7}438

one can see in the above ayahs immediately a few points. Today, Islam is an identity of the religion which is accepted by the Creator, Allah ﷻ. It has the inclusive perfect original authentic core of imān, belief. If one wants to please the Creator and make a choice to find the purpose in one's life and after death, the current identified religion as Islam is the choice as clearly stated in the communication sent to humans by God. I really strongly believe that the above verses are very clear, explicit, unambiguous, and obvious if someone is trying to look and search for the purpose. In a religion, the communication is between the person and a Divine Being one can call Allah, God, the Creator or with other names. If the Creator communicates clearly to tell this is what I want

---

435. 9:74 [The hypocrites] swear by God that they have said nothing [wrong]; yet most certainly have they uttered a saying which amounts to a denial of the truth,[102] and have [thus] denied the truth after [having professed] their self-surrender to God: for they were aiming at something which was beyond their reach. And they could find no fault [with the Faith] save that God had enriched them and [caused] His Apostle [to enrich them] out of His bounty! Hence, if they repent, it will be for their own good. but if they turn away, God will cause them to suffer grievous suffering in this world and in the life to come, and they will find no helper on earth, and none to give [them] succour.

436. (30:22) And among his wonders is the creation of the heavens and the earth, and the diversity of your tongues and colours: for in this, behold, there are messages indeed for all who are possessed of [innate] knowledge!

437. (49:17) Many people think that they have bestowed a favour upon thee [O Prophet] by having surrendered [to thee]. Say thou: "Deem not your surrender a favour unto me: nay, but it is God who bestows a favour upon you by showing you the way to faith—if you are true to your word!"

438. 61:7 And who could be more wicked than one who invents [such] a lie about [a message from] God, seeing that he is [but] being called to self-surrender unto Him? But God does not bestow His guidance upon evil-doing folk.

you to follow and this is the true explanation of your purpose, then there is no interpretation for a seeker but submit themselves. Then, they are called as Muslim. In this perspective, the identity of Muslim is the person who carries these core teachings of imān.

This does not mean that experience, mind or the previous teachings of ahlu-kitāb would not have a value. Rather, it is going to stand on a very strong framework of genuine teachings of Islam. Therefore, a lot of times, a person becoming a new Muslim has often the statements as "now, I understand much better…It makes sense…I used to always have problem with this concept but now it makes perfect sense…I always felt spiritual but I asked guidance…etc." In this perspective, the popular trends of spirituality and cosmology at our times can be authenticated with the frame work of the Qurān and hadith if someone is really at a position of seeking the purpose then naturally submission and surrender stage occurs, الله اعلم.

The expressions such as لَا يَعْلَمُونَ [439] as in this ayah and others, especially in the ending of ayahs as أَفَلَا تَعْقِلُونَ [440] {البقرة/44} , أَفَلَا تَعْقِلُونَ {البقرة/76}, أَفَلَا تَعْقِلُونَ {آل عمران/65}[441], أَفَلَا تَتَفَكَّرُونَ {الأنعام/50}, أَفَلَا تَتَذَكَّرُونَ[442] {الأنعام/80}, أَفَلَا تَتَّقُونَ [443] {الأعراف/65} encourages to person to learn and to know, with يَعْلَمُونَ, then use the mind as mentioned consecutively in Sûrah Baqarah and al'Imrān with أَفَلَا تَعْقِلُونَ and then use the critical thinking as mentioned in {الأنعام/50}. أَفَلَا تَتَفَكَّرُونَ. Then, after this stage a person take an action, make decision and perform the dhikr, salah and remembrance of Allah ﷻas mentioned in {الأنعام/80}. أَفَلَا تَتَذَكَّرُونَ. Then, it is hoped that inshAllah this dhikr will lead the person to taqwa as mentioned {الأعراف/65}. أَفَلَا تَتَّقُونَ. One can review the above rendering or analysis in the Qurān that it reveals itself with the word أَفَلَا how it is used at the end of each ayah consecutively, الله اعلم. This shows and encourages each person who has a sound mind, logic and reasoning to look into the teachings of Islam, الله اعلم. In other words, Islam is a very logical religion.

If one continues with the word أَفَلَا at the endings of the aysahs after the above mentioned surahs, then the order and process of using mind with constant critical thinking restarts again as mentioned in أَفَلَا تَعْقِلُونَ

---

439. Will you not then, use your reason?"
440. Then will you not reason?
441. Then will you not give thought?
442. Will you not, then, keep this in mind?
443. Then will you not fear Him?

{الأعراف/169}, أَفَلاَ تَذَكَّرُونَ {يونس/3}, أَفَلاَ تَعْقِلُونَ {يونس/16}, أَفَلاَ تَتَّقُونَ {يونس/31}, it is suggested after this stage to critical think and make dhikr. When one embodies this stage, then taqwa with imān can be embodied in person. For this person, what this person sees and hears become different than others as mentioned أَفَلاَ يُبْصِرُونَ {السجدة/26}[444] and أَفَلاَ يَسْمَعُونَ {السجدة/27}[445]. This person looks, hears, feels and experiences everything with the Nūr of imān but not with the darkness of kufr. Then, this person can be at the gist or essence of imān as a person of gratitude as mentioned in أَفَلاَ يَشْكُرُونَ {يس/35}. أَفَلاَ يَشْكُرُونَ {يس/73}[446] As Sûrah Yāsîn is the core of the Qurān (26) (22), the core of imān is the station of shukr or hamd to Allah ﷻ.

In the above renderings, as the above endings are repeated constantly, the cycles of struggle or the effort of increasing one's relationship with Allah ﷻ increases with aqil, critical thinking applied on all the signs of Allah ﷻ as mentioned with the phrase أَفَلاَ تَعْقِلُونَ[447], then with this disposition remembrance of Allah ﷻ as mentioned with the phrase أَفَلاَ[448] تَذَكَّرُونَ, and reaching to taqwa as mentioned with the phrase أَفَلاَ تَتَّقُونَ, embodying this in all life with all senses as mentioned أَفَلاَ يَسْمَعُونَ and أَفَلاَ يُبْصِرُونَ and finally reaching to the station of shukr and hamd as mentioned with أَفَلاَ يَشْكُرُونَ، الله اعلم.

It is interesting to look at the munafiqûn with the next ayah. When they meet with believers they say we believed as mentioned وَإِذَا لَقُوا[449] الَّذِينَ آمَنُوا قَالُوا آمَنَّا. Yet, at the same time, perhaps when they are told again to believe as mentioned وَإِذَا قِيلَ لَهُمْ آمِنُوا كَمَا آمَنَ النَّاسُ[450], then they don't like the concept of renewal and constancy of imān as mentioned in the form of mudari in قَالُوا أَنُؤْمِنُ[451]. In the previous case, they may have viewed imān as something an action that when it is done then it is over as mentioned قَالُوا آمَنَّا[452] in their other proclaim. When they are reminded that imān is a continuous venture, they don't seem to like it, الله اعلم.

---

444. [But) can, then, they [who deny the truth] learn no lesson
445. Can they not, then, see [the truth of resurrection]?
446. Will they not, then, be grateful?
447. Then will you not reason?
448. Will you not, then, keep this in mind?
449. And when they found those who believe, they said we believe.
450. And when it is said to them, "Believe as the people have believed,"
451. They say, "Should we believe.
452. They say, "We believe."

The word السُّفَهَاء[453] can allude to the specific group of people as mentioned in the ayah's sabab nuzûl. On another perspective, the Prophet ﷺ mentions in a hadith with a meaning that a person will not be a true believer until he is tagged as an outcast in the society (9). In this perspective, others calling the real believers as السُّفَهَاء can in reality authenticate their belief as the hadith mentions, الله اعلم.

It can be also important to understand why they call the believers and early sahabah as السُّفَهَاء from what they see and observe. If people have certain value system defined by the norms of the society then going out of these norms can be considered in the category of السُّفَهَاء. For example, believers showing altruism, donating their wealth to please Allah ﷻ, preferring themselves over the poor or needy or preferring hunger over feeding others with the limited food of theirs can be considered as السُّفَهَاء in the society at that time and in most societies still today, الله اعلم. So, from reference point of one value system others' acts can be considered irrational or funny as mentioned with the word السُّفَهَاء. Today, there is an evolving methodology of understanding different value systems with the modern discourses of biased free or non-discriminatory attitudes in academic epistemology.

As mentioned before the word السُّفَهَاء can be referred for a person who has limitations in grasping, realizing and understanding the basic notions that others can normally grasp, realize and understand easily as mentioned in وَاخْتَارَ مُوسَى قَوْمَهُ سَبْعِينَ رَجُلاً لِّمِيقَاتِنَا فَلَمَّا أَخَذَتْهُمُ الرَّجْفَةُ قَالَ رَبِّ لَوْ شِئْتَ أَهْلَكْتَهُم مِّن قَبْلُ وَإِيَّايَ أَتُهْلِكُنَا بِمَا فَعَلَ السُّفَهَاء مِنَّا إِنْ هِيَ إِلاَّ فِتْنَتُكَ تُضِلُّ بِهَا مَن تَشَاء وَتَهْدِي مَن تَشَاء أَنتَ وَلِيُّنَا فَاغْفِرْ لَنَا وَارْحَمْنَا وَأَنتَ خَيْرُ الْغَافِرِينَ {الأعراف/155}[454]. As an Islamic legal term, it may mean for a person who don't follow the guidelines of mind and reasoning as mentioned in وَلاَ تُؤْتُواْ السُّفَهَاء أَمْوَالَكُمُ الَّتِي جَعَلَ اللَّهُ لَكُمْ قِيَاماً وَارْزُقُوهُمْ فِيهَا وَاكْسُوهُمْ وَقُولُواْ لَهُمْ قَوْلاً مَّعْرُوفًا {النساء/5}[455]. In its popular usage, this word may mean the lowly classes or the poor in a society as it is used this ayah by munãfiqs وَإِذَا قِيلَ لَهُمْ آمِنُواْ كَمَا آمَنَ النَّاسُ

---

453. The foolish.

454. 7:55 Call unto your Sustainer humbly, and in the secrecy of your hearts. Verily, He loves not those who transgress the bounds of what is right.

455. And do not give the weak-minded your property, which Allah has made a means of sustenance for you, but provide for them with it and clothe them and speak to them words of appropriate kindness.

قَالُواْ أَنُؤْمِنُ كَمَا آمَنَ السُّفَهَاءُ أَلا إِنَّهُمْ هُمُ السُّفَهَاءُ وَلَكِن لاَ يَعْلَمُونَ {البقرة/13}[456]. However, when Allah ﷻ mentions in the same ayah the same word السُّفَهَاءُ as إِنَّهُمْ هُمُ السُّفَهَاءُ وَلَكِن لاَ يَعْلَمُونَ {البقرة/13}[457], this has the first other two meanings but not the understanding of munafiqûn about what they mean with this word, الله اعلم. Because Allah ﷻ is far from mocking of people as these lowly people do.

In this perspective, the expression أَلا إِنَّهُمْ هُمُ السُّفَهَاءُ وَلَكِن لاَ يَعْلَمُونَ {البقرة/13} alludes to importance of knowing, especially knowing oneself. Knowing oneself, the purpose, our relation with our surroundings is the beginning point. In other words, when we say "I", "the self" it is not even our physical body, organs, hands, ears, legs or feet. There is something in us called self which makes decisions, feels emotions such as pain or happiness. One can call this as mind, heart, or conscience but here, rather than these terms, one can call this as nafs or self, other than our physical body although we are located in this frame of the physical body. The body becomes as an external dress of the self which can change. So, knowing as mentioned with the word يَعْلَمُونَ is the key. This knowing starts with the realization of the existence of the self, then understanding its purpose, potentials, and weaknesses. This then can be the transition point as a measure stick to know Allah ﷻ. The ayah وَلاَ تَكُونُوا كَالَّذِينَ نَسُوا اللَّهَ فَأَنسَاهُمْ أَنفُسَهُمْ أُوْلَئِكَ هُمُ الْفَاسِقُونَ {الحشر/19}[458] can allude the importance of this knowledge called as I'lm, الله اعلم. In this perspective, there is no basis of knowledge or sound methodology of learning in the claims of munafiqûn .

One can analyze the sequence of epistemology from the ayahs that follow: {البقرة/13}[460] لاَ يَعْلَمُونَ, مَا يَشْعُرُونَ {البقرة/9}[459], لاَ يَشْعُرُونَ {البقرة/12}. In the case of {البقرة/9} مَا يَشْعُرُونَ, the word مَا (nafyi-hal) can indicate thay they don't have the basic recognition skills of cognition at that time or at the present time. If this becomes a regular pattern, then the word لاَ (nafyi-istiqbal) in the expression لاَ يَشْعُرُونَ [461]{البقرة/12} can indicate

---

456. And when it is said to them, "Believe as the people have believed," they say, "Should we believe as the foolish have believed?" Unquestionably, it is they who are the foolish, but they know [it] not.
457. Unquestionably, it is they who are the foolish, but they know [it] not.
458. (59:19) and be not like those who are oblivious of God, and whom He therefore causes to be oblivious of [what is good for] their own selves: [for] it is they, they who are truly depraved!
459. And perceive [it] not.
460. But they know [it] not.
461. And perceive [it] not.

that their inability to recognize can become a chronic and permanent disease. Then this overall effect can lead to {البقرة/13} [462] لاً يَعْلَمُونَ that they won't understand and know properly because for basic knowing (I'lm) the first step is recognition (shuur), الله اعلم.

The above three level inability of not recognition or knowing can also have projection on another three levels. If a person doesn't know about something, then this can be due to a simple or raw illiteracy of this person about this knowledge. If the person does not know that he or she doesn't know about something, then this can be due to a twofold heedlessness of this person about this knowledge. If the person does not know about something and argues or claims that he or she knows without any simple and basic methodology, then this can be due to a threefold ignorance of this person about this knowledge. The threefold ignorance is unlikely or difficult to change or learn compared to the one who has simple or raw illiteracy, الله اعلم.

Now, one can review the scriptural literature that there was an expectation by the ahlu kitāb for a Prophet. This was mentioned in their books. Then, why still the Prophet ﷺ was not accepted fully if there were clear signs in their books and scholarship? The answer can be due to the group identity attachments as a social phenomenon. From the perspective of tasawwuf, it can due to hasad[463], علم الله.

In another perspective, the expression {البقرة/13} [464] وَلَكِن لاً يَعْلَمُونَ can be a reassuring and comforting statement from Allah ﷻ for Rasulullah ﷺ. When one reviews the ayah وَإِذَا قِيلَ لَهُمْ آمِنُوا كَمَا آمَنَ النَّاسُ قَالُوا أَنُؤْمِنُ كَمَا آمَنَ السُّفَهَاء أَلا إِنَّهُمْ هُمُ السُّفَهَاء وَلَكِن لاً يَعْلَمُونَ {البقرة/13} [465] there is discomforting attitude of munafiqûn in their engagements with the sahabah and the Prophet ﷺ. Especially, if one considers the above renderings of ahlu-kitāb when they find the Prophet in their scriptural scholarship but still not accepting the Prophet can really hurt the feelings of the Prophet ﷺ. Therefore, Allah ﷻ comforts the Prophet ﷺ and the Muslims with the expression {البقرة/13} وَلَكِن لاً يَعْلَمُونَ[466].

---

462. They know [it] not.
463. Envy.
464. But they know [it] not.
465. And when it is said to them, "Believe as the people have believed," they say, "Should we believe as the foolish have believed?" Unquestionably, it is they who are the foolish, but they know [it] not.
466. But they know [it] not.

On another perspective, Islam is the religion of critical thinking, science, logic, reason and cognition. In this regards, the people who don't have this genuine approach or methodology of Islam, would not be able to understand and accept the teachings of Islam as indicated with the expression وَلَٰكِنَّ لاَ يَعْلَمُونَ {13/البقرة}, الله اعلم.

On another note, there is a teaching here for the Muslims as well. As Islam is the religion of critical thinking, science, logic, reason and cognition, then a Muslim is the person of reason, logic, cognition and science. Even though, they don't have these qualities, a Muslim is expected to embody these qualities.

[14]

وَإِذَا لَقُواْ الَّذِينَ آمَنُواْ قَالُواْ آمَنَّا وَإِذَا خَلَوْاْ إِلَى شَيَاطِينِهِمْ قَالُواْ إِنَّا مَعَكُمْ إِنَّمَا نَحْنُ مُسْتَهْزِؤُونَ [467]{14/البقرة}

In the previous ayahs, there was the evil of munafiqûn with fasad as mentioned وَإِذَا قِيلَ لَهُمْ لاَ تُفْسِدُواْ فِي الأَرْضِ[468]. Now, another type of evil is of their discourse, broadcast and attitude of mockery and sarcasm about the believers as mentioned إِنَّمَا نَحْنُ مُسْتَهْزِؤُونَ[469]{14/البقرة}.

In the expression وَإِذَا لَقُواْ الَّذِينَ آمَنُواْ قَالُواْ آمَنَّا وَإِذَا خَلَوْاْ[470], both إِذَا show that they encounter and meet with the believers and their own cliques very often and frequently. Also, the word إِذَا can show the certainity of their meeting both with the believers and their own cliques.

In the above ayah, the word خَلَوْ has a key stance. In tasawwuf, the word خَلَوْ[471], khalwah used to be in solitude for self-reflection, muraqaba. This shows the reality of one's essence being when the person is in solitude in reflection alone. On the other hand, the word خَلَوْ can allude to their effort of hiding their real dispositions. They cannot really show their real face but they need to reveal it in secrecy, الله اعلم.

A person is constantly in distraction. One cannot truly, sincerely and genuinely know Allah ﷻ if the person does not know oneself. In other words, the person should learn, know and practice listening to

---

467. And when they meet those who believe, they say, "We believe"; but when they are alone with their evil ones, they say, "Indeed, we are with you; we were only mockers."
468. And when it is said to them, "Do not cause corruption on the earth"
469. We were only mockers."
470. And when they meet those who believe, they say, "We believe"; but when they are alone.
471. They are alone.

oneself. These self-dialogue can be inspirational in a positive sense. Or, it can be a temptation in a negative sense due to the greasy parts of the heart and with the external effects of the shaytan. In both cases, the detection is the first step. In other words, self-dialogue is the first step. This is the place where all the positive inspirations, come from Allah ﷻ. This is the place where all the Satanic thoughts and feelings can come and gather as well.

So, after this self-dialogue, the person should master how to clean, fight and remove the constant dust occurring due to temptations from Satan. This dust can also be similar to an oil. If it is not cleaned immediately, it may stick and become more difficult to clean unless with a harsh tool with squealing noise of pain, trials, and tests. So, before these stages, one should always look at one's heart to listen constantly and see where Allah ﷻ is.

One should remember, the heart will be occupied with either Allah ﷻ with positive light feelings and inspirations of imān. Or, it will be occupied with shaytan in the form of worldly attachments, useless occupations and temptations with dark depressing feelings of kufr. The heart does not stay empty.

In the case of munafiqûn, since Allah ﷻ is not in their hearts then there is the other agent, shaytan comes in as mentioned in the expression وَإِذَا خَلَوْاْ إِلَى شَيَاطِينِهِمْ[472].

Depending on the level of imān, a believer, a Muslim can have partial occupations. Therefore, the dhikr of la ilaha illa Allah ﷻ is a key and constant practice to remove, discharge, and empty the grease, puss, and dust from heart and then to attach, fill, and charge with Allah ﷻ. The five times prayer is in their essence has all this purpose. The Sûrah Fātiha with constant repetition has this purpose. The dhikrs in ruku and sujud have this purpose. The soul of all the prayers, and rituals have this purpose, الله اعلم.

Also as mentioned before, as lying is a major disease of the disease of the heart as explained in detail before so as the negative group identities or identity politics with the expressions in the following ayahs as وَإِذَا لَقُواْ الَّذِينَ آمَنُواْ قَالُواْ آمَنَّا وَإِذَا خَلَوْاْ إِلَى شَيَاطِينِهِمْ قَالُواْ إِنَّا مَعَكُمْ إِنَّمَا نَحْنُ مُسْتَهْزِؤُونَ {البقرة/14}[473].

---

472. But when they are alone with their evil ones.
473. And when they meet those who believe, they say, "We believe"; but when they are alone with their evil ones, they say, "Indeed, we are with you; we were only mockers."

One of the hikmahs of itnab that the ayahs about munafiqûn comes in detail that as they believe spend most of their time with the Muslims, they constantly hear the bad traits of a munāfiq. Then, it is hoped that they start disliking these traits of theirs. Finally, there may be some drops of imān that may come to their hearts. In this perspective, the Qurān teaches us some practical ways how to deal with them. For example, doing continuous itnab as the Qurān does in social engagements can inshAllah bring some drops to their hearts. In other words, talking and discussing constantly and regularly about the traits of munafiqûn with them without losing hope but with the intention of following way of the Qurān can be one of the methods, الله اعلم.

One of the distinctions between the munāfiq and kāfir is that munāfiq has the traits of mockery, humiliating others, deceit, dishonesty, dublicity and ostentation. On the contrary, kāfir may not have those traits as the munāfiq. Therefore, the Qurān uses itnab, explaining in detail their character compared to kāfir.

One of the other possible reasons of itnab could be when a person knows something and mixes with something wrong then it is more difficult distinguish the truth from falsehood. In other words, if a person does not know anything it can be easier to teach this person compared to the one who knows some but knows it with mistakes. Sometimes, we find builders instead of fixing or repairing a house, they just demolish the entire house and a build a new one. Because, it takes really effort and time to fix each problem and adapt it. Similarly, the people of the book, ahlu kitāb, know some of the true and correct knowledge about the religion of Allah ﷻ. Due to the various reasons historically, the current knowledge of theirs are mixed with mistakes and problems. In this case, if there are especially munāfiqs from them, it really needs a lot of time, effort and explanation to handle these cases as the Qurān makes itnab, detailed style of explaining this case, الله اعلم.

In the expression إِنَّمَا نَحْنُ مُسْتَهْزِؤُونَ[474], one can use takid, إِنَّمَا, about something known or somewhat agreed upon. In both cases they use either إِنَّمَا نَحْنُ مُصْلِحُونَ[475] as before or إِنَّمَا نَحْنُ مُسْتَهْزِؤُونَ as in this ayah. So, their first takid, إِنَّمَا, as in إِنَّمَا نَحْنُ مُصْلِحُونَ is only for the purpose of

---

474. We were only mockers.
475. We are but reformers.

istihza when they mention their real disposition as إِنَّمَا نَحْنُ مُسْتَهْزِؤُونَ,[476] الله اعلم.

When a person faces an evil, or difficulty, there are some parts of imān, belief that activates itself. One is the protection of one's dignity. In these difficult situations and when facing evil, the person still does not want to show him or herself lowly or humiliated to others. In other words, a person who has imān always maintains a true factual powerlessness, weakness, humbleness and humility in their relationship with Allah ﷻ. On the other hand, the person maintains a sense of honor and dignity with an attitude of kindness and niceness in their relationship with people.

Another faculty of imān that reveals itself is kindness and caring. The original term in the language can be shawkah. A person who has shawkah, kindness, and caring does not show an attitude of mocking, humiliating and making fun of others.

Another faculty of imān that reveals itself is showing respect and humbleness when the truths are presented to this person. In other words, this can be the disposition of not arguing, making excuses and diving into demagogical discourses but respecting, listening and try to deduce in a such way that to benefit oneself. It is narrated that one of the titles of Omar ra was al-waqqaf, the one who stops immediately when a truth was presented to him from the Qurān and hadith. As one can know Omar ra that he has a reputation of his firm stance against injustice. When someone used to challenge his disposition and presented counter arguments, he immediately stopped his discourse and went into self-check mode, الله اعلم.

The opposite of imān is nifāq. It also has some signs. One is the notion of having no sincerity in the relationship with Allah ﷻ and having no dignity when engaging with others. For example, if this person lies and people find out this then, he or she doesn't not have any feeling of guilt or shame. Therefore, this person can take the habit of lying as a trait and does not mind what others think about him or her. In this perspective, this person can generate lies constantly publicly or privately. As he or she indulges in this as a habit sometimes this person's lies contradict with their other lies and so, people realize and humiliate and mock about them about these obvious opposing and piling lies. Yet,

---

476. We were only mockers.

this person doesn't mind and continues to lie. In the minds of these people, lying is normalized and is not an issue of unethical, or immoral behavior.

Another trait that reveals from nifāq is the person's inclination towards fasad. In other words, the person likes, enjoys and takes the habit of making fasad, mischief, and disunity among people, groups, families, and societies. This was mentioned in the above ayahs as their obvious trait as {البقرة/11} [477] وَإِذَا قِيلَ لَهُمْ لاَ تُفْسِدُواْ فِي الأَرْضِ قَالُواْ إِنَّمَا نَحْنُ مُصْلِحُونَ.

Another trait that reveals from nifāq is humiliating, demeaning, dishonoring, insulting, and mocking others and taking pleasure from this. It is interesting to analyze the sabab nuzûl of the ayahs 10-14. The lead person in nifāq Abdullah ibn Salul sees Abu Bakr ra, Omar ra and Ali ra while walking. He tells his friends that they should witness how he will mock them. Then, he utters some true statements individually to their face about what they did for Islam. Then, he leaves them and tells his friends how he made fun of them. This is really interesting. He says things that are true but it is with a intention and attitude of mockery. Again, this reveals the importance and key factor of intention and attitude in Islam. In other words, imān and belief is intention and attitude. Ama'l or actions solidify the imān and make the person embody the imān. Therefore, in Islamic canonized teachings and creed, a person with imān but without any good action or ibadah can be saved and go to Jannah but a person with tons of amal, good actions or even worship without correct intention and attitude may not be saved, الله اعلم. In this case, the munāfiqs had a wrong intention by proclaiming themselves as a Muslim. For this reason, a person who may have imān but incorrect attitude such as arrogance may not directly go to Jannah as mentioned by the Prophet (9) ﷺ.

The dispositions of imān and kufur or nifāq are opposite to each other. Imān necessitates humility in front of Allah ﷻ but dignity and honor in front of other creation. In other words, a person of imān has an honor and dignity in front of people of nifāq and kufur but at the same time, he or she maintains merciful and caring disposition towards the believers and all creation due to having humility in front of Allah ﷻ. Nifāq and kufr don't have proper recognition of Allah ﷻ.

---

477. And when it is said to them, "Do not cause corruption on the earth," they say, "We are but reformers."

Therefore, the people who have nifāq and kufr can often seek disgrace and low character in front of others in order to reach their purpose. Then, this is called riya, ostentation or showing off because the person acts to please others in order to reach to a goal or purpose instead of having intention to please Allah ﷻ. Riya, ostentation and showing off necessitates lies, الله اعلم. Therefore, the expression وَإِذَا لَقُوا الَّذِينَ آمَنُو [478] shows this type of riya, or show off that they embody in themselves. At the same time nifāq can entail humiliating and mocking others.

In the internal dispositions, nifāq puts the hearts in the spiritual state of fasad. Therefore, in the external world, the munāfiqs symbolize the cause of fasad among people in societies. The person who has fasad in his or heart can be in the disposition of spiritual darkness of orphanage. In other words, he or she assumes oneself alone in these actions and states of heart that there is no Creator, Watcher, Protector, Merciful, and all the different Names and Attributes of Allah ﷻ. Then, this person becomes in a chaotic state of not knowing his or her true self, and the purpose and his or her relation with other creation, universe and systems. This is another name for kufr. Therefore, nifāq and kufr are interrelated.

The dispositions of chaotic and spiritual dark states of having no purpose, orphanage, and solitude to transform this person in a fearful state. This fearful state can make this person to run, to hide, to be secretive with his cliques as mentioned in وَإِذَا خَلَوْا, الله اعلم [479].

One of the results of nifāq is to severe the sila-rahìm, kinship. This removes caring and love among the loved ones. When caring and love is not present, then there is fasad and fitnah. Fitnah can lead to improper distribution of rights among people called khiyanah, injustice. Khiyanah, injustice, can lead to weakness. Weakness necessitates to refuge in something. In this case, they refuge in their shayatin as mentioned [480] وَإِذَا خَلَوْا إِلَى شَيَاطِينِهِمْ. This causality relationship can be valid in personal lives as well as the social lives of communities or systems. In other words, as one can analyze the misguidance of a person with this causality. One can analyze the cases of fall or collapse of systems, empires, or governments with this causal relationship as well, الله اعلم.

---

478. And when they meet those who believe.
479. But when they are alone.
480. But when they are alone with their evil ones.

Opposite to imān, nifāq has uncertainty, skepticism, and doubt. A munāfiq does not have a certain, clear, sure, and confident disposition. This can lead to inconsistent and conflicting dispositions. Then, this can lead to the traits and peculiarities of untrustworthiness, dishonesty, disloyalty and treachery. The overall result of this temperament and personalities require the person to be assured on their path if they want to keep this as a character or manner. Therefore, they get reassured and encouraged regularly by their cliques or shayatin when they get together as mentioned وَإِذَا خَلَوْاْ إِلَى شَيَاطِينِهِمْ[481]. In other words, when they say قَالُواْ إِنَّا[482] مَعَكُمْ, the expression إِنَّا مَعَكُمْ can indicate their continuous renewal of their commitment with them. The expression إِنَّا مَعَكُمْ[483] as jumla ismiyyah can allude to this continuity. A true believer needs to renew their imān with La ilaha illa Allah as suggested by the Prophet (22) ﷺ. On the opposite pole, a munāfiq renews their belief with the Shayatain as this expression قَالُواْ إِنَّا مَعَكُمْ indicates, الله اعلم.

In the expression قَالُواْ إِنَّا مَعَكُمْ, there is a tak'id and swearing with the words إِنَّا and also مَعَكُم. They feel that they need to swear to their real friends from shayatin to eliminate any misunderstandings because they are hanging around with Muslims. If there is any doubt they want to remove it from their real friends' mind that they are not in reality with Muslims. To make their point stronger, they swear again with tak'id with the words إِنَّمَا[484] and نَحْنُ[485] in the expression إِنَّمَا نَحْنُ مُسْتَهْزِؤُونَ[486] that they hang around with Muslims only to humiliate and make fun of them as mentioned with the word مُسْتَهْزِؤُونَ[487].

The Real and Pseudo Self with أُوقُلَّ and أُوْلَخَ

One can analyze two key words or expressions in this ayah of إِذَا لَقُواْ الَّذِينَ آمَنُواْ قَالُواْ آمَنَّا وَإِذَا خَلَوْاْ إِلَى شَيَاطِينِهِمْ قَالُواْ إِنَّا مَعَكُمْ إِنَّمَا نَحْنُ مُسْتَهْزِؤُونَ[488] {البقرة/14}.

---

481. But when they are alone with their evil ones.
482. They say, "Indeed, we are with you.
483. We are with you.
484. We are.
485. We.
486. We were only mockers.
487. Mockers.
488. And when they meet those who believe, they say, "We believe"; but when they are alone with their evil ones, they say, "Indeed, we are with you; we were only mockers."

These are إِذَا لَقُو[489] and إِذَا خَلَوْ ا[490]. The first word لَقُو can mean to meet with someone or people. In other words, this word can allude any type of engagements that when we meet with others. This can be social, kindship or professional engagements. These engagements can be temporary in their nature. It may be difficult to display and control one's real identity or real-self in these engagements due to different social dynamics. For example, a person may do something because he or she may not want to upset someone or others etc. It may be difficult to reveal ones' own self, the inclinations, or the desires in a group engagement.

The second word خَلَوْ ا can mean being in solitude with your real self. In this case, the real tendencies, desires, emotions and inclinations reveal and the person can be in a self-dialogue mode. This is a permanent state compared to first case of لَقُو which is a temporary state. In the temporary state, there may not be the real self but partial or opposite of the real self. Therefore, imãn or kufr is in the second case of خَلَوْ ا when the real self is revealed with self-dialogue. In this case, the only witness of the real-self other than the person is Allah ﷻ.

Therefore, the first state is a temporary state with لَقُو which can be a state of sins or mistakes. A true believer can make mistakes and sins in different engagements. As long as when he or she is in in the state of خَلَوْ ا in self-dialogue, self-accountability with repentance and regret, then Allah ﷻ can forgive this person. Because his real self does not approve this unreal self's mistake in different engagements. Therefore, the Prophet ﷺ mentions when a believer makes a sin, imãn is not with that person at that moment (9) (3). So this can be called a pseudo or unreal or temporary self with the word لَقُو. All the cases of sins instilled with gadab, wrong judgment or instantaneous change of the real-self can be an example of this pseudo self. The moments of "what did I do? why did I get angry? why did I say this? I was not right . . . etc." as the cases of self-dialogue with the word خَلَو can show the disposition of the real self. This can be called in religious terms as tawbah, regret, repentance, or istighfãr when this real self-verbalizes and embodies to the next step of asking forgiveness for this person's pseudo self's actions.

One can analyze this discussion with the case of the hadith killer of ninety-nine people and asking for repentance (9). For whatever reason,

---

489. And when they meet.
490. And when they are alone.

there was this evil act but this person was bothered with this. One can also analyzes the cases of pseudo self in the cases of anger or gadab in marital, parent-children, or student-teacher relationships. As long as the real-self does not approve the outcomes excuted by the pseudo-self then the relationships can be fixed with the fadl, rahmah and tawfiq of Allah ﷻ.

Overall, as one can see munāfiqs has the opposite disposition their pseudo self has the dialogues of imān in the state of لَقُوا but their real self has the disposition of kufr in the state of خَلَوَ. The dangerous point reveals itself for everyone and all of us if the real self loses this trait of regret, tawbah and repentance to Allah ﷻ.

May Allah ﷻ protect us from the evils of our own selves, pseudo or real. Amìn

When one analyzes the word إِذَا, in the expression وَإِذَا لَقُوا الَّذِينَ[491] آمَنُوا قَالُوا آمَنَّا وَإِذَا خَلَوْا إِلَى شَيَاطِينِهِمْ, there can be possibility of intentional meeting of the munāfiqs with the believers. In other words, they may look the ways to meet with the believers in order to humiliate or mock them. According to some of the muffassirun, the harf-i jar إِلَى[492] has the meaning of مع[493] in this ayah. In other words, the state of munāfiqs is not a temporary but permanent state with the shayatin.

On the other hand, the reason that إِلَى is used instead of مع can have different possibilities. One possibility is that the harf-i jar إِلَى entails the meaning of taking refuge. In this case, they take refuge into their shayatin. The harf-i jar إِلَى can also indicate the transfer of knowledge, and the intimidate affairs of Muslims to their real friends.

In the expression وَإِذَا لَقُوا الَّذِينَ آمَنُوا قَالُوا آمَنَّا وَإِذَا خَلَوْا إِلَى شَيَاطِينِهِمْ, the word شَيَاطِينِهِمْ[494] is plural. The singular form is لِشَّيْطَانُ. This word can have a proper noun or a common noun meaning On the other hand, when one reviews the ayah وَإِذْ قُلْنَا لِلْمَلَائِكَةِ اسْجُدُوا لِآدَمَ فَسَجَدُوا إِلاَّ إِبْلِيسَ أَبَى وَاسْتَكْبَرَ وَكَانَ مِنَ الْكَافِرِينَ {البقرة/34} وَقُلْنَا يَا آدَمُ اسْكُنْ أَنتَ وَزَوْجُكَ الْجَنَّةَ وَكُلاَ مِنْهَا رَغَداً حَيْثُ شِئْتُمَا وَلاَ تَقْرَبَا هَذِهِ الشَّجَرَةَ فَتَكُونَا مِنَ الظَّالِمِينَ{البقرة/35} فَأَزَلَّهُمَا الشَّيْطَانُ عَنْهَا فَأَخْرَجَهُمَا مِمَّا كَانَا

---

491. And when they meet those who believe, they say, "We believe"; but when they are alone with their evil ones.

492. To.

493. With.

494. Their evil ones.

فِيهِ وَقُلْنَا اهْبِطُواْ بَعْضُكُمْ لِبَعْضٍ عَدُوٌّ وَلَكُمْ فِي الأَرْضِ مُسْتَقَرٌّ وَمَتَاعٌ إِلَى حِينٍ {البقرة/36[495]}.
The word إِبْلِيسَ can be the proper name and title of الشَّيْطَانُ is given to
إِبْلِيسَ representing evil, rebellion and fasad, الله اعلم. To support this stand
point, when Allah ﷻ addresses directly this being as[496] قَالَ يَا إِبْلِيسُ مَا لَكَ أَلَّا أَ
{الحجر/32} تَكُونَ مَعَ السَّاجِدِينَ, the word إِبْلِيسُ is used as possibly the proper
name. Then, إِبْلِيسُ gets the lead title of الشَّيْطَانُ as representing the evil,
rebellion and fasad. Any person, persons, being or beings representing
the evil, rebellion and fasad can carry this title of الشَّيْطَانُ or الشَّيَاطِينِ, الله
اعلم as mentioned in إِنَّ الْمُبَذِّرِينَ كَانُواْ إِخْوَانَ الشَّيَاطِينِ وَكَانَ الشَّيْطَانُ لِرَبِّهِ كَفُورًا
{الإسراء/27}[497]. In this case, there is the language that there are human
shaytans and jinn shaytans to represent this notion of evil embodiment
through humans and jinns, الله اعلم.

Even, one can realize this notion of the interaction of animals with
the realms of shaytan as mentioned in the hadiths of the Prophet ﷺ.
For example, the camels followed by some of the shayatin (27) (28), the
incidents of dogs' barking at the time of adhan, the incident of donkeys'
screams (3) (hadith # 3303) or the case of Omar ra visiting Damascus
(8) and riding on a horse can be some examples (9).

One of the interpretations for the root word of الشَّيْطَانُ is شطن which
means to be far from. In this regard, it can be said that shaytan is far
from the Rahmah of Allah ﷻ. When one reviews the tawfiz the person
chooses the side of Allah ﷻ by taking refuge and at the same time, puts
shaytan on another pole to be away from or distanced from its evil. In
some of the discourses of ahlu-tasawwuf, there are depictions of shaytan.
I think some of these statements are expressed in some spiritual states
of sakr, that the person may not be aware of what he or she is saying in
their conscious or awake state of mind or heart. These interpretations

---

495. 2:34And when We told the angels, "Prostrate yourselves before Adam!"—they all
prostrated themselves, save Iblis, who refused and gloried in his arrogance: and thus he
became one of those who deny the truth
2:35 And We said: "O Adam, dwell thou and thy wife in this garden, and eat freely thereof,
both of you, whatever you may wish; but do not approach this one tree, lest you become
wrongdoers."2:36 But Satan caused them both to stumble therein, and thus brought about
the loss of their erstwhile state. And so We said: "Down with you, [and be henceforth] enemies
unto one another; and on earth you shall have your abode and your livelihood for a while!"
496. 22:32 This is [to be borne in mind]. And anyone who honours the symbols set up by God
[shall know that,] verily, these [symbols derive their value] from the God-consciousness in the
[believers'] hearts.
497. (17:27) Behold, the squanderers are, indeed, of the ilk of the satans—inasmuch as Satan
has indeed proved most ungrateful to his Sustainer.[33]

if taken literally can cause major problems with the clear teachings of the religion and mislead many in their aqidah. Actually it did. As one can see the projection of these interpretations in traditional eastern religions and also in some of the groups which claim to be under the umbrella of Islam but clear opposing views of in their aqidah with the clear teachings, والله اعلم.

In the expression وَإِذَا لَقُوا الَّذِينَ آمَنُوا[498], instead of مُؤْمِنُون[499], the expression الَّذِينَ آمَنُو is used. The word الَّذِينَ آمَنُو allude to the quality of iman in a human being besides many other qualities. This can indicate that munāfiqs meet and engage the people of imān with this quality of theirs. Also, this quality can be the most important quality in a human besides other qualities, والله اعلم.

In the expression وَإِذَا لَقُوا الَّذِينَ آمَنُوا قَالُو[500], the word قَالُو[501] can indicate that they verbalize

something that they really don't believe. The word قَالُو can also allude that they need to say something in order to remove and clarify the existing claims about them that they are involved in fasad and mischief. The word قَالُو can also signify that they want to utter some words in order to be aware of about the intimate discourses of Muslims, والله اعلم.

In addition, in the expression وَإِذَا لَقُوا الَّذِينَ آمَنُوا قَالُوا آمَنَّا[502] can require more emphasis or takid with the word آمَنَّا. Although there is some doubt about the disposition of munāfiqs in their relationships with Muslims, there is still not much emphasis. Yet, one can expect more emphasis. This shows that they just say it but it really does not show their true stance, والله اعلم.

In another perspective, a takid in this case with the word آمَنَّا can also possibly reveal their real identity. Sometimes, if they are hiding their real identity with something superficial, too much emphasis on this light, thin and superficial curtain can possibly tear it. Because, takid and emphasis removes the doubt. The process of removing the doubts entail investigation, inquiry and analysis. If this is process is applied then, their real identity would be revealed. Therefore, they don't prefer the method of taki'd, والله اعلم.

---

498. And when they meet those who believe.
499. Believers.
500. And when they meet those who believe, they say.
501. They say.
502. And when they meet those who believe, they say, "We believe".

In addition the word اٰمَنَّا[503] is a jumla fiiliyah which is a transitory state compared to a jumla ismiyyah which is a permanent state. In that perspective, their imān is only superficial and temporary verbal discourse. In this perspective, in the expression [504]وَإِذَا لَقُوا الَّذِينَ آمَنُوا قَالُوا آمَنَّا وَإِذَا خَلَوْا إِلَى شَيَاطِينِهِم can show immature character traits as changing according to the conditions.

In the expression [505]وَإِذَا لَقُوا الَّذِينَ آمَنُوا, the phrase الَّذِينَ آمَنُو[506] can indicate that the believers were among you before. But, they separated from your clique by making their choice in the true belief. The expression الَّذِينَ آمَنُو can show with the word sila الَّذِينَ that there is a dynamic process of people increasing on the side of imān. In other words, the people of imān are increasing constantly, الله اعلم.

The word شَيَاطِينِهِم[507] in the expression [508]وَإِذَا خَلَوْا إِلَى شَيَاطِينِهِمْ can indicate that as the shaytans are invisible not easy to detect, their leaders are not easy to detect and point out, الله اعلم. When one reviews this ayah with its initial sabab nuzûl, one can see that there was an interaction between the munāfiqs and the people from ahlu-kitāb who had obstinacy not in believing the message of the Prophet ﷺ although they knew the Prophet from their scriptures like they knew their own children. This can show that the munāfiqs can see them as their leaders in order to receive some ideas and strength in their disposition, الله اعلم.

When one compares the expressions of munāfiqs how they talk to the believers and how they talk to their real friends is interesting. In the ayah [509]وَإِذَا لَقُوا الَّذِينَ آمَنُوا قَالُوا آمَنَّا وَإِذَا خَلَوْا إِلَى شَيَاطِينِهِمْ قَالُوا إِنَّا مَعَكُمْ إِنَّمَا نَحْنُ, when they meet with the believers they say [510]وَإِذَا لَقُوا الَّذِينَ آمَنُوا قَالُوا آمَنَّا. But, when they are with their real friends they say [511]قَالُوا إِنَّا مَعَكُمْ. There is a taki'd إِنَّا which shows their real enthusiasm in the second case compared to very dull expression of the first case with the believers.

---

503. "We believe."
504. And when they meet those who believe, they say, "We believe"; but when they are alone with their evil ones.
505. And when they meet those who believe.
506. Those who believe.
507. Their evil ones.
508. But when they are alone with their evil ones.
509. And when they meet those who believe, they say, "We believe"; but when they are alone with their evil ones, they say, "Indeed, we are with you.
510. And when they meet those who believe, they say, "We believe".
511. They say, "Indeed, we are with you.

In the expression قَالُواْ إِنَّا مَعَكُمْ إِنَّمَا نَحْنُ مُسْتَهْزِؤُونَ[512], there is no atf or any connecter between إِنَّا مَعَكُمْ and إِنَّمَا نَحْنُ مُسْتَهْزِؤُونَ[513]. For an atf or connector, if something is exactly same with another or opposite to another, then an atf may not be used. But, if there is an intermediary level of connection, one can use an atf or connector to bond those similarities. Yet, in this case when one has a function of badal then, as in this case, إِنَّا مَعَكُمْ إِنَّمَا نَحْنُ مُسْتَهْزِؤُونَ[514], then this can serve as a purpose of taki'd to emphasize their real position is in nifãq. At the same time, the expression إِنَّمَا نَحْنُ مُسْتَهْزِؤُونَ show the betrayal of munafiqûn to the believers. The expression of إِنَّا مَعَكُمْ can show some type of doubt for their real disposition among their real friends. Therefore, possibly they question them and they need to proclaim and renew their stance with the expression إِنَّا مَعَكُمْ, الله اعلم.

From above discussions, one can also understand the importance of following or belonging to a school. This can be positive or negative. The negative case be the munãfiqs as mentioned also in مُذَبْذَبِينَ بَيْنَ ذَلِكَ لاَ إِلَى هَؤُلاء وَلاَ إِلَى هَؤُلاء وَمَن يُضْلِلِ اللَّهُ فَلَن تَجِدَ لَهُ سَبِيلاً {143/النساء}[515]. They go back and forth with skepticism, interest based engagements and judgmental traits. They don't establish a group identity. These are the ones who are in between and can have sometimes hard time to situate themselves. In our current times, one can call this as lost-wanderers, the ones who cannot really differentiate right from wrong or false from the truth.

There can be two extremes of group identities. One is approving everything whether evil or good as the result of the emerging liberal trends. On the other hand, being so conservative with one's values that the person may not be aware of with the needs of his or her time. In other words, a person who is disconnected some of the realities of his or her time, culture and social trends can be an example of this extreme.

There can be another group of between as mentioned وَبَيْنَهُمَا حِجَابٌ وَعَلَى الأَعْرَافِ رِجَالٌ يَعْرِفُونَ كُلاًّ بِسِيمَاهُمْ وَنَادَوْاْ أَصْحَابَ الْجَنَّةِ أَن سَلاَمٌ عَلَيْكُمْ لَمْ يَدْخُلُوهَا

---

512. Hey say, "Indeed, we are with you; we were only mockers."
513. We were only mockers.
514. "Indeed, we are with you; we were only mockers."
515. (4:143) Wavering between them, [belonging] neither to the believers nor to the disbelievers. And whoever Allah leaves astray—never will you find for him a way.

وَ هُمْ يَطْمَعُونَ {الأعراف/46}[516]. These people can have certain stance of ethical, moral behavior and some type of stance with the believers. Yet, due to some reasons, they were not able to truly identify their group identity in the world. Then, Allah ﷻ gives them another chance of recognition to identify their real disposition as mentioned in the ayah.

As the sabab-nuzûl of the ayahs can cite specific incidents, the Qurãn's golden and diamond rules are valid for all the times. In this perspective, there will be such people who would mention true statements about other Muslims and proclaim themselves as Muslims but yet, they will engage with them with the intention of mockery, May Allah ﷻ protect all of us being in these situations, Amin.

[15]

{ اللّٰهُ يَسْتَهْزِئُ بِهِمْ وَيَمُدُّهُمْ فِي طُغْيَانِهِمْ يَعْمَهُونَ [517]{البقرة/15}

After the detailed explanations of the dispositions of the munãfiqs, then their retribution is explained.

If one reviews the ideal character of a Muslim instilled by the Qurãn and the teachings of the Prophet ﷺ that one can realize some of the traits as follows:

وَعِبَادُ الرَّحْمَٰنِ الَّذِينَ يَمْشُونَ عَلَى الْأَرْضِ هَوْنًا وَإِذَا خَاطَبَهُمُ الْجَاهِلُونَ قَالُوا سَلَامًا {الفرقان/63}[518]

وَالَّذِينَ لَا يَشْهَدُونَ الزُّورَ وَإِذَا مَرُّوا بِاللَّغْوِ مَرُّوا كِرَامًا {الفرقان/72}[519]

A Muslim has a perspective to please Allah ﷻ and concerns for akhirah. An ignorant or a jahil bothering him or her, he or she does not deal or respond this person in their own way of belligerence. Yet,

---

516. 7:46 And between the two there will be a barrier. And there will be persons who [in life] were endowed with the faculty of discernment [between right and wrong], recognizing each by its mark. And they will call out unto the inmates of paradise, "Peace be upon you!"- not having entered it themselves, but longing [for it].

517. [But] Allah mocks them and prolongs them in their transgression [while] they wander blindly.

518. (25:63) For, [true] servants of the Most Gracious are [only] they who walk gently on earth, and who, whenever the foolish address them, reply with [words of] peace;

519. 25:72 And [know that true servants of God are only] those who never bear witness to what is false, and [who], whenever they pass by [people engaged in] frivolity, pass on with dignity;

at the same time as a human being, he or she may be affected with the belligerence of these ignorant ones. In this perspective, Allah ﷻ comforts the believers and mentions { اللّٰهُ يَسْتَهْزِىءُ بِهِمْ وَيَمُدُّهُمْ فِي طُغْيَانِهِمْ يَعْمَهُونَ [520]{البقرة/15. In this case, the expression اللّٰهُ يَسْتَهْزِىءُ بِهِمْ[521] should be understood as Allah ﷻ accounts them with retribution in this dunya and afterlife. In this perspective, their statement of اِنَّمَا نَحْنُ مُسْتَهْزِؤُونَ[522] is nullified, terminated, reversed and abolished with the reality of اللّٰهُ يَسْتَهْزِىءُ بِهِمْ.

At the same time, if a person makes the istihza of someone whose status is clearly established, then this person in reality can be humiliating himself in front of others. For example, Rasulullah ﷺ's noble traits and character is obvious, clear and accepted by people. If a person makes the istihza of Rasulullah ﷺ, then in reality the person is humiliating him or herself in front of others.

One should understand the last expression وَيَمُدُّهُمْ فِي طُغْيَانِهِمْ يَعْمَهُونَ[523] with the discussions of free choice and free will of the person. As they had the choice of an evil and insisted on their stance, then Allah ﷻ created the means for their choice. This expression also alludes to the notion about some of the extreme opinions about free choice, kasb/acquirement of person and destiny. Allah ﷻ creates everything. If a person wants an evil or good then the means are created by Allah ﷻ to enable the free choice execution of the individual. But at the end, the person is responsible with his or her choice in front of Allah ﷻ.

As one can realize the word يَمُدُّهُمْ [524] does not mean "to cause" something. It has the meanings of help when a person is already in one situation. In other words, the word "madat" has the meaning of asking help from someone to do something. In this case, as they desire and ask help do more evil, the it is given to them as mentioned وَيَمُدُّهُمْ فِي طُغْيَانِهِمْ[525].

---

520. [But] Allah mocks them and prolongs them in their transgression [while] they wander blindly.
521. [But] Allah mocks them.
522. We were only mockers.
523. And prolongs them in their transgression [while] they wander blindly.
524. Prolongs them.
525. Prolongs them in their transgression.

At the end, to eliminate any type of misunderstandings the word طُغْيَانِهِمْ[526] has the izafah to هم[527] making it as a takid and clear that it is their rendering of evil through kasb/acquiring.

In the part اللهُ يَسْتَهْزِىءُ بِهِمْ, the expression يَسْتَهْزِىءُ بِهِم[528] is jumla fiiliyah compared to the the previous expression for the stance of munāfiqs as إِنَّمَا نَحْنُ مُسْتَهْزِءُونَ{البقرة 14/}[529]. In this perspective, jumla fiiliyah can indicate that Allah restitutes them as an action due to their evil action. On the other hand, jumla ismiyyah in the second expression can allude to the permanent state of their evil and sarcasm disposition. Therefore, there is no name of Allah as Mustahzi and it is not correct to call or think in aqidah with this perspective. Allah restitutes as a result of their action as mentioned in the form of a jumla fiiliyah.

When one makes istihza with the believers due to their belief then, they in reality do not respect the guidelines of the religion as sent by Allah . Therefore, the expression اللهُ يَسْتَهْزِىءُ بِهِم[530] shows that Allah responds to them.

The word يَمُدُّهُمْ[531] can show that their stance in fitnah is a long-life trait. The word يَمُدُّهُمْ can mean a type of elongation. This word can signify the cases of overflow in the sea or river at certain times. The word طُغْيَانِهِمْ in this case can show how one can exceed one's limits with one's relationship with Allah . The word طُغْيَانِهِمْ is also used in order to express overflowing water in the sea or a river. The word يَعْمَهُونَ[532] can show the disposition of recklessness and aimlessness.

In the full expression of وَيَمُدُّهُمْ فِي طُغْيَانِهِمْ يَعْمَهُونَ[533], each word can support the other word in this phrase to depict a character who is belligerent, vulgar, and yet do not know and realize what they are doing.

In the expression اللهُ يَسْتَهْزِىءُ بِهِمْ[534], there is no atf or connection to the previous parts. In this perspective, it shows that Allah does not give their retribution due to their immediate evil act but due to their continuous evil disposition as a natural trait of theirs. In other words,

---

526. Their transgression.
527. Them.
528. Mocks them.
529. We were only mockers.
530. [But] Allah mocks them.
531. Prolongs them.
532. Blindly.
533. And prolongs them in their transgression [while] they wander blindly.
534. [But] Allah mocks them.

Allah ﷻ does not penalize a person similar to humans of due to immediate anger etc. These are deficient human qualities. Allah ﷻ as Al-Awwal[535] and Al-Akhir[536], Al-Batin[537] and Al-Zahir[538], and as Al-Alîm[539] know their true reality. Accordingly, their outcomes reveal accordingly. In this perspectives, Allah ﷻ do not penalize them with their evil immediately yet they still engage and continue with it.

On another note, the retribution of Allah ﷻ can be hidden as the expression اللّٰهُ يَسْتَهْزِىءُ بِهِم can allude. One can call this istidraj that they may think that they are in a triumph but in reality they are not.

In the expression وَيَمُدُّهُمْ فِي طُغْيَانِهِمْ يَعْمَهُونَ[540], since they request and ask constantly to be in what they want to do, then Allah ﷻ enables the means for them. The increase as mentioned يَمُدُّهُمْ[541] reveals itself when Allah ﷻ does not immediately punish them in their immediate engagements. Then their evil engagements exponentially increase and they get the false conclusion that they are the guided people because there is no intervention for their evil. This may be called as istidraj in tasawwuf.

When one reviews the two expressions قَالُوا إِنَّا مَعَكُمْ إِنَّمَا نَحْنُ مُسْتَهْزِؤُونَ {البقرة/14}[542] and immediately following أللّٰهُ يَسْتَهْزِىءُ بِهِم وَيَمُدُّهُمْ فِي طُغْيَانِهِمْ يَعْمَهُونَ {البقرة/15}[543], one can witness very live sentence structure. After their disposition of munafiqûn in ayah 14, the following ayah in 15 could have had different possibilities. But, it is presented in such a dynamic way that the reader keeps the flow and asks what is next. Then, the person gets an awe, self-check, self-balance and caution with the style and content. Other possibilities of wordings could have been chosen. Yet, it can also depict a human inclinations of dynamism قَالُوا إِنَّا مَعَكُمْ إِنَّمَا نَحْنُ مُسْتَهْزِؤُونَ {البقرة/14} then

immediately أللّٰهُ يَسْتَهْزِىءُ بِهِم[544] follows. This can show how Transendent Realities of the Words of Allah ﷻ can project and take some colors in the dimension of human reference point. Therefore, in many places of

---

535. The First.
536. The Last.
537. The Hidden.
538. The Manifest.
539. The All-Knowing.
540. And prolongs them in their transgression [while] they wander blindly.
541. Prolong.
542. They say, "Indeed, we are with you; we were only mockers."
543. [But] Allah mocks them and prolongs them in their transgression [while] they wander blindly.
544. [But] Allah mocks them.

the Qurān Allah ﷻ alludes to the fact that for humans there is a human messenger as some people claimed to have an extraordinary agent such as angels to be a prophet or messenger of God.

The word طُغْيَانِهِمْ[545] can show that their mischief can be life a storm that it may devastate things. This word can allude to these inner meanings, الله اعلم. The word يَعْمَهُونَ[546] can show that they don't have a meaningful goal and purpose. When especially combined with the word طُغْيَانِهِمْ, it can show that mischiefs don't have a meaningful goal and purpose.

In the expression طُغْيَانِهِمْ يَعْمَهُونَ[547], one can ask "does being in tugyan, mischief lead to heedlessness and impetuousness as the word يَعْمَهُونَ can allude? When a person is out of his or her limits with طُغْيَانِهِمْ, then it is easy to make mistakes in the state of not following any guidelines and lose his or her real purpose and goal.

One should also note the importance of not to take anything light related with the guidelines sent by Allah ﷻ. One can realize that for example in the case of Sālih as, when they make fun of a shiar, a sacred item as mentioned وَيَا قَوْمِ هَذِهِ نَاقَةُ اللَّهِ لَكُمْ آيَةً فَذَرُوهَا تَأْكُلْ فِي أَرْضِ اللَّهِ وَلاَ تَمَسُّوهَا بِسُوءٍ فَيَأْخُذَكُمْ عَذَابٌ قَرِيبٌ {هود/64}[548] then a whole nation was destroyed.

[16]

أُوْلَئِكَ الَّذِينَ اشْتَرَوُاْ الضَّلاَلَةَ بِالْهُدَى فَمَا رَبِحَت تِّجَارَتُهُمْ وَمَا كَانُواْ مُهْتَدِينَ {البقرة/16}[549]

This ayah has a conclusion stance of the previous notions. It has the style of using a business transaction terminology. As early people who encounter the discourses of the Qurān were businessman and women, business or trade is an inevitable engagement of humans in their social life at different levels.

On another perspective, a person's life is a business that one either invests makes a profit or becomes bankrupted in one's relationship with Allah ﷻ. The term bankruptcy as muflis is mentioned by the Prophet (9) ﷺ. in one narration. As the person's most important asset in this

---

545. Their transgression.
546. They wander blindly.
547. In their transgression [while] they wander blindly.
548. 11:64 And [then he said]: "O my people! This she camel belonging to God shall be a token for you: so leave her alone to pasture on God's earth, and do her no harm, lest speedy chastisement befall you!"
549. (2:16) [for] it is they who have taken error in exchange for guidance; and neither has their bargain brought them gain, nor have they found guidance [elsewhere].

life is time, a wise person constantly evaluates how he or she spends his or her time. Because it is limited, using in the most profitable way at different times, places, and contexts is a sign of a wise person. A person trying to situate his or her position in the struggle of the path of Allah ﷻ constantly takes the first step to gain. Sometimes, changing situations, and aging can require the person adapt one's habits and optimize this trade in one's relationship with Allah ﷻ. The word اِشْتَرُو[550] can be to exchange something with another thing according to the many muffisurun. Yet, this meaning does not fully give the meaning of اِشْتَرُو. Because, in the word شْتَرُو, there is a trade between two parties. With the meaning of exchange, there is no need for two parties. A person can go and change an item without the need of the other party or individual.

Also, the word شْتَرُو is in mādi, past form. This can allude to the discussions of qadar, qada and kasb, acquirement as discussed previously. In this regard, their acquirement of mischief leads to their stance and disposition in the realms of qadar and qada with the word شْتَرُو, الله اعلم.

There are two sources of stress either being in dalālah or not being in hidāyah as mentioned[551] الضَّلَالَةَ بِالْهُدَى. In other words, being in dalālah is a source of stress. The other source is when the person loses the hidāyah and knowing and realizing losing of this guidance, may Allah ﷻ protect us. The word الضَّلَالَةَ[552] can mean not clearly seeing one's path. This word can have different meanings of misguidance among the people who call them Muslims or non-Muslims. Therefore, Rasulullah ﷺ mentions that his ummah will have seventy-two different sects and only one would be guided, may Allah ﷻ protect us from any type of misguidance and have us hold the Qurān and Sunnah of Rasullullah ﷺ very tightly.

A person may ask why أُوْلَئِكَ[553] is used although the munāfiqs are not easily identifiable. One possibility can be that because the Qurān describes their qualities much in detail, now one can actually picture them as if they see them.

When one looks the terminology in the فَمَا رَبِحَت تِّجَارَتُهُمْ وَمَا كَانُوا[554] مُهْتَدِينَ, one can realize that there are some business terms. One can also analyze this ayah within the rules and terms of doing business. In other

---

550. Purchased.
551. Error [in exchange] for guidance.
552. Error.
553. Those are [the ones].
554. So their transaction has brought no profit, nor were they guided.

words, business or trade can be defined as exchanging something for
something else. In this case as munāfiqs exchange, hidāyah with dalālah
and have dalālah as their final asset. The fitrah of a person is on hidāyah
that is how munāfiqs make this exchange. The believers exchange dalālah
with hidāyah and have hidāyah final asset. The state of increasing one's
imān compared to its previous state can be called a relative dalālah for
believers.

On one perspective, trade or business is suggested by the Prophet
ﷺ as an occupation as also the Prophet ﷺ was himself taking care of
business of Khadijah رضى الله عنها. A smart businessman does not invest
in transactions when there is no profit as the word رَبِحَت[555] can allude to.
On the other hand, the main asset of a person when he or she is born
is the ability and potential of fitrah to choose hidāyah with his or her
free choice. Yet, when the person does not make the right investment
by not choosing the hidāyah as mentioned وَمَا كَانُواْ مُهْتَدِينَ[556], then there
is no profit as mentioned مَا رَبِحَت تِّجَارَتُهُمْ although his or her initial asset
of fitrah had the huge potential of the hidāyah. May Allah ﷻ protect us.

When one analyses the initial expression هُدًى لِّلْمُتَّقِينَ[557] that came in
the beginning of this Sūrah with وَمَا كَانُواْ مُهْتَدِينَ[558], this can show that
Allah ﷻ gave the Qurān as the hidāyah but they did not accept it and be
muhtadin.

On another level, if one analyzes this ayah أُوْلَئِكَ الَّذِينَ اشْتَرَوُاْ الضَّلاَلَةَ
بِالْهُدَى فَمَا رَبِحَت تِّجَارَتُهُمْ وَمَا كَانُواْ مُهْتَدِينَ {البقرة/16}[559], both the word أُوْلَئِكَ and
الَّذِينَ[560] can allude to the oddity, strangeness and irrational disposition
of these people. The word أُوْلَئِكَ can indicate the meaning of farness
pointing to this strangeness. The word الَّذِينَ can indicate the meaning of
the necessity of detailing this case with the sentence structure of sila in
Arabic because this is an odd and strange case but not a clear, explicit
and immediately understandable case, الله اعلم.

The letter ف is fa sababiyah. In this case, since they preferred dalālah
over hidāyah, then their engagement did not cause them to benefit them.
From the perspective of sabab nuzūl, the early makkans were adept in

---

555. Profit.
556. Nor were they guided.
557. A guidance for those conscious of Allah
558. Nor were they guided.
559. (2:16) [for] it is they who have taken error in exchange for guidance; and neither has their
bargain brought them gain, nor have they found guidance [elsewhere].
560. Those who.

trade. In addition, ahlu kitāb and munafiqûn were skillful in trade. They knew well these terms of profit, gain, and loss. This type of language contextualized the early as well as the later generalizations for their level of understandings.

When one analyzes the expression وَمَا كَانُوْا مُهْتَدِين, the word كَانُو can indicate some continuity in their stance either being in dalālah in this case or its opposite for others in hidāyah. This can show that being in dalālah or hidāyah as an attribute of a person can come as a habitual and continuous disposition of a person in one's life. There can be some externally seeming exceptions to this rule. Yet, we don't know the internal case of a person that only Allah ﷻ knows the inner, batin and outer, zahir realities. This habitual or continuous stance can also allude to one's engagement with amal or actions, either amal Sālih leading to hidāyah or amal su-i leading to dalālah, الله اعلم.

[17]

مَثَلُهُمْ كَمَثَلِ الَّذِي اسْتَوْقَدَ نَاراً فَلَمَّا أَضَاءتْ مَا حَوْلَهُ ذَهَبَ اللهُ بِنُورِهِمْ وَتَرَكَهُمْ فِي ظُلُمَاتٍ لاَّ يُبْصِرُونَ ﴿البقرة/17﴾561

One of the biggest painful positions is to taste a nimah and then to lose it. Because, since the person knows that nimah and experienced and tasted, now without this habit the person can be in real bitter and distressed state. Especially, if the person had some ingredients of imān as the biggest nimah, then the person can be in the highest state of depression in its loss. This itself can make the person in multiple darknesses. Therefore, the highest and expected state is to embody the full state of imān all the time with ihsan in order to remove all the black points of darkness and to form a continuous and uninterrupted line of imān. In tasawwuf, the dhikrs performed with La ilaha illa Allah has the purpose of embodying this continuity.

Yes, imān is the biggest nimah for existence. One second or less time of the state of kufr can put the person in a very deep and devastating states of darkness. Therefore, the dua of the Prophet ﷺ as asking to Allah ﷻ not leaving the person in the state of kufr for the time period of blinking of an eye or less can also show this dangerous state of darkness

---

561. Their example is that of one who kindled a fire, but when it illuminated what was around him, Allah took away their light and left them in darkness [so] they could not see.

of times without Allah ﷻ which can be called kufr. May Allah ﷻ protect us, because this is the biggest punishment for the person even in this dunya.

On another perspective, the phrase اسْتَوْقَدَ نَار [562] can be similar to ignition systems that we see in our daily lives in cars, ovens, light switches or other devices. If we take a car as an example, when a car is ignited with a key or a button, then with a huge initial power of ignition, the car starts and gets going. Imãn in a person can be similar to this initial ignition as mentioned with the light or fire in the expression اسْتَوْقَدَ نَار. Once, it enters then the person can keep going and speed up quickly or slowly depending on the person in one's relationship with Allah ﷻ, increasing one's imãn. One can imagine a car starting and stopping, how displeasing it is. Car doesn't move although it may make some noise. In this case, when the person does not ignite his or her systems or if there is a problem in the alternator system in car terms then the car may stop. This can be similar to the expected change or alternation in one's life when the imãn enters to one's heart and mind. If there is a problem in this expected change in one's life, then, the person may not embody the imãn.

In this perspective, kãfir is different than a munãfiq. Kãfir does not have an opportunity to be exposed to the lights of imãn because he or she may not be around the believers. Therefore, if a kãfir does not have a substantiated prejudice, as soon as he or she is exposed to the lights of imãn as the initial ignition, then they may not leave their state of imãn compared to munãfiqs.

In this regard, kãfir after becoming a believer can appreciate all the states of imãn because of the full awareness of contrasting all the agents of darkness with light, kufur with imãn. In other words, when a munãfiq is in persistent heedlessness for the routine practices of imãn called gaflah, then, he or she may not realize and appreciate the golden life vests of imãn. On the other hand, when a kãfir comes from hunger, poverty, destitute of imãn, then this person fully realizes, embodies and enjoys all the transforming effects of imãn. Yet, here the case is fully submission with humbleness and humility with open-mindedness without any prejudice to these golden teachings.

---

562. Who kindled a fire.

To prove the above argument, one can witness the quantity and quality of the zeal or the boost in people's imān after becoming Muslim from different backgrounds compared to the Muslims born in Muslim countries. The latter case may not realize what they have due to being born into these teachings. On the other hand, the new Muslims may appreciate imān more due to their contrasting past and present, الله اعلم.

Sometimes there can be special type of ignition given by Allah ﷺ such as إِذْ قَالَ مُوسَى لِأَهْلِهِ إِنِّي آنَسْتُ نَارًا سَآتِيكُم مِّنْهَا بِخَبَرٍ أَوْ آتِيكُم بِشِهَابٍ قَبَسٍ لَّعَلَّكُمْ تَصْطَلُونَ {النمل/7}[563]. In this case, Musa as is given the ignition of Prophethood when Allah ﷺ communicated with Musa as.

In this perspective, if one relates this ayah with the previous one, then one can realize that imān is the hidāyah. Yet, they made a choice with their own free will not to invest in it similar to business transaction as explained in the above ayah.

In the ayah above, there is a very vivid description that one's imagination and faculties of emotions can be triggered in order to understand, then picture and finally contextualize the meanings and feelings in this very colorful depiction. One should remember that in the depictions of the Qurān and hadith, there is no extravagancy or exaggeration. In literature, when humans use metaphorical language or parables, they like to exaggerate as much as possible to get attention. Especially, with our current times of novel writing industry, the writers may not have concern of exaggeration and ungrounded cases due to their main concern of being the best seller in the market. On the other hand, in Islam teachings.

On another perspective, one can understand the existence of metaphorical and figurative language through parables in scriptures. Among many reasons, one is to expand this vivid depiction to get the attention of imaginative and other faculties of person. This also shows the possible effects of pictures in human's mind and emotional faculties. This can be positive or negative.

Sometimes, one's imagination accepts and depicts unusual cases quicker. In other words, once imagination may tend to reject immediately and rationally accessible cases due to being ordinary or

---

563. [Mention] when Moses said to his family, "Indeed, I have perceived a fire. I will bring you from there information or will bring you a burning torch that you may warm yourselves."

cliché. Therefore, one can see here an interesting case of depicting the inner position of munāfiqs.

Sometimes, the language that is directing to the mind and logic does not have the capacity to describe the details of inner dispositions of feelings and emotions. In this case, the figurative and metaphorical language in parables can be more close to explaining these details in emotions and feelings. The ayah is very vividly depicting their inner faculties and emotions of fear, pessimism, uncertainty, anxiety, stress, darkness, panic, gloominess, nervousness and uneasiness, SubhanAllah! As one can realize in the previous ayahs, the inner dynamics, intentions and the drive of munāfiqs are very complex. It is not easy to understand and decipher them. In this regards, giving examples help to go into details of some of this complexity.

In Arabic language, there are different reasons of using similitude or metaphorical language. Some are to explain the possibility of the reality of the topic of discussion, to identify the discussed case, to identify its quantity, to clarify the case in one's mind, to attract the reader's attention and to make the reader to focus on the case (29).

Here, another interesting concept is the trend that when a person does not have a Nûr, he or she may benefit from the ones who has it. In this case, one can review this ayah with other the Quranic ayahs when Allah ﷻ mentions even in the scenes of akhirah as: يَوْمَ يَقُولُ الْمُنَافِقُونَ وَالْمُنَافِقَاتُ لِلَّذِينَ آمَنُوا انظُرُونَا نَقْتَبِسْ مِن نُّورِكُمْ قِيلَ ارْجِعُوا وَرَاءكُمْ فَالْتَمِسُوا نُورًا فَضُرِبَ بَيْنَهُم بِسُورٍ لَّهُ بَابٌ بَاطِنُهُ فِيهِ الرَّحْمَةُ وَظَاهِرُهُ مِن قِبَلِهِ الْعَذَابُ 564{الحديد/13}. Munāfiqs in the dunya used to benefit from the Nûr, light, of the imān and its reflections. As the munafiqûn were and are living with the ahlu-imān, they have been getting some benefit of this imān. If an evil person sits and hangs around with good people, there will be some good effect on him or her even though he or she maintains the evilness. This ayah mentioned in Sûrah hadid shows that they want to continue with this attitude even in the akhirah, الله اعلم.

This ayah on another level shows that with all the mischief and evil renderings of munafiqûn, they are still under the control and allowance of Allah ﷻ. Sometimes, a person can become pessimistic or hopeless as

564. (57:13)On the [same] Day the hypocrite men and hypocrite women will say to those who believed, "Wait for us that we may acquire some of your light." It will be said, "Go back behind you and seek light." And a wall will be placed between them with a door, its interior containing mercy, but on the outside of it is torment.

one follows the news and watches the mischief happenings on the earth. In this regard, this is a reminder to the person that Allah ﷻ is in control with the Divine Mashiyyah and Allowance.

On another reflection, in this ayah مَثَلُهُمْ كَمَثَلِ الَّذِي اسْتَوْقَدَ نَاراً فَلَمَّا أَضَاءتْ مَا حَوْلَهُ ذَهَبَ اللّهُ بِنُورِهِمْ وَتَرَكَهُمْ فِي ظُلُمَاتٍ لاَّ يُبْصِرُونَ {البقرة/17}[565], the expression اسْتَوْقَدَ نَاراً[566] can allude to the fitnah they started. They may have a very false or transient type of success or light in these mischiefs that they may feel happy. Yet, when Allah ﷻ removes this pseudo or fake light of joy or happiness due to their mischief as mentioned ذَهَبَ اللّهُ بِنُورِهِمْ[567]. Then, they are again in their normal and continuous state of darkness of lack of iman and full of mischief renderings as mentioned وَتَرَكَهُمْ فِي ظُلُمَاتٍ[568] لاَّ يُبْصِرُونَ {البقرة/17}.

One can ask why their light was gone sometime after them tasting the light or the light of iman? Can they have no light from the beginning? When a person tastes a nimah, there is more pain when the person loses it as mentioned with the word فَلَمَّا[569].

One can argue that there is a hidden (mahzuf) sentence between فَلَمَّا أَضَاءتْ مَا حَوْلَهُ[570]and ذَهَبَ اللّهُ بِنُورِهِمْ[571]. This can be that when they had the fire or light of iman that they did not maintain the necessary means to keep this fire. Then, it disappeared or vanished overtime. When there is a fire for warming up in the woods, someone needs to take the necessary means to maintain so that it doesn't disappear. Similarly, iman's existence depends on amalu Sālih, and learning. If they are not present then, one's iman can be endangered. The Prophet صلى الله عليه وسلم mentions that the boundary between iman and kufr is salah, one's prayers (9).

When one analyzes the expression وَتَرَكَهُمْ فِي ظُلُمَاتٍ لاَّ يُبْصِرُونَ[572], the first part وَتَرَكَهُمْ فِي ظُلُمَاتٍ[573] can indicate a deeper and another level of distress and uneasiness when the person is left in darkness. Yet, in darkness if the people see their friends and their surroundings, they

---

565. Their example is that of one who kindled a fire, but when it illuminated what was around him, Allah took away their light and left them in darkness [so] they could not see.

566. Kindled a fire.

567. Allah took away their light

568. And left them in darkness [so] they could not see.

569. But when.

570. But when it illuminated what was around him.

571. Allah took away their light.

572. And left them in darkness [so] they could not see.

573. And left them in darkness.

may have some relief, but they cannot see them as well as mentioned in
لَا يُبْصِرُونَ[574]. This induces another type of distress, fear and uneasiness
on the person's psychology. May Allah ﷻ protect us, Amin.

When one looks at the phrase of مَثَلُهُمْ كَمَثَلِ[575], the word misal is used
twice. Although one can argue that this usage is due to the sentence
or word usage in Arabic, yet, this can show the importance of giving
examples, missal in explanations, الله اعلم. If one reviews the previous
ayah, there were some specific character traits of munāfiqs explained
before. Now, with this ayah and later, by giving examples, the explained
concept is solidified and substantiated. Nowadays, one can see a similar
teaching method in our modern times: first explaining the knowledge/
theory and then giving examples, الله اعلم. The examples given here are
not very specific and limited but it can be also generalized depending on
the time, context, people and cases.

In different places in the Qurān, the word مثل is used for giving
examples. In some of the places, it comes with the word ضرب for example
وَضَرَبَ اللَّهُ مَثَلًا رَّجُلَيْنِ أَحَدُهُمَا أَبْكَمُ لَا يَقْدِرُ عَلَى شَيْءٍ وَهُوَ كَلٌّ عَلَى مَوْلَاهُ أَيْنَمَا يُوَجِّههُّ لَا
يَأْتِ بِخَيْرٍ هَلْ يَسْتَوِي هُوَ وَمَن يَأْمُرُ بِالْعَدْلِ وَهُوَ عَلَى صِرَاطٍ مُّسْتَقِيمٍ {النحل/76}[576]. In
some other places, this word is not used but one can understand this is
a similitude, a missal, as well. In language, the examples or similitudes
have more power to describe the details and to engage the feelings and
emotions of the person with the content and gist of the message.

Here, harfu tashbih كـ is not mahzuf, hidden. With its explicit
presence, it is possibly due to the emphasis to focus the reader to the
tasbih, similitude. Harfu tashbih كـ also suggests the necessity of one to
one correspondence in similitude with parallelism.

Although the munāfiqs are Jamā'ah, a group, in the expression مَثَلُهُمْ[577]
كَمَثَلِ الَّذِي اسْتَوْقَدَ نَارًا the sila word الَّذِي[578] is singular but not plural. This can
show that in the engagements of fitnah, the effect of one person's causing
fitnah can be equivalent of many occurrences and chain reactions of
fitnah. In other words, a person making fitnah can represent a huge
group in the effects of its destruction.

---

574. [So] they could not see.
575. Their example is that of one who
576. And Allah presents an example of two men, one of them dumb and unable to do a thing,
while he is a burden to his guardian. Wherever he directs him, he brings no good. Is he equal
to one who commands justice, while he is on a straight path?
577. Their example is that of one who kindled a fire.
578. Who.

Alternatively, when a person is part of a jammah, the effect of one person can be like the entire jammah, group. This can be something both for good or bad.

The letter س in the word اِسْتَوْقَدَ[579] can indicate the difficulty of them making fitnah. In other words, they choose to make fitnah or mischief, but they are not forced to do it. Sometimes, without his or her choice, a person can find oneself in the middle of a fitnah. This case is different than the one who by choice and will does the fitnah.

In the expression اِسْتَوْقَدَ نَاراً[580], the word نَاراً can indicate that although the fire can give light yet, it can burn the person if one touches it. Similarly, most of the time fitnahs instigated by the munāfiqs can externally look reasonable and give light, yet once one gets involved and touches it then the person can be destroyed. Therefore, Rasulullah ﷺ suggests at the time of fitnah, although the person seem to agree with one side, it is better not to touch but be passive without being involved, اﷲ اعلم (9). In the phrase اِسْتَوْقَدَ نَاراً[581], the nakra, undefinite article in the word نَاراً can indicate their rush to get any type of fire.

In the phrase فَلَمَّا أَضَاءتْ مَا حَوْلَهُ[582], the letter of ف can allude to the concept of the cycle of darkness and light in their relation with imān.

In the expression فَلَمَّا أَضَاءتْ مَا حَوْلَهُ ذَهَبَ اللهُ بِنُورِهِمْ وَتَرَكَهُمْ فِي ظُلُمَاتٍ لاَّ يُبْصِرُونَ[583] shows that they lit the fire not for the purpose of warming up but for seeing as mentioned أَضَاءتْ[584]. They don't have the Nûr, light of imān so that they can see and use it as the source of guidance. Yet, Musa as wanted fire to warm up as mentioned إِذْ قَالَ مُوسَى لِأَهْلِهِ إِنِّي آنَسْتُ نَارًا سَآتِيكُم مِّنْهَا بِخَبَرٍ أَوْ آتِيكُم بِشِهَابٍ قَبَسٍ لَّعَلَّكُمْ تَصْطَلُونَ[585] {النمل/7}. because Musa as has the imān.

Another interesting point is that in the expression اِسْتَوْقَدَ نَاراً فَلَمَّا[586] أَضَاءتْ مَا حَوْلَهُ ذَهَبَ اللهُ بِنُورِهِمْ both the underlined words nar, fire and Nûr, light comes from the same root. As one can see in the previous

---

579. Kindled.
580. Kindled a fire.
581. Kindled a fire.
582. But when it illuminated what was around him.
583. But when it illuminated what was around him, Allah took away their light and left them in darkness [so] they could not see.
584. It illuminated.
585. [Mention] when Moses said to his family, "Indeed, I have perceived a fire. I will bring you from there information or will bring you a burning torch that you may warm yourselves."
586. Who kindled a fire, but when it illuminated what was around him, Allah took away their light.

paragraph, how the same thing can become a source of darkness, fithnah, evil and loss for one group, munafiqûn compared to the other group it can become the light, source of guidance, goodness, ethical, and triumph for the other group, the people of imān.

The word حَوْلَهُ مَا[587] can indicate the entire directions or volume surrounding the person. Then, one can imagine the contrast between existence of light and its absence in totality.

The word ظُلُمَاتٍ[588] can indicate that they are in multitude of spiritual and mental darkness due to the word ظُلُمَاتٍ being plural but not singular.

In the expression ذَهَبَ أللهُ بِنُورِهِمْ[589], the harf jar ب of the word بِنُورِهِم can indicate that something has a potential benefit. The revealing of this potentiality also depends on Allah ﷻ's Mashiyyah, Will. In the expression ذَهَبَ اللهُ بِنُورِهِمْ, when Allah ﷻ takes out the benefit from something no one can bring it back. This can add more hopelessness in the state and expectations of munafiqûn .

[18]

صُمٌّ بُكُمٌ عُمْيٌ فَهُمْ لاَ يَرْجِعُونَ [590] {البقرة/18/}

When a person is in difficulty, he or she can be in expectation with different means and engagements. In search of hope, one can sometimes say something, hear something, say something or see something then, he or she may become hopeful. Yet, if the person cannot use these faculties in oneself, there may not be any hope at all, الله اعلم.

The expression لاَ يَرْجِعُونَ[591] can indicate that there are sometimes cases and evil involvements that the person can be involved by choice. Then, if the person changes his or her mind to leave that evil, that evil may not let the person leave. So, this person can become hopeless as mentioned with لاَ يَرْجِعُونَ, الله اعلم. May Allah ﷻ protect us, Amìn.

The overall picture can show that without any means of help, they are fully in a hopeless and pessimistic states of darkness.

---

587. What was around him.
588. Darkness.
589. Allah took away their light.
590. Deaf, dumb and blind—so they will not return [to the right path].
591. Will not return [to the right path].

[30]

وَإِذْ قَالَ رَبُّكَ لِلْمَلَائِكَةِ إِنِّي جَاعِلٌ فِي الأَرْضِ خَلِيفَةً قَالُواْ أَتَجْعَلُ فِيهَا مَن يُفْسِدُ فِيهَا

وَيَسْفِكُ الدِّمَاء وَنَحْنُ نُسَبِّحُ بِحَمْدِكَ وَنُقَدِّسُ لَكَ قَالَ إِنِّي أَعْلَمُ مَا لاَ تَعْلَمُونَ[592]

The word إِنِّي[593] indicates that Allah ﷻ creates without any means or mediators. There is no mediator, angel, vehicle or means when Allah ﷻ creates. On the other hand, when Allah ﷻ communicates with humans for example [97,1] إِنَّا أَنزَلْنَاهُ فِي لَيْلَةِ الْقَدْرِ[594], in the word أَنزَلْنَاهُ[595], the plural form نَا indicates that Allah ﷻ sends the revelation through an angel. Also, the suffix نَا can also signify the Majestic Authority of the Divinity where the Arabic linguistically necessitates the plural form similar to other languages to emphasize the Majesty for establishing respect and awe in the person's heart and mind in one's relationship with Allah ﷻ.

In the expression إِنِّي أَعْلَمُ مَا لَا تَعْلَمُونَ[596] the word إِنِّي can include different possibilities with the emphasis:

► The angels, malaikah, tell to Allah ﷻ some of the possible evil outcomes of humans' livelihood and responsibility on the earth. However, Allah ﷻ creates and gives them the responsibility, khilafah, on the earth with a wisdom and an outcome of good. This can show a principle that an outcome of a complete good should not be left out due to the possible outcome of some smaller evils.

► The responsibility and abilities of the humans are not fully known to angels, malaikah. But it is known by Allah ﷻ. In others words, angels' lack of knowledge should not necessitate or invalidate the nonexistence of responsibility, khilafah of humans.

---

592. And [mention, O Muhammad], when your Lord said to the angels, "Indeed, I will make upon the earth a successive authority." They said, "Will You place upon it one who causes corruption therein and sheds blood, while we declare Your praise and sanctify You?" He [Allah] said, "Indeed, I know that which you do not know."
593. I am.
594. Indeed, We sent it [i.e., the Qurān] down during the Night of Decree.
595. We sent it [i.e., the Qurān].
596. "Indeed, I know that which you do not know."

In the above verse, the word جَاعِلٌ[597] comes instead of خَالِق[598]. This can be due to the reason that the angels, malaikah, do not have any issue about the creation of humans but they question that humans are given the responsibility of خَلِيفَة. The angels question that humans, by becoming the khalifah on earth, can be a possible source of mischief.

The preposition فِي is used for فِي الأَرْض instead of عَلَى. This can be due to humans' ability to infuse through the earth through different mining technologies. In some implicit meanings, the earth can be a body for humans and the humans themselves can be the soul of the earth. When the humans die the earth will die with it.

قَالَ and قَالُو shows that Allah ﷻ teaches humans the etiquettes of conversation and consultation. Allah ﷻ Exalted is far beyond the consultations and Allah ﷻ is far beyond for the need of asking opinions.

[31-33][599]

وَعَلَّمَ آدَمَ الأَسْمَاء كُلَّهَا ثُمَّ عَرَضَهُمْ عَلَى الْمَلَائِكَةِ فَقَالَ أَنبِئُونِي بِأَسْمَاء هَؤُلاء إِن كُنتُمْ صَادِقِينَ {البقرة/31} قَالُواْ سُبْحَانَكَ لاَ عِلْمَ لَنَا إِلاَّ مَا عَلَّمْتَنَا إِنَّكَ أَنتَ الْعَلِيمُ الْحَكِيمُ {البقرة/32} قَالَ يَا آدَمُ أَنبِئْهُم بِأَسْمَآئِهِمْ فَلَمَّا أَنبَأَهُمْ بِأَسْمَآئِهِمْ قَالَ أَلَمْ أَقُل لَّكُمْ إِنِّي أَعْلَمُ غَيْبَ السَّمَاوَاتِ وَالأَرْضِ وَأَعْلَمُ مَا تُبْدُونَ وَمَا كُنتُمْ تَكْتُمُونَ

The importance of naming things, differentiating them and explaining them with different sciences can be expressed with the word بِأَسْمَاء[600]. Also, the importance of knowledge and learning is expressed with بِأَسْمَاء. One of the scholars (1) says i'lm is the wealth of scholar: buys it with knowledge, retains and owns it with naming it and disciplining it with different sciences and methodologies. One of the advancements in the modern physics especially comes with different representations. For example, if one reviews the concepts in quantum physics one can understand most of the representations and symbolizations are due to the detailing of the information and naming them. Then, one can look at mathematical and physical representations that may not mean anything

---

597. I will make.
598. I will create.
599. (2:31) And He taught Adam the names—all of them. Then He showed them to the angels and said, "Inform Me of the names of these, if you are truthful." (2:32) They said, "Exalted are You; we have no knowledge except what You have taught us. Indeed, it is You who is the Knowing, the Wise."
600. Names.

to a regular person but can have a lot of meanings for a theoretical physicist.

The names can refer to different sciences as their possible peak levels were demonstrated by the miracles mentioned in the Qurãn. The miracles have two possible purposes: to make the people accept the messengers of God and also, to sample possible scientific advancements for humanity in order to encourage them to achieve these levels. As one can realize in natural sciences, for example in experimental physics, a physicist always works with samples. One of the Quranic logic that is presented often is that God mentions if God created as a sample on the earth, it is easier to duplicate the sample in the afterlife for recreation. In the Qurãn, this is a logic presented especially to the ones who view death as extinction and impossibility in recreation.

For some people, the word الأَسْمَاء can signify the different languages and ways of communication among humans, different species, and all of the creation from the past to future. In other words, medias of communication can entail the meanings. The codes, cultures, emotions, physiological states, and genres that are not meaningful for some people but it can be meaningful for the ones who know all these mediums of communication as one may call this as language. In this regard, one can think about Sulayman as communicating with the birds, the mountains and stones making dhikr of Allah, understanding the scripture with its proper meanings and positions etc.

Once the person understands then the person can take a position. In that regard, the Prophet has the means of communicating what is expected from Allah and how this knowledge and expectation can be actualized in the human realm. Therefore, the Prophet had the highest station of knowing all the لأَسْمَاء and applied this in His's own life and was a role model for all the creation. One can remember in this regard, the Prophet's position towards women, children, stones, crying wooden piece in the mosque, a complaining donkey etc. With this perspective, the Prophet صلى الله عليه وسلم knew لأَسْمَا with their true meaning and purpose.

In addition, an important methodology in the aqaidah is that knowing something, i'lm follows the knowledge, malum. In other words, when someone knows something, it is a discovery of a reality that is already there. If the person does not know or does know discover, the reality, the existing knowledge, and the science, i'lm, are still there.

Therefore, the title of this book is al-istinbatu is knowing, and discovering what is there. The authors' and the people's discovery does not make a change to the reality of the ocean of the Qurān. Similarly, in the essence of creation, Allah ﷻ created humans so that they can discover and do istinbāt, synthesis and analysis from what is already there. So that, the person can reveal this fact to oneself and others. In short, there is no invention but discovery.

Therefore, asma is used in the Qurān that Allah ﷻ taught to Adam as. Name of something, isim or asma, does not add a value to that reality, and to this science. Humans' knowing does not add anything but it is the effort of discovery. In this effort, all synthetizes, critical thinking and discovery can all happen. We can call this science today. If there is the conservation of energy in physics for example, we did not make this law but it is there. Allah ﷻ made it. We discovered it. We are using it in different applications of engineering. Then, we can call this theoretical science, knowing the conservation of energy. Applying this discovery, on an appliance such as refrigerator can be called applied science. We are using and synthesizing what is already there.

Finally, knowing Allah ﷻ truly can be related with one of the statements believed to be Hadis Qudsi although not cited in authentic hadith books, about the Kanz can possibly support this notion (16), الله اعلم [601]. Allah ﷻ is always there, Present, Al-Hayy and Al-Kayyum. Humans' knowing Allah ﷻ is the purpose of creation. The positive sciences are the steps to serve this ultimate goal of knowing the Creator, the One, Allah ﷻ. If a person does not truly know Allah جل جلاله then, it does not change anything from reality but a miserable and incorrect rendering of the meanings and purpose of life and afterlife for that person. If a person knows Allah ﷻ then it still does not change anything but a happy, falāh, and true renderings of the meanings and purpose in this life and afterlife for that purpose. In short, knowing, learning, struggle on the path, doing synthesis and critical thinking in the worldly dimensions can help us learn the methodologies and do istinbāt, synthesis, analytical thinking and critical approach with all advancing sciences so that we

---

601. Allah knows best.

can truly find Allah ﷻ. Nothing changes the reality. Allah ﷻ is One and Unique, Al-Hayy[602], Al-Ahad[603], Al-Qayyum[604].

[36-37]

فَأَزَلَّهُمَا الشَّيْطَانُ عَنْهَا فَأَخْرَجَهُمَا مِمَّا كَانَا فِيهِ وَقُلْنَا اهْبِطُواْ بَعْضُكُمْ لِبَعْضٍ عَدُوٌّ وَلَكُمْ فِي الأَرْضِ مُسْتَقَرٌّ وَمَتَاعٌ إِلَى حِينٍ {البقرة/36} فَتَلَقَّى آدَمُ مِن رَّبِّهِ كَلِمَاتٍ فَتَابَ عَلَيْهِ إِنَّهُ هُوَ التَّوَّابُ الرَّحِيمُ {البقرة/37}[605]

الأعراف [19-20]

وَيَا آدَمُ اسْكُنْ أَنتَ وَزَوْجُكَ الْجَنَّةَ فَكُلاَ مِنْ حَيْثُ شِئْتُمَا وَلاَ تَقْرَبَا هَذِهِ الشَّجَرَةَ فَتَكُونَا مِنَ الظَّالِمِينَ {الأعراف/19} فَوَسْوَسَ لَهُمَا الشَّيْطَانُ لِيُبْدِيَ لَهُمَا مَا وُورِيَ عَنْهُمَا مِن سَوْءَاتِهِمَا وَقَالَ مَا نَهَاكُمَا رَبُّكُمَا عَنْ هَذِهِ الشَّجَرَةِ إِلاَّ أَن تَكُونَا مَلَكَيْنِ أَوْ تَكُونَا مِنَ الْخَالِدِينَ {الأعراف/20}[606]

When the person is prohibited not to do something, the temptation or waswasa of human nature or tendencies can make the person incline towards that prohibited item, may Allah ﷻ protect us. It is natural or normal to fall into sin, error, or do something harmful even though one can instruct this person or a child the harmful outcomes of this engagement. As mentioned by the Prophet (صلى الله عليه وسلم) [26] it is normal to make mistakes, sins or errors but the best one is the one who accepts one's mistakes and turns to Allah ﷻ with repentance and humbleness as exemplified by Adam as. There is the normalization of human's tendencies to error and to make mistakes. So, this approach can be important in both adult and child education, the emphasis of normalizing the mistakes but the most important thing is asking forgiveness from Allah ﷻ and connecting again and again. The

---

602. The Living.
603. The Unique.
604. The Independent.
605. 2:36 But Satan caused them both to stumble therein, and thus brought about the loss of their erstwhile state. And so We said: "Down with you, [and be henceforth] enemies unto one another; and on earth you shall have your abode and your livelihood for a while!" 2:37 Then Adam received from his Lord [some] words, and He accepted his repentance. Indeed, it is He who is the Accepting of repentance, the Merciful.
606. 7:19 And [as for thee], O Adam, dwell thou and thy wife in this garden, and eat, both of you, whatever you may wish; but do not approach this one tree, lest you become evildoers!" (7:20) Thereupon Satan whispered unto the two with a view to making them conscious of their nakedness, of which [hitherto] they had been unaware; and he said: "Your Sustainer has but forbidden you this tree lest you two become [as] angels, or lest you live forever."

knowledge of not being perfect as a human being should be deliberated but the teaching of what to do if one makes a mistake in child and adult education is critical in the methodology of self-development.الأعراف 21-22]]

وَقَاسَمَهُمَا إِنِّي لَكُمَا لَمِنَ النَّاصِحِينَ {الأعراف/21} فَدَلَّاهُمَا بِغُرُورٍ فَلَمَّا ذَاقَا الشَّجَرَةَ بَدَتْ لَهُمَا سَوْءَاتُهُمَا وَطَفِقَا يَخْصِفَانِ عَلَيْهِمَا مِن وَرَقِ الْجَنَّةِ وَنَادَاهُمَا رَبُّهُمَا أَلَمْ أَنْهَكُمَا عَن تِلْكُمَا الشَّجَرَةِ وَأَقُل لَّكُمَا إِنَّ الشَّيْطَانَ لَكُمَا عَدُوٌّ مُّبِينٌ {الأعراف/22} قَالَ رَبَّنَا ظَلَمْنَا أَنفُسَنَا وَإِن لَّمْ تَغْفِرْ لَنَا وَتَرْحَمْنَا لَنَكُونَنَّ مِنَ الْخَاسِرِينَ 607

As seen in the above ayah, for Shaytan, it was not easy to make zalla to Adam as. Shaytan took an oath that he was saying the truth. Adam as did not know if a being like Satan can take an oath and then lie. Possibly, Adam as could have forgotten the command of Allah ﷻ that he should not approach that tree, as the name of a human is al-insaan in Arabic which means that the one who forgets. الله اعلم. Again, the role model attitude of Adam as and our mother Hawwa as comes as فَتَلَقَّى آدَمُ مِن رَّبِّهِ 608 كَلِمَاتٍ in Sûrah Baqarah 37 that they immediately turned back to Allah ﷻ as the dua of theirs follow as:

قَالَ رَبَّنَا ظَلَمْنَا أَنفُسَنَا وَإِن لَّمْ تَغْفِرْ لَنَا وَتَرْحَمْنَا لَنَكُونَنَّ مِنَ الْخَاسِرِينَ 609

This should be the approach to learn and to teach in the relationship with Allah ﷻ for the offspring of Adam as. The approach resets one's position with the Creator, Rabbul Alamin, and asking forgiveness. One can see possibly that Adam as may have wanted to worship like angels and forget the prohibition of Allah ﷻ about that the tree when فَوَسْوَسَ إِلَيْهِ الشَّيْطَانُ قَالَ يَا آدَمُ هَلْ أَدُلُّكَ عَلَى شَجَرَةِ الْخُلْدِ وَمُلْكٍ لَّا يَبْلَى {طه/120} 610

---

607. 7:21 And he swore unto them, "Verily, I am of those who wish you well indeed! (22)—and thus he led them on with deluding thoughts. But as soon as the two had tasted [the fruit] of the tree, they became conscious of their nakedness; and they began to cover themselves with pieced-together leaves from the garden. And their Sustainer called unto them: "Did I not forbid that tree unto you and tell you, 'Verily, Satan is your open foe'?"
7:23 The two replied: "O our Sustainer! We have sinned against ourselves—and unless Thou grant us forgiveness and bestow Thy mercy upon us, we shall most certainly be lost!"
608. Then Adam received from his Lord.
609. The two replied: "O our Sustainer! We have sinned against ourselves—and unless Thou grant us forgiveness and bestow Thy mercy upon us, we shall most certainly be lost!"
610. 20:120But Satan whispered unto him, saying: "O Adam! Shall I lead thee to the tree of life eternal; and [thus] to a kingdom that will never decay?"

In addition, the expression فَتَلَقَّى آدَمُ مِن رَّبِّهِ كَلِمَاتٍ shows that when a person is in a deep intizar or dua or in a state of heart and mind of regret and asking forgiveness then, Allah ﷻ teaches that person how and what to say properly to transform those feelings or spiritual states into words. One can call this inspiration or revealation for the Prophets. In other words, the person does his or her part then Allah ﷻ guides that person as always. The ilhamat or inspirations of the waliy of Allah ﷻ in their writings or litanies can be another example of this. In other words, they live these words in their heart and mind then, Allah ﷻ inspires them in words what to write, الله اعلم. Another example of this is the hadith from Anas Ibn Malik about the yawmul qiyamah that the Prophet ﷺ mentions that Allah ﷻ inspires the Prophet how to make thana, praise, of Allah ﷻ. Then, after staying long at sajdah, the Prophet asks and begs for the shafaah for the people in Jahannam (9). This is again the state of the Prophet and Allah ﷻ inspires him. ﷺ, الله اعلم

[41]

وَآمِنُواْ بِمَا أَنزَلْتُ مُصَدِّقاً لِّمَا مَعَكُمْ وَلاَ تَكُونُواْ أَوَّلَ كَافِرٍ بِهِ وَلاَ تَشْتَرُواْ بِآيَاتِي ثَمَناً قَلِيلاً وَإِيَّايَ فَاتَّقُونِ {البقرة/41}[611]

One can review the expression وَلاَ تَشْتَرُواْ بِآيَاتِي ثَمَناً قَلِيلاً[612] in the Qurān that it comes in different contexts and places. One of the context is the case that ahlu-kitāb hides the knowledge from the books of Allah ﷻ revealed to them for different motifs. On the other hand, especially today, when one looks efforts of Christians inviting people to church with different advertisement tools but yet, the churches are empty. In these efforts, one can see the genuine calls by using the words God, scripture, prayer, sins or repentance. Yet, the results does not seem to be strong although there are different means of communication. In these cases, these genuine words can be بِآيَاتِي yet, the content of the tawhid and worship principles and following the guidelines has been changed therefore, the outcome is not much fruitful due to وَلاَ تَشْتَرُواْ بِآيَاتِي ثَمَناً قَلِيلاً. In these perspectives, it is not uncommon to find people in the West to be repelled or distanced

---

611. 2:41 Believe in that which I have [now] bestowed from on high, confirming the truth already in your possession, and be not foremost among those who deny its truth; and do not barter away My messages for a trifling gain; and of Me, of Me be conscious!
612. And do not barter away My messages for a trifling gain.

from the religion due to non-genuine calls of people to religion. This may lead a person to think about cheap advertising and marketing tools about the high values of religion can also be in the discussions of وَلَا تَشْتَرُواْ بِآيَاتِي ثَمَناً قَلِيلاً. الله اعلم

[49]

The below verses outline the interaction of the previous believers of their time. There is a relationship between not appreciating the favors of Allah ﷻ, and not having imān, disbelief. It is always easy to fall into this danger of attitude, the attitude of not appreciation. This attitude can cause major deviation in one's relationship with Allah ﷻ.

وَإِذْ نَجَّيْنَاكُم مِّنْ آلِ فِرْعَوْنَ يَسُومُونَكُمْ سُوَءَ الْعَذَابِ يُذَبِّحُونَ أَبْنَاءكُمْ وَيَسْتَحْيُونَ نِسَاءكُمْ وَفِي ذَلِكُم بَلاء مِّن رَّبِّكُمْ عَظِيمٌ ⁶¹³

  After the help of Allah ﷻ that they were saved from the oppression in Egypt, but they started worshipping the cow.

[55]

وَإِذْ قُلْتُمْ يَا مُوسَى لَن نُّؤْمِنَ لَكَ حَتَّى نَرَى اللَّهَ جَهْرَةً فَأَخَذَتْكُمُ الصَّاعِقَةُ وَأَنتُمْ تَنظُرُونَ ⁶¹⁴

The attitude of arrogance and disrespect by saying "we won't believe till we see Allah ﷻ."

---

613. And [recall] when We saved you [i.e., your forefathers] from the people of Pharaoh, who afflicted you with the worst torment, slaughtering your [newborn] sons and keeping your females alive. And in that was a great trial from your Lord.
614. And [recall] when you said, "O Moses, we will never believe you until we see Allah outright"; so the thunderbolt took you while you were looking on.

[61]

وَإِذْ قُلْتُمْ يَا مُوسَى لَن نَّصْبِرَ عَلَىَ طَعَامٍ وَاحِدٍ فَادْعُ لَنَا رَبَّكَ يُخْرِجْ لَنَا مِمَّا تُنبِتُ الأَرْضُ
مِن بَقْلِهَا وَقِثَّآئِهَا وَفُومِهَا وَعَدَسِهَا وَبَصَلِهَا قَالَ أَتَسْتَبْدِلُونَ الَّذِي هُوَ أَدْنَى بِالَّذِي هُوَ خَيْرٌ
اهْبِطُواْ مِصْراً فَإِنَّ لَكُم مَّا سَأَلْتُمْ وَضُرِبَتْ عَلَيْهِمُ الذِّلَّةُ وَالْمَسْكَنَةُ وَبَآؤُواْ بِغَضَبٍ مِّنَ اللّهِ
ذَلِكَ بِأَنَّهُمْ كَانُواْ يَكْفُرُونَ بِآيَاتِ اللّهِ وَيَقْتُلُونَ النَّبِيِّينَ بِغَيْرِ الْحَقِّ ذَلِكَ بِمَا عَصَواْ وَّكَانُواْ
يَعْتَدُونَ 615

Not being happy what Allah gave them but asking more and being greedy
in worldly matters can be one perspective. The preference of lower than
higher is mentioned in this verse. One can understand, the plants or
vegetables planted in the lower levels of ground such as onion or garlic.
In that perspective, the word, بَقْلِهَا 616, can refer the vegetables coming
from the ground. According to the interpretation, if their preferences
of food was due to their eating habits while they were slaves in Egypt,
then this can allude to the notion of longing or nostalgia of the past
memories embedded in human nature even though sometimes it may
be good or bad, الله اعلم.

[67-71]

وَإِذْ قَالَ مُوسَى لِقَوْمِهِ إِنَّ اللّهَ يَأْمُرُكُمْ أَنْ تَذْبَحُواْ بَقَرَةً قَالُواْ أَتَتَّخِذُنَا هُزُواً قَالَ أَعُوذُ بِاللّهِ أَنْ
أَكُونَ مِنَ الْجَاهِلِينَ {البقرة/67} قَالُواْ ادْعُ لَنَا رَبَّكَ يُبَيِّن لَّنَا مَا هِيَ قَالَ إِنَّهُ يَقُولُ إِنَّهَا بَقَرَةٌ
لاَّ فَارِضٌ وَلاَ بِكْرٌ عَوَانٌ بَيْنَ ذَلِكَ فَافْعَلُواْ مَا تُؤْمَرونَ {البقرة/68} قَالُواْ ادْعُ لَنَا رَبَّكَ
يُبَيِّن لَّنَا مَا لَوْنُهَا قَالَ إِنَّهُ يَقُولُ إِنّهَا بَقَرَةٌ صَفْرَاء فَاقِعٌ لَّوْنُهَا تَسُرُّ النَّاظِرِينَ {البقرة/69}

---

615. And [recall] when you said, "O Moses, we can never endure one [kind of] food. So call
upon your Lord to bring forth for us from the earth its green herbs and its cucumbers and its
garlic and its lentils and its onions." [Moses] said, "Would you exchange what is better for what
is less? Go into [any] settlement and indeed, you will have what you have asked." And they
were covered with humiliation and poverty and returned with anger from Allah [upon them].
That was because they [repeatedly] disbelieved in the signs of Allah and killed the prophets
without right. That was because they disobeyed and were [habitually] transgressing.
616. Its green herbs.

قَالُواْ ادْعُ لَنَا رَبَّكَ يُبَيِّن لَّنَا مَا هِيَ إِنَّ الْبَقَرَ تَشَابَهَ عَلَيْنَا وَإِنَّا إِن شَاءَ اللَّهُ لَمُهْتَدُونَ
{البقرة/70} قَالَ إِنَّهُ يَقُولُ إِنَّهَا بَقَرَةٌ لاَّ ذَلُولٌ تُثِيرُ الأَرْضَ وَلاَ تَسْقِي الْحَرْثَ مُسَلَّمَةٌ لاَّ
شِيَةَ فِيهَا قَالُواْ الآنَ جِئْتَ بِالْحَقِّ فَذَبَحُوهَا وَمَا كَادُواْ يَفْعَلُونَ {البقرة/71}[617]

One may ponder as he or she reads the above ayahs what can be the possible hikmahs of the above ayahs for today besides their canonized teachings in classical and valuable scholarship of tafasir? In other words, how the ayahs of the Qurãn open themselves according to people, context, region, culture and time? As we are living at a time of globalized world, the physical boundaries are becoming less definitive in the interactions of culture and people due to internet and other means of instant and wide communication and data transfer tools. The second means of difference marking our era is the ongoing huge diaspora of Muslims being forced to migrate and leave their hometowns. There is a substantial migration and settlement of Muslims in non-Muslim countries.

The above two perspectives can bring some new openings of the Qurãn for Muslims to contextualize the pearls and diamonds of the Qurãn. One of the perspectives that one can witness is the context of the above ayahs. If a person lives in a Muslim country, the above ayahs can be really difficult to understand. In other words, one cannot imagine a person or a group that would dare to have even thoughts not even words about one's relationship with Allah ﷻ.

In Muslim countries, a person may not practice the teachings of the religion, yet, when it comes to the religion they tend to defend these teachings. There are famous stories among people. For example, if one

---

617. 2:67 AND LO! Moses said unto his people: "Behold, God bids you to sacrifice a cow." They said: "Dost thou mock at us?" He answered: "I seek refuge with God against being so ignorant!"
2:68 Said they: "Pray on our behalf unto thy Sustainer that He make clear to us what she is to be like." [Moses] replied: "Behold, He says it is to be a cow neither old nor immature, but of an age in-between. Do, then, what you have been bidden!"
2:69 Said they: "Pray on our behalf unto thy Sustainer that He make clear to us what her colour should be." [Moses] answered: "Behold; He says it is to be a yellow cow, bright of hue, pleasing to the beholder."
2:70 Said' they: "Pray on our behalf unto thy Sustainer that He make clear to us what she is to be like, for to us all cows resemble one another; and then, if God so wills, we shall truly be guided aright!"
2:71 [Moses] answered: "Behold, He says it is to be a cow not broken-in to plough the earth or to water the crops, free of fault, without markings of any other colour." Said they: "At last thou hast brought out the truth!"—and thereupon they sacrificed her, although they had almost left it undone.[55]

tells the people in the bar in a Muslim country that people are destroying the mosque they may get up and immediately to stop it while they are drunk.

On the other hand, the jokes with the sacred notions and items seem to be normalized over time in a non-Muslim country. Maybe, this can be due to the effect of philosophy, the changes of original scriptures, the loss of trust in clergy and religious authorities, and possibly due to some other reasons. Therefore, there was an unfathomable discord in cartoon crisis (30) about understanding the Muslim position and attitude towards the sacred compared to the non-Muslim position towards it. Due to this this discord and not understanding these two different positions, there were a lot of conflicts.

In addition, there is a substantial understanding that one of the reasons that the Qurān, the Prophet Muhammad صلى الله عليه وسلم and Islam have been sent by Allah ﷻ to all humans is to instill this lost intrinsic quality universally until the end of days. This intrinsic and essential quality is to have adab and respect for the sacred.

[76]

وَإِذَا لَقُواْ الَّذِينَ آمَنُواْ قَالُواْ آمَنَّا وَإِذَا خَلاَ بَعْضُهُمْ إِلَىَ بَعْضٍ قَالُواْ أَتُحَدِّثُونَهُم بِمَا فَتَحَ اللّهُ عَلَيْكُمْ لِيُحَآجُّوكُم بِهِ عِندَ رَبِّكُمْ أَفَلاَ تَعْقِلُونَ618

Promoting hypocrisy, and deceit among people is one of the perspectives here.

[79]

فَوَيْلٌ لِّلَّذِينَ يَكْتُبُونَ الْكِتَابَ بِأَيْدِيهِمْ ثُمَّ يَقُولُونَ هَذَا مِنْ عِندِ اللّهِ لِيَشْتَرُواْ بِهِ ثَمَناً قَلِيلاً فَوَيْلٌ لَّهُم مِّمَّا كَتَبَتْ أَيْدِيهِمْ وَوَيْلٌ لَّهُمْ مِّمَّا يَكْسِبُونَ619

To change the Scriptures by Allah ﷻ is another ingratitude towards Allah ﷻ.

---

618. And when they meet those who believe, they say, "We have believed"; but when they are alone with one another, they say, "Do you talk to them about what Allah has revealed to you so they can argue with you about it before your Lord?" Then will you not reason?

619. So woe to those who write the "scripture" with their own hands, then say, "This is from Allah," in order to exchange it for a small price. Woe to them for what their hands have written and woe to them for what they earn.

[97]

قُلْ مَن كَانَ عَدُوًّا لِّجِبْرِيلَ فَإِنَّهُ نَزَّلَهُ عَلَى قَلْبِكَ بِإِذْنِ اللّهِ مُصَدِّقاً لِّمَا بَيْنَ يَدَيْهِ وَهُدًى وَبُشْرَى لِلْمُؤْمِنِينَ[620]

To slander even to the unseen beings such as angels is another attitude of negative disposition.

[114]

وَمَنْ أَظْلَمُ مِمَّن مَّنَعَ مَسَاجِدَ اللّهِ أَن يُذْكَرَ فِيهَا اسْمُهُ وَسَعَى فِي خَرَابِهَا أُوْلَئِكَ مَا كَانَ لَهُمْ أَن يَدْخُلُوهَا إِلاَّ خَآئِفِينَ لهُمْ فِي الدُّنْيَا خِزْيٌ وَلَهُمْ فِي الآخِرَةِ عَذَابٌ عَظِيمٌ {البقرة/114}[621]

The expression مَا كَانَ لَهُمْ أَن يَدْخُلُوهَا إِلاَّ خَآئِفِينَ[622] can allude that whenever we have any type of fear we need to run to the masjid to comfort ourselves. Sometimes, we have fears from different things or our own sins that we would receive punishment from Allah ﷻ. Then, running to masjid can be similar to running to Allah ﷻ. This can be similar to a child when he doesn't listen to his mother then he can just go and hug her mother crying about what he did. A mother would immediately hug the child and forgive him. As one should be careful with the analogies with Allah ﷻ with adab and respect that when a creation translated as a'bd, running to Allah ﷻ in the form of running to a masjid with fear and staying there and asking forgiveness then can for sure make this person be forgiven by Allah ﷻ. As Allah ﷻ is more Merciful and Forgiving than a human mother towards her own child. Therefore, when the person is overwhelmed with the feelings of frustrations, fear, pessimism, hopelessness and other downsizing feelings, running to masjid, staying there and enjoying the protection, and forgiveness of Allah ﷻ with tears can be very practically important solution, الله اعلم.

---

620. Say, "Whoever is an enemy to Gabriel—it is [none but] he who has brought it [i.e., the Qurān] down upon your heart, [O Muhammad], by permission of Allah, confirming that which was before it and as guidance and good tidings for the believers."

621. 2:114 Hence, who could be more wicked than those who bar the mention of God's name from [any of] His houses of worship and strive for their ruin, [although] they have no right to enter them save in fear [of God]? For them, in this world, there is ignominy in store; and for them, in the life to come, awesome suffering.

622. They have no right to enter them save in fear [of God]?

[147]

الْحَقُّ مِن رَّبِّكَ فَلاَ تَكُونَنَّ مِنَ الْمُمْتَرِينَ 623{البقرة/147}

الْحَقُّ مِن رَّبِّكَ فَلاَ تَكُن مِّن الْمُمْتَرِينَ 624{آل عمران/60}

وَالَّذِينَ آتَيْنَاهُمُ الْكِتَابَ يَعْلَمُونَ أَنَّهُ مُنَزَّلٌ مِّن رَّبِّكَ بِالْحَقِّ فَلاَ تَكُونَنَّ مِنَ الْمُمْتَرِينَ 625{الأنعام/114}

قَبْلِكَ لَقَدْ جَاءكَ الْحَقُّ مِن رَّبِّكَ فَلاَ تَكُونَنَّ مِنَ الْمُمْتَرِينَ 626{يونس/94}

According the verses above, if one applies the rules of logic if either the book is from Allah or it is not. If the book is not from Allah ☙, then there will be a lot of contradictions. If there are not contradictions that means that the Book **is** from Allah ☙, (referring to another verse), so don't be among the ones who have doubt.

[155]

وَلَنَبْلُوَنَّكُمْ بِشَيْءٍ مِّنَ الْخَوفِ وَالْجُوعِ وَنَقْصٍ مِّنَ الأَمَوَالِ وَالأنفُسِ وَالثَّمَرَاتِ وَبَشِّرِ الصَّابِرِينَ 627{البقرة/155}

It is very interesting to note that Allah ☙ mentions that the person will be tested from the things that the person has fear of it. Therefore, the ayah starts with وَلَنَبْلُوَنَّكُمْ بِشَيْءٍ مِّنَ الْخَوفِ anything that the person has fear from it, can be a potential test or trial for the person. A way of medicine to this can be the embodiment of the phrase, لَا إله إلا الله, la ilaha illa Allah. This phrase is the entrance of a person to Islam. In its true practice, anything that is overpowering and causing fear in the person should be removed as the la ilaha can imply. The expression illa can signify a forceful removal of these fears through the tests and trials because the person is attached to this and holds fear of losing it. Therefore, removing

---

623. The truth is from your Lord, so never be among the doubters.
624. The truth is from your Lord, so do not be among the doubters.
625. And those to whom We [previously] gave the Scripture know that it is sent down from your Lord in truth, so never be among the doubters.
626. Before you. The truth has certainly come to you from your Lord, so never be among the doubters.
627. 2:155 And most certainly shall We try you by means of danger, and hunger, and loss of worldly goods, of lives and of [labour's] fruits. But give glad tidings unto those who are patient in adversity

can entail a painful surgery of tests and trials until nothing is attached in one's heart except Allah ﷻ as the expression ends with this Lafzu Mubarak, illa Allah.

This process on the other hand necessitates patience. In other words, the successful ones will be the ones who show patience as mentioned وَبَشِّرِ الصَّابِرِينَ. Not the ones, complaining, stopping the connection with Allah ﷻ, blaming, astagfirullah, na'athu billah Allah ﷻ but the ones being patient and saying and practicing Alhamdulillah, the appreciation of Allah ﷻ.

One can see different avenues in the Qurān when the word الْخَوْف is explicitly mentioned:

قَالَ إِنِّي لَيَحْزُنُنِي أَن تَذْهَبُواْ بِهِ وَأَخَافُ أَن يَأْكُلَهُ الذِّئْبُ وَأَنتُمْ عَنْهُ غَافِلُونَ 628{يوسف/13

قَالَ رَبِّ إِنِّي أَخَافُ أَن يُكَذِّبُونِ 629{الشعراء/12

In the above cases, one can analyze this word about the Prophets of Allah ﷻ. It is interesting to note that Yaqub as was given the same argument by his sons. In the case of Musa as, they denied him as but he as still fulfilled the mission of prophethood.

لَئِن بَسَطتَ إِلَيَّ يَدَكَ لِتَقْتُلَنِي مَا أَنَاْ بِبَاسِطٍ يَدِيَ إِلَيْكَ لَأَقْتُلَكَ إِنِّي أَخَافُ اللَّهَ رَبَّ الْعَالَمِينَ 630{المائدة/28}

In the above ayah, khaf is positive trait. It is a fear in order not to fall in sin. So, when the khaf is used for Allah ﷻ it is a positive disposition.

قُلْ إِنِّيَ أَخَافُ إِنْ عَصَيْتُ رَبِّي عَذَابَ يَوْمٍ عَظِيمٍ 631{الأنعام/15}

The case of inzar, that most of the Prophets warned their people about a fearful end in this world and in the akhirah.

So, the fear, khaf can be a positive or negative disposition for the person.

---

628. [Jacob] said, "Indeed, it saddens me that you should take him, and I fear that a wolf would eat him while you are of him unaware."
629. He said, "My Lord, indeed I fear that they will deny me.
630. If you should raise your hand against me to kill me—I shall not raise my hand against you to kill you. Indeed, I fear Allah, Lord of the worlds.
631. Say, "Indeed I fear, if I should disobey my Lord, the punishment of a tremendous Day."

[185]

شَهْرُ رَمَضَانَ الَّذِيَ أُنزِلَ فِيهِ الْقُرْآنُ هُدًى لِّلنَّاسِ وَبَيِّنَاتٍ مِّنَ الْهُدَى وَالْفُرْقَانِ فَمَن شَهِدَ
مِنكُمُ الشَّهْرَ فَلْيَصُمْهُ وَمَن كَانَ مَرِيضًا أَوْ عَلَى سَفَرٍ فَعِدَّةٌ مِّنْ أَيَّامٍ أُخَرَ يُرِيدُ اللهُ بِكُمُ
الْيُسْرَ وَلاَ يُرِيدُ بِكُمُ الْعُسْرَ وَلِتُكْمِلُواْ الْعِدَّةَ وَلِتُكَبِّرُواْ اللّهَ عَلَى مَا هَدَاكُمْ وَلَعَلَّكُمْ تَشْكُرُونَ
{البقرة/185[632]}

As we get more dependent on food and drinks in our contemporary time, one can ask through the dialogues of nafs that why Allah ﷻ ordered fasting? Astagfirullah, does Allah ﷻ want difficulty for us? Immediately, Allah ﷻ answers this dialogue of the nafs as يُرِيدُ اللّه بِكُمُ الْيُسْرَ وَلاَ يُرِيدُ[633] بِكُمُ الْعُسْر "No, Allah ﷻ does not want difficulty for you but Allah ﷻ wants easiness for you." Astagfirullah, one of the most difficult things for the nafs is fasting, deprived from food and drink.

As humans are intrinsically not grateful and thankful as mentioned إِنَّ الْإِنسَانَ لِرَبِّهِ لَكَنُودٌ[634]{العاديات/6}, most of the time people develop this trait of gratefulness over time by training. This training is achieved mostly when the person is deprived of what they have. The ayah mentions that وَلَنَبْلُوَنَّكُم بِشَيْءٍ مِّنَ الْخَوفِ وَالْجُوعِ وَنَقْصٍ مِّنَ الأَمْوَالِ وَالأَنفُسِ وَالثَّمَرَاتِ وَبَشِّرِ الصَّابِرِينَ[635]{البقرة/155}. This deprivation can come either with shocking loses of the loved ones or items, trials, tests, accidents, illnesses, financial difficulties, divorces, trials of the children, family or friends etc.

The second way is to train oneself deliberately and consciously through the executions of the free will and free choice for attaining the trait of gratitude. This can be through deliberate prayers, fasting or charity. For example, in the case fasting one deliberately choose not to eat with his or her free will in order to appreciate and have gratitude for Allah ﷻ for the constant bounties. In charity, one tries to detach oneself and appreciate and have gratitude to Allah ﷻ for financial stability.

---

632. 2:185 It was the month of Ramadan in which the Qur'an was [first] bestowed from on high as a guidance unto man and a self-evident proof of that guidance, and as the standard by which to discern the true from the false. Hence, whoever of you lives to see this month shall fast throughout it; but he that is ill, or on a journey, [shall fast instead for the same] number of other days. God wills that you shall have ease, and does not will you to suffer hardship; but [He desires] that you complete the number [of days required], and that you extol God for His having guided you aright, and that you render your thanks [unto Him].
633. God wills that you shall have ease, and does not will you to suffer hardship.
634. Indeed mankind, to his Lord, is ungrateful.
635. And We will surely test you with something of fear and hunger and a loss of wealth and lives and fruits, but give good tidings to the patient.

Finally, in five times prayer one deliberately make a choice to pray and to remind him or herself this essence of gratitude for Allah ﷻ as Sûrah Fātiha starts with {الفاتحة/2} 636 الْحَمْدُ لِلَّهِ رَبِّ الْعَالَمِينَ.

If one chooses to take and follow the second route, the painful and shocking discourses of the first route can be minimized inshAllah as mentioned in the ayah مَّا يَفْعَلُ اللَّهُ بِعَذَابِكُمْ إِن شَكَرْتُمْ وَآمَنتُمْ وَكَانَ اللَّهُ شَاكِرًا عَلِيمًا {النساء/147} 637. Here in this ayah, the word بِعَذَابِكُمْ 638 can also refer to these trials in this world, الله اعلم. Similarly, another ayah as وَإِذْ تَأَذَّنَ رَبُّكُمْ لَئِن شَكَرْتُمْ لَأَزِيدَنَّكُمْ وَلَئِن كَفَرْتُمْ إِنَّ عَذَابِي لَشَدِيدٌ {إبراهيم/7} 639 can indicate that when a person chooses the second route then Allah ﷻ increases the bounties as mentioned with the expression لَئِن شَكَرْتُمْ لَأَزِيدَنَّكُمْ 640 . Yet, if the person chooses the first route then, the expression وَلَئِن كَفَرْتُمْ إِنَّ عَذَابِي لَشَدِيدٌ 641 can allude to the difficulties of these trials and unfortunate outcomes in this dunia and akhirah, may Allah ﷻ protect us. The word تَأَذَّنَ in tafsîr of Imam Maturidi is mentioned as wa'ad as a promise from Allah (31)ﷻ.

There can be another category for the elect such as the Prophets and awliyaullah. They follow the second route but the trials can be given to them to increase their level. Yet, in their spiritual state of their relationship with Allah ﷻ, they always embody the notion of gratitude and hamd to Allahﷻ, الله اعلم.

[231]

وَإِذَا طَلَّقْتُمُ النِّسَاءَ فَبَلَغْنَ أَجَلَهُنَّ فَأَمْسِكُوهُنَّ بِمَعْرُوفٍ أَوْ سَرِّحُوهُنَّ بِمَعْرُوفٍ وَلَا تُمْسِكُوهُنَّ ضِرَارًا لِتَعْتَدُوا وَمَن يَفْعَلْ ذَلِكَ فَقَدْ ظَلَمَ نَفْسَهُ وَلَا تَتَّخِذُوا آيَاتِ اللَّهِ هُزُوًا وَاذْكُرُوا نِعْمَتَ اللَّهِ عَلَيْكُمْ وَمَا أَنزَلَ عَلَيْكُم مِّنَ الْكِتَابِ وَالْحِكْمَةِ يَعِظُكُم بِهِ وَاتَّقُوا اللَّهَ وَاعْلَمُوا أَنَّ اللَّهَ بِكُلِّ شَيْءٍ عَلِيمٌ (231 642)

---

636. All praise is due to Allah, lord of both worlds.
637. What would Allah do with [i.e., gain from] your punishment if you are grateful and believe? And ever is Allah Appreciative and Knowing.
638. With your punishment.
639. And [remember] when your Lord proclaimed, 'If you are grateful, I will surely increase you [in favor]; but if you deny, indeed, My punishment is severe.'
640. 'If you are grateful, I will surely increase you.
641. But if you deny, indeed, My punishment is severe.'
642. 2:231 And so, when you divorce women and they are about to reach the end of their waiting-term, then either retain them in a fair manner or let them go in a fair manner. But do not retain them against their will in order to hurt [them]: for he who does so sins indeed against himself. And do not take [these] messages of God in a frivolous spirit; and remember the blessings with which God has graced you, and all the revelation and the wisdom which He has bestowed on you from on high in order to admonish you thereby; and remain conscious of God, and know that God has full knowledge of everything.

It is very interesting to analyze the expression وَلَا تَتَّخِذُوا اٰيَاتِ اللهِ هُزُوًا[643] especially the word هُزُوًا[644] about what it can mean in our time. If one can review the related verses, Allah ﷻ mentions the guidelines of shariah and fiqh to follow. In this case, there are some rules and guidelines to follow in Islam. Then, the expression comes as وَلَا تَتَّخِذُوا اٰيَاتِ اللهِ هُزُو. Especially in our modern times, the current learning epistemology is based on mind if it doesn't make sense we tend to provide alternative interpretations with especially social scientist approach of academia. Then, one can look at these biased and not genuine discussions of orientalism which happened before but not much today. Allah ﷻ mentions to respect and to follow these guidelines in these verses but not making explicitly or implicitly making fun of them because it does not fit the current trends in the discourses of philosophy or social science.

In other words, as discussed before, religion is an attitude of humbleness, submission and gratitude to Allah ﷻ. Historically, Allah ﷻ made elevated all the respect for the scholars who kept this balance of following the religion with its external rules, fiqh, shariah and guidelines but at the same internalizing with their essence through practice with a check and balance system of heart and mind.

On another note, following these guidelines are considered as respecting the shiar that what Allah ﷻ told us to follow rather as mere intellectualizing with mockery. One can realize that the above ayah is mentioned after immediately the mention of the consecutive fiqh rulings. In other words, following the Aqidah is important, critical and essence. Yet, at the same if the person does not give importance and respect these rulings outlined by Allah ﷻ then, the person can again put oneself in risk of endangering one's relationship with Allah ﷻ which is called imān. Here is the case of talaq in the above verse mentioned with all the rules.

In this regard, the next step is to leave the people who has a negative attitude towards sacred teachings as mentioned in Sûrah Maidah:

يَا اَيُّهَا الَّذِينَ اٰمَنُوا لَا تَتَّخِذُوا الَّذِينَ اتَّخَذُوا دِينَكُمْ هُزُوًا وَلَعِبًا مِنَ الَّذِينَ اُوتُوا الْكِتَابَ مِنْ قَبْلِكُمْ وَالْكُفَّارَ اَوْلِيَاءَ وَاتَّقُوا اللهَ اِنْ كُنْتُمْ مُؤْمِنِينَ (57)[645]

---

643. And do not take [these] messages of God in a frivolous spirit.

644. Frivolous spirit.

645. 5:57 O you who have attained to faith! Do not take for your friends such as mock at your, faith and make a jest of it—be they from among those who have been vouchsafed revelation before your time, or [from among] those who deny the truth [of revelation as such]—but remain conscious of God, if you are [truly] believers

Another example is mentioned in Sûrah Jasiya:

وَإِذَا عَلِمَ مِنْ آيَاتِنَا شَيْئًا اتَّخَذَهَا هُزُوًا أُولَئِكَ لَهُمْ عَذَابٌ مُهِينٌ(9)‏ 646

[186]

وَإِذَا سَأَلَكَ عِبَادِي عَنِّي فَإِنِّي قَرِيبٌ أُجِيبُ دَعْوَةَ الدَّاعِ إِذَا دَعَانِ فَلْيَسْتَجِيبُوا لِي وَلْيُؤْمِنُوا بِي لَعَلَّهُمْ يَرْشُدُونَ {البقرة/186}‏ 647

When the person sincerely opens her or his hands, Allah ﷻ is right there.
The person can connect with Allah ﷻ immediately.

[255]

اللَّهُ لاَ إِلَهَ إِلاَّ هُوَ الْحَيُّ الْقَيُّومُ لاَ تَأْخُذُهُ سِنَةٌ وَلاَ نَوْمٌ لَهُ مَا فِي السَّمَاوَاتِ وَمَا فِي الْأَرْضِ مَن ذَا الَّذِي يَشْفَعُ عِنْدَهُ إِلاَّ بِإِذْنِهِ يَعْلَمُ مَا بَيْنَ أَيْدِيهِمْ وَمَا خَلْفَهُمْ وَلاَ يُحِيطُونَ بِشَيْءٍ مِّنْ عِلْمِهِ إِلاَّ بِمَا شَاء وَسِعَ كُرْسِيُّهُ السَّمَاوَاتِ وَالأَرْضَ وَلاَ يَؤُودُهُ حِفْظُهُمَا وَهُوَ الْعَلِيُّ الْعَظِيمُ {البقرة/255}‏ 648

As one can ponder upon why this ayah is considered as the
greatest ayah as mentioned in the hadith (26). One can review different
explanations in the tafâsir. In addition, when one really reads this ayah
with it is true and real meanings, the knowledge is not related with
humans and human realities. This knowledge is related with Allah ﷻ.

On another perspective, the meanings are reduced to human
understanding. For example,

The Creator is Allah ﷻ. This necessitates oneness as mentioned لاَ 649
إِلَهَ إِلاَّ هُوَ. Then, this necessitates All Alive and All Continuous Existence
as mentioned الْحَيُّ الْقَيُّومُ 650. This necessitates having no human deficient

---

646. Allah has promised those who believe and do righteous deeds [that] for them there is forgiveness and great reward.
647. 2:186 AND IF My servants ask thee about Me—behold, I am near; I respond to the call of him who calls, whenever he calls unto Me: let them, then, respond unto Me, and believe in Me, so that they might follow the right way.
648. 2:255 GOD—there is no deity save Him, the Ever-Living, the Self-Subsistent Fount of All Being. Neither slumber overtakes Him, nor sleep. His is all that is in the heavens and all that is on earth. Who is there that could intercede with Him, unless it be by His leave? He knows all that lies open before men and all that is hidden from them, whereas they cannot attain to aught of His knowledge save that which He wills [them to attain]. His eternal power overspreads the heavens and the earth, and their upholding wearies Him not. And he alone is truly exalted, tremendous.
649. There is no deity save Him.
650. The Ever-Living, The Self-Subsistent.

qualities of sleep, heedlessness or unawareness even less than a second as mentioned لَا تَأْخُذُهُ سِنَةٌ وَلَا نَوْمٌ[651]. This necessitates ownership of everything and all the creation as mentioned لَّهُ مَا فِي السَّمَاوَاتِ وَمَا فِي الْأَرْضِ[652]. After this, who can claim any power, authority, or influence next to Allah ﷻ except if Allah ﷻ gives permission as mentioned مَن ذَا الَّذِي يَشْفَعُ عِنْدَهُ إِلَّا بِإِذْنِهِ[653]. After this, Allah ﷻ knows everything past, future, secret or public as mentioned يَعْلَمُ مَا بَيْنَ أَيْدِيهِمْ وَمَا خَلْفَهُمْ[654]. After this who can claim any knowledge from Allah ﷻ's knowledge except for whom Allah enables and selects as mentioned وَلَا يُحِيطُونَ بِشَيْءٍ مِّنْ عِلْمِهِ إِلَّا بِمَا شَاءَ[655].

When the person is need of constant intervention in one's life, the Names of Allah الْحَيُّ الْقَيُّومُ[656] ﷻ saves the person from the oppression and darkness of each second. Therefore, the dua of the Prophet ﷺ as "يا حي يا قيوم ،برحمتك أستغيث ، أصلح لي شأني كله ، ولا تكلني إلى نفسي طرفة عين"[657] (26) shows the need of constant connection with Allah ﷻ at the level of each second or even each less time quantities. On another perspective, this shows that the person should be constantly, every second, self-dealing with him or herself to check the existence of this connection and to refresh this connection that if the person is at that second connected to Allah ﷻ. Each disconnection is a darkness, a black hole, and a seed for depression, darkness and anxiety. Then, other duas of the Prophet ﷺ as[658] "اللهم يا مقلب القلوب ثبت قلبي على دينك," complements this important notion.

On another perspective, in the ayah اتْلُ مَا أُوحِيَ إِلَيْكَ مِنَ الْكِتَابِ وَأَقِمِ الصَّلَاةَ إِنَّ الصَّلَاةَ تَنْهَى عَنِ الْفَحْشَاءِ وَالْمُنكَرِ وَلَذِكْرُ اللَّهِ أَكْبَرُ وَاللَّهُ يَعْلَمُ مَا تَصْنَعُونَ[659]{العنكبوت/45} the expression وَلَذِكْرُ اللَّهِ أَكْبَرُ can show this ultimate constant and regular connection more than the five-times prayers. The goal of fardh prayers is to instill the notion of regular connection with Allah ﷻ but the ideal state is to spread this in one's all daily minutes and seconds with notion

---

651. Neither slumber overtakes Him, nor sleep.

652. His is all that is in the heavens and all that is on earth.

653. Who is there that could intercede with Him, unless it be by His leave?

654. He knows all that lies open before men and all that is hidden from them.

655. Whereas they cannot attain to aught of His knowledge save that which He wills [them to attain].

656. The Ever-Living, The Self-Subsistent.

657. Oh The Ever-Lasting, Oh The Sustainer and Protector of all that exists, with your mercy I seek aid, correct for me all my matters and do not entrust me to my own self even for the blink of an eye, ever.

658. Oh turner of the hearts, confirm our hearts on your religion.

659. Recite, [O Muhammad], what has been revealed to you of the Book and establish prayer. Indeed, prayer prohibits immorality and wrongdoing, and the remembrance of Allah is greater. And Allah knows that which you do.

of presence in front of Allah ﷻ. Ahlu tasawwuf can call this khudur, the presence, readiness and awareness in one's relationship with Allah ﷻ.

[258][660]

أَلَمْ تَرَ إِلَى الَّذِي حَاجَّ إِبْرَاهِيمَ فِي رَبِّهِ أَنْ آتَاهُ اللَّهُ الْمُلْكَ إِذْ قَالَ إِبْرَاهِيمُ رَبِّيَ الَّذِي يُحْيِي وَيُمِيتُ قَالَ أَنَا أُحْيِي وَأُمِيتُ قَالَ إِبْرَاهِيمُ فَإِنَّ اللَّهَ يَأْتِي بِالشَّمْسِ مِنَ الْمَشْرِقِ فَأْتِ بِهَا مِنَ الْمَغْرِبِ فَبُهِتَ الَّذِي كَفَرَ وَاللَّهُ لاَ يَهْدِي الْقَوْمَ الظَّالِمِينَ

This verse tells us that at the time of Ibrahim as there was much worshipping of the stars. As a challenge, Ibrahim as again brings an example related with the sun. In the previous case of his as own father and people, he (as) also brought the similar examples, with the dialogues of [661] "لَا احب الافلين ....", the moon, the sun, the stars, coming and appearing and disappearing.

660. 2:258 ART THOU NOT aware of that [king] who argued with Abraham about his Sustainer, [simply] because God had granted him kingship? Lo! Abraham said: "My Sustainer is He who grants life and deals death." [The king] replied: "I [too] grant life and deal death!" Said Abraham: "Verily, God causes the sun to rise in the east; cause it, then, to rise in the west!" Thereupon he who was bent on denying the truth remained dumbfounded: for God does not guide people who [deliberately] do wrong.
661. like not those that set [i.e., disappear]."

3

Sûrah Al-Imrãn

[1-2][662]

الم {آل عمران/1} اللّٰهُ لَا إِلَهَ إِلاَّ هُوَ الْحَيُّ الْقَيُّومُ {آل عمران/2}

Allah starts this ayah similar to Sûrah Baqara with Alif, Lam Mim. Then, a similar part, a verse in the second ayah as اللّٰهُ لَا إِلَهَ إِلاَّ هُوَ الْحَيُّ[663] الْقَيُّومُ like in ayatul kursi is mentioned. Here, the Names of Allah as الْحَيُّ الْقَيُّومُ[664] are considered as some of the greatest names of Allah by many scholars.

[31][665]

قُلْ إِنْ كُنْتُمْ تُحِبُّونَ اللّٰهَ فَاتَّبِعُونِي يُحْبِبْكُمُ اللّٰهُ وَيَغْفِرْ لَكُمْ ذُنُوبَكُمْ وَاللّٰهُ غَفُورٌ رَحِيمٌ

When one looks this ayah from it is opposite, it can be as : if you don't follow the Prophet then you really don't love Allah . Even though the person can claim that he or she loves Allah but if the Prophet is not in this love then the real love for Allah is not there. Therefore, one can find a lot of discussions in Islamic scholarship if one can be saved without following the path of Rasulullah or the Sunnah although he or she may belief of One and Unique Creator, Allah اعلم الله, . Another ayah in Sûrah Nisã 14:

وَمَنْ يَعْصِ اللّٰهَ وَرَسُولَهُ وَيَتَعَدَّ حُدُودَهُ يُدْخِلْهُ نَارًا خَالِدًا فِيهَا وَلَهُ عَذَابٌ مُهِينٌ

---

662. 3:1 Alif. Lam. Mim. 3:2 GOD—there is no deity save Him, the Ever-Living, the Self-Subsistent Fount of All Being!

663. There is no deity save Him, The Ever-Living, The Self-Subsistent Fount of All Being!

664. The Ever-Living, The Self-Subsistent Fount of All Being!

665. 3:31 Say [O Prophet]: "If you love God, follow me, [and] God will love you and forgive you your sins; for God is much-forgiving, a dispenser of grace."

[37-40][666]

فَتَقَبَّلَهَا رَبُّهَا بِقَبُولٍ حَسَنٍ وَأَنبَتَهَا نَبَاتًا حَسَنًا وَكَفَّلَهَا زَكَرِيَّا كُلَّمَا دَخَلَ عَلَيْهَا زَكَرِيَّا الْمِحْرَابَ وَجَدَ عِندَهَا رِزْقًا قَالَ يَا مَرْيَمُ أَنَّى لَكِ هَذَا قَالَتْ هُوَ مِنْ عِندِ اللَّهِ إِنَّ اللَّهَ يَرْزُقُ مَن يَشَاء بِغَيْرِ حِسَابٍ {آل عمران/37}

هُنَالِكَ دَعَا زَكَرِيَّا رَبَّهُ قَالَ رَبِّ هَبْ لِي مِن لَّدُنْكَ ذُرِّيَّةً طَيِّبَةً إِنَّكَ سَمِيعُ الدُّعَاء {آل عمران/38} فَنَادَتْهُ الْمَلاَئِكَةُ وَهُوَ قَائِمٌ يُصَلِّي فِي الْمِحْرَابِ أَنَّ اللَّهَ يُبَشِّرُكَ بِيَحْيَى مُصَدِّقًا بِكَلِمَةٍ مِّنَ اللَّهِ وَسَيِّدًا وَحَصُورًا وَنَبِيًّا مِّنَ الصَّالِحِينَ {آل عمران/39} قَالَ رَبِّ أَنَّى يَكُونُ لِي غُلاَمٌ وَقَدْ بَلَغَنِيَ الْكِبَرُ وَامْرَأَتِي عَاقِرٌ قَالَ كَذَلِكَ اللَّهُ يَفْعَلُ مَا يَشَاء {آل عمران/40}

Above ayah is another example of the power of dua as Zakariya as did. Especially, when the person is in old age and all the means of strength are gone, the person can still get what he or she wants with the power of dua, prayer and with the power of connection with Allah ﷻ.

The above ayahs can be a proof that when Zakariya as witnessed the bounties given to Maryam as, he as also made dua as the word هُنَالِكَ can signify. In these good cases, one does not view this as a jealousy but as something to have something in one's relationship with Allah ﷻ. This is called gibta.

---

666. 3:37 And thereupon her Sustainer accepted the girl-child with goodly acceptance, and caused her to grow up in goodly growth, and placed her in the care of Zachariah.[26] Whenever Zachariah visited her in the sanctuary, he found her provided with food. He would ask: "O Mary, whence came this unto thee?" She would answer: "It is from God; behold, God grants sustenance unto whom He wills, beyond all reckoning."

3:38 In that self-same place, Zachariah prayed unto his Sustainer, saying: "O my Sustainer! Bestow upon me [too], out of Thy grace, the gift of goodly offspring; for Thou, indeed, hearest all prayer."

3:39 Thereupon, as he stood praying in the sanctuary, the angels called out unto him: "God sends thee the glad tiding of [the birth of] John, who shall confirm the truth of a word from God, and [shall be] outstanding among men, and utterly chaste, and a prophet from among the righteous."

3:40 [Zachariah] exclaimed: "O my Sustainer! How can I have a son when old age has already overtaken me, and my wife is barren?" Answered [the angel]: "Thus it is: God does what He wills."

[42]⁶⁶⁷

وَإِذْ قَالَتِ الْمَلاَئِكَةُ يَا مَرْيَمُ إِنَّ اللَّه اصْطَفَاكِ عَلَى نِسَاء الْعَالَمِينَ {آل عمران/42}

The above is interesting to point out to show the level of Maryam as. Firstly, the clear and explicit expression of her position with وَاصْطَفَاكِ عَلَى نِسَاء الْعَالَمِينَ. Secondly, the explicit use of the word اصْطَفَاكِ twice in the same ayah to show her level. At the same time, to show a method of teaching of with repetition who may be in trials or difficulties. Thirdly, the usage of very praising words explicitly such as اصْطَفَاكِ وَطَهَّرَكِ. Fourthly, the mention of her name as recognition and honor as يَا مَرْيَمُ. Lastly, the repetition of the personal pronoun of كِ in all the words of كِ to show her close and high relationship with Allah ﷻ الله اعلم. I think we lack in transferring these Quranic realities to the Christian world to show the level of Maryam as in our tradition.

[55]⁶⁶⁸

إِذْ قَالَ اللَّهُ يَا عِيسَى إِنِّي مُتَوَفِّيكَ وَرَافِعُكَ إِلَيَّ وَمُطَهِّرُكَ مِنَ الَّذِينَ كَفَرُواْ وَجَاعِلُ الَّذِينَ اتَّبَعُوكَ فَوْقَ الَّذِينَ كَفَرُواْ إِلَى يَوْمِ الْقِيَامَةِ ثُمَّ إِلَيَّ مَرْجِعُكُمْ فَأَحْكُمُ بَيْنَكُمْ فِيمَا كُنتُمْ فِيهِ تَخْتَلِفُونَ {آل عمران/55}

الم {الروم/1} غُلِبَتِ الرُّومُ {الروم/2} فِي أَدْنَى الْأَرْضِ وَهُم مِّن بَعْدِ غَلَبِهِمْ سَيَغْلِبُونَ {الروم/3} فِي بِضْعِ سِنِينَ لِلَّهِ الْأَمْرُ مِن قَبْلُ وَمِن بَعْدُ وَيَوْمَئِذٍ يَفْرَحُ الْمُؤْمِنُونَ {الروم/4} بِنَصْرِ اللَّهِ يَنصُرُ مَن يَشَاء وَهُوَ الْعَزِيزُ الرَّحِيمُ {الروم/5}

The above ayahs, الله اعلم can signify the position of Christian dominance in the world over the kuffar as the European, Rum, descendants of Europe. The ayah does not say Muslims but it says اتَّبَعُوكَ فَوْقَ الَّذِينَ كَفَرُو. In that perspective, الله اعلم, it can show the implicit notions of justice of Christian dominant countries, such as Europe, America and others with their dominance. Dominance may have representation of justice,

---

667. 3:42 AND LO! The angels said: "O Mary! Behold, God has elected thee and made thee pure, and raised thee above all the women of the world."

668. 3:55 Lo! God said: "O Jesus! Verily, I shall cause thee to die, and shall exalt thee unto Me, and cleanse thee of [the presence of] those who are bent on denying the truth; and I shall place those who follow thee [far] above those who are bent on denying the truth, unto the Day of Resurrection. In the end, unto Me you all must return, and I shall judge between you with regard to all on which you were wont to differ.

اللہ اعلم. Muslims in that sense can live in these countries safely compared to other places, اللہ اعلم.

[79]⁶⁶⁹

مَا كَانَ لِبَشَرٍ أَن يُؤْتِيَهُ اللّهُ الْكِتَابَ وَالْحُكْمَ وَالنُّبُوَّةَ ثُمَّ يَقُولَ لِلنَّاسِ كُونُواْ عِبَادًا لِّي مِن دُونِ اللّهِ وَلَكِن كُونُواْ رَبَّانِيِّينَ بِمَا كُنتُمْ تُعَلِّمُونَ الْكِتَابَ وَبِمَا كُنْتُمْ تَدْرُسُونَ {آل عمران/79}

The above is an interesting ayah that shows a rational argument to show and refute the claims of people giving divinity to other humans or saints who were preaching to believe in God. In other words, if Allah ﷻ sends a prophet with a book or scripture, with an understanding and wisdom of guiding the people to Allah ﷻ, then it does not make sense that this same human claims to worship to him or herself other than God. This conflicts with the original mission that this person was sent for. What this prophet of God can say is that worship and remember Allah ﷻ that they would be accountable with their existing guidance and wisdom presented in their scriptures as mentioned كُونُواْ رَبَّانِيِّينَ بِمَا كُنتُمْ تُعَلِّمُونَ الْكِتَابَ وَبِمَا كُنْتُمْ تَدْرُسُونَ {آل عمران/79}.

[134]⁶⁷⁰

{ الَّذِينَ يُنفِقُونَ فِي السَّرَّاء وَالضَّرَّاء وَالْكَاظِمِينَ الْغَيْظَ وَالْعَافِينَ عَنِ النَّاسِ وَاللّهُ يُحِبُّ الْمُحْسِنِينَ {آل عمران/134}

In this ayah, one can see a definition of muhsin who has the qualities of ihsan. All the three cases mentioned in the ayah have something in common. The person is doing something but his or her nafs wants the opposite but still the person holds and controls his or her desires and does what is recommended by Allah ﷻ. It is very difficult to do. The person still uses his or her reason but not the emotions.

It is very difficult share what you have with others. The natural tendency is being stingy. When the person gives away what he or she

---

669. 3:79 It is not conceivable that a human being unto whom God had granted revelation, and sound judgment, and prophethood, should thereafter have said unto people, "Worship me beside God"; but rather [did he exhort them], "Become men of God by spreading the knowledge of the divine writ, and by your own deep study [thereof]."
670. (3:134) who spend [in His way] in time of plenty and in time of hardship, and hold in check their anger, and pardon their fellow-men because God loves the doers of good;

likes the person feels uneasy about it but still does it for the pleasure of Allah ﷻ.

Lastly, the person holds and controls his or her anger although one can be right in a situation. His or her nafs wants to shout and be mean but still the person controls oneself although it is very difficult. He or she does it only for the pleasure of Allah ﷻ.

The person does not take revenge or even does not apply justice against oneself but forgives the vulgarity of others although it is very difficult to do. He or she does it only for the pleasure of Allah ﷻ.

When one implements these in real life situations then the person can have the qualities of a muhsin, inshAllah.

[135][671]

وَالَّذِينَ إِذَا فَعَلُواْ فَاحِشَةً أَوْ ظَلَمُواْ أَنْفُسَهُمْ ذَكَرُواْ اللّهَ فَاسْتَغْفَرُواْ لِذُنُوبِهِمْ وَمَن يَغْفِرُ الذُّنُوبَ إِلاَّ اللّهُ وَلَمْ يُصِرُّواْ عَلَى مَا فَعَلُواْ وَهُمْ يَعْلَمُونَ {آل عمران/135}

As all of us can do mistakes by being a human, the ayah suggests not to insist on it once the person understands that this is a mistake or sin as mentioned {آل عمران/135}[672] وَلَمْ يُصِرُّواْ عَلَى مَا فَعَلُواْ وَهُمْ يَعْلَمُونَ. In other words, after anger and games of one's own nafs and shaytan as mentioned وَالْكَاظِمِينَ الْغَيْظَ وَالْعَافِينَ عَنِ النَّاسِ وَاللّهُ يُحِبُّ الْمُحْسِنِينَ[673]{آل عمران/134}, when the person understands he or she is wrong then immediately, it is important ask forgiveness from Allah ﷻ and from the parties involved in this engagement.

[145][674]

وَمَا كَانَ لِنَفْسٍ أَنْ تَمُوتَ إِلاَّ بِإِذْنِ اللهِ كِتَابًا مُّؤَجَّلاً وَمَن يُرِدْ ثَوَابَ الدُّنْيَا نُؤْتِهِ مِنْهَا وَمَن يُرِدْ ثَوَابَ الآخِرَةِ نُؤْتِهِ مِنْهَا وَسَنَجْزِي الشَّاكِرِينَ {آل عمران/145}

---

671. (3:135) and who, when they have committed a shameful deed or have [otherwise] sinned against themselves, remember God and pray that their sins be forgiven—for who but God could forgive sins?—and do not knowingly persist in doing whatever [wrong] they may have done.

672. And do not knowingly persist in doing whatever [wrong] they may have done.

673. And hold in check their anger, and pardon their fellow-men because God loves the doers of good;

674. 3:145 And no human being can die save by God's leave, at a term pre-ordained. And if one desires the rewards of this world, We shall grant him thereof; and if one desires the rewards of the life to come, We shall grant him thereof; and We shall requite those who are grateful [to Us].

It is interesting to note that Allah ﷻ specifically mentions that death occurs not randomly but with the permission and qadar, destined by Allah ﷻ as in the expression وَمَا كَانَ لِنَفْسٍ أَنْ تَمُوتَ إِلاَّ بِإِذْنِ الله كِتَابًا مُّؤَجَّلًا[675]. Most of the time, the evil looking incidents are defined as evil because they seem to happen randomly. But, it is not the case, especially with the random looking cases of death. Everything, especially something critical like death happens with the permission of Allah. Therefore, Allah ﷻ mentions the expression إِلاَّ بِإِذْنِ الله[676] so that people, do not worship and idolize the worldly reasons that causes a person's death, الله اعلم.

One can see similar encounters in the Qurān for other evil looking incidents with the expression إِلاَّ بِإِذْنِ الله. For example, the verse below clearly indicates this in any type of tests, trials or difficult situations as:

مَا أَصَابَ مِن مُّصِيبَةٍ إِلَّا بِإِذْنِ اللَّهِ وَمَن يُؤْمِن بِاللَّهِ يَهْدِ قَلْبَهُ وَاللَّهُ بِكُلِّ شَيْءٍ عَلِيمٌ[677]{التغابن/11}

{ إِنَّمَا النَّجْوَى مِنَ الشَّيْطَانِ لِيَحْزُنَ الَّذِينَ آمَنُوا وَلَيْسَ بِضَارِّهِمْ شَيْئًا إِلَّا بِإِذْنِ اللَّهِ وَعَلَى اللَّهِ فَلْيَتَوَكَّلِ الْمُؤْمِنُونَ[678]{المجادلة/10}

وَاتَّبَعُواْ مَا تَتْلُواْ الشَّيَاطِينُ عَلَى مُلْكِ سُلَيْمَانَ وَمَا كَفَرَ سُلَيْمَانُ وَلَكِنَّ الشَّيْاطِينَ كَفَرُواْ يُعَلِّمُونَ النَّاسَ السِّحْرَ وَمَا أُنزِلَ عَلَى الْمَلَكَيْنِ بِبَابِلَ هَارُوتَ وَمَارُوتَ وَمَا يُعَلِّمَانِ مِنْ أَحَدٍ حَتَّى يَقُولاَ إِنَّمَا نَحْنُ فِتْنَةٌ فَلاَ تَكْفُرْ فَيَتَعَلَّمُونَ مِنْهُمَا مَا يُفَرِّقُونَ بِهِ بَيْنَ الْمَرْءِ وَزَوْجِهِ وَمَا هُم بِضَارِّينَ بِهِ مِنْ أَحَدٍ إِلاَّ بِإِذْنِ اللَّهِ وَيَتَعَلَّمُونَ مَا يَضُرُّهُمْ وَلاَ يَنفَعُهُمْ وَلَقَدْ عَلِمُواْ لَمَنِ اشْتَرَاهُ مَا لَهُ فِي الآخِرَةِ مِنْ خَلاَقٍ وَلَبِئْسَ مَا شَرَوْاْ بِهِ أَنفُسَهُمْ لَوْ كَانُواْ يَعْلَمُونَ[679]{البقرة/201}

---

675. And no human being can die save by God's leave, at a term pre-ordained.

676. By God's leave.

677. No disaster strikes except by permission of Allah. And whoever believes in Allah—He will guide his heart. And Allah is Knowing of all things.

678. Private conversation is only from Satan that he may grieve those who have believed, but he will not harm them at all except by permission of Allah. And upon Allah let the believers rely.

679. And they followed [instead] what the devils had recited during the reign of Solomon. It was not Solomon who disbelieved, but the devils disbelieved, teaching people magic and that which was revealed to the two angels at Babylon, Hārūt and Mārūt. But they [i.e., the two angels] do not teach anyone unless they say, "We are a trial, so do not disbelieve [by practicing magic]." And [yet] they learn from them that by which they cause separation between a man and his wife. But they do not harm anyone through it except by permission of Allah. And they [i.e., people] learn what harms them and does not benefit them. But they [i.e., the Children of Israel] certainly knew that whoever purchased it [i.e., magic] would not have in the Hereafter any share. And wretched is that for which they sold themselves, if they only knew.

وَمَا كَانَ لِنَفْسٍ أَن تُؤْمِنَ إِلاَّ بِإِذْنِ اللّهِ وَيَجْعَلُ الرِّجْسَ عَلَى الَّذِينَ لاَ يَعْقِلُونَ [680]{يونس/100}
as one can see the kufr is the biggest musibah.

One can also see that this expression إِلاَّ بِإِذْنِ اللّهِ comes in when there is a possibility of doubt about truthfulness or genuineness of the Divine message. For example:

قُلْ مَن كَانَ عَدُوًّا لِّجِبْرِيلَ فَإِنَّهُ نَزَّلَهُ عَلَى قَلْبِكَ بِإِذْنِ اللّهِ مُصَدِّقاً لِّمَا بَيْنَ يَدَيْهِ وَهُدًى وَبُشْرَى لِلْمُؤْمِنِينَ [681]{البقرة/97}

} وَمَا أَرْسَلْنَا مِن رَّسُولٍ إِلاَّ لِيُطَاعَ بِإِذْنِ اللّهِ وَلَوْ أَنَّهُمْ إِذ ظَّلَمُواْ أَنفُسَهُمْ جَآؤُوكَ فَاسْتَغْفَرُواْ اللّهَ وَاسْتَغْفَرَ لَهُمُ الرَّسُولُ لَوَجَدُواْ اللّهَ تَوَّابًا رَّحِيمًا [682]{النساء/64}

الآنَ خَفَّفَ اللّهُ عَنكُمْ وَعَلِمَ أَنَّ فِيكُمْ ضَعْفًا فَإِن يَكُن مِّنكُم مِّئَةٌ صَابِرَةٌ يَغْلِبُواْ مِئَتَيْنِ وَإِن يَكُن مِّنكُمْ أَلْفٌ يَغْلِبُواْ أَلْفَيْنِ بِإِذْنِ اللّهِ وَاللّهُ مَعَ الصَّابِرِينَ [683]{الأنفال/66}

وَلَقَدْ أَرْسَلْنَا رُسُلاً مِّن قَبْلِكَ وَجَعَلْنَا لَهُمْ أَزْوَاجًا وَذُرِّيَّةً وَمَا كَانَ لِرَسُولٍ أَن يَأْتِيَ بِآيَةٍ إِلاَّ بِإِذْنِ اللّهِ لِكُلِّ أَجَلٍ كِتَابٌ [684]{الرعد/38}

الَر كِتَابٌ أَنزَلْنَاهُ إِلَيْكَ لِتُخْرِجَ النَّاسَ مِنَ الظُّلُمَاتِ إِلَى النُّورِ بِإِذْنِ رَبِّهِمْ إِلَى صِرَاطِ الْعَزِيزِ الْحَمِيدِ (Ibrahim 1)

وَدَاعِيًا إِلَى اللَّهِ بِإِذْنِهِ وَسِرَاجًا مُّنِيرًا [685]{الأحزاب/46}

Or, if there is a possibility of shirk that when people see if they don't give the full authority to Allahﷻ. الله اعلم.

---

680. And it is not for a soul [i.e., anyone] to believe except by permission of Allah, and He will place defilement upon those who will not use reason.
681. Say, "Whoever is an enemy to Gabriel—it is [none but] he who has brought it [i.e., the Qurān] down upon your heart, [O Muhammad], by permission of Allah, confirming that which was before it and as guidance and good tidings for the believers."
682. And We did not send any messenger except to be obeyed by permission of Allah. And if, when they wronged themselves, they had come to you, [O Muhammad], and asked forgiveness of Allah and the Messenger had asked forgiveness for them, they would have found Allah Accepting of repentance and Merciful.
683. Now, Allah has lightened [the hardship] for you, and He knows that among you is weakness. So if there are from you one hundred [who are] steadfast, they will overcome two hundred. And if there are among you a thousand, they will overcome two thousand by permission of Allah. And Allah is with the steadfast.
684. And We have already sent messengers before you and assigned to them wives and descendants. And it was not for a messenger to come with a sign except by permission of Allah. For every term is a decree.
685. And one who invites to Allah, by His permission, and an illuminating lamp.

اللّهُ لاَ إِلَهَ إِلاَّ هُوَ الْحَيُّ الْقَيُّومُ لاَ تَأْخُذُهُ سِنَةٌ وَلاَ نَوْمٌ لَّهُ مَا فِي السَّمَاوَاتِ وَمَا فِي الأَرْضِ مَن ذَا الَّذِي يَشْفَعُ عِنْدَهُ إِلاَّ بِإِذْنِهِ يَعْلَمُ مَا بَيْنَ أَيْدِيهِمْ وَمَا خَلْفَهُمْ وَلاَ يُحِيطُونَ بِشَيْءٍ مِّنْ عِلْمِهِ إِلاَّ بِمَا شَاء وَسِعَ كُرْسِيُّهُ السَّمَاوَاتِ وَالأَرْضَ وَلاَ يَؤُودُهُ حِفْظُهُمَا وَهُوَ الْعَلِيُّ الْعَظِيمُ 686{البقرة/255}

This is especially very vivid, emphasized, repeated and apparent in the case of Isa as due to his followers as:

وَرَسُولاً إِلَى بَنِي إِسْرَائِيلَ أَنِّي قَدْ جِئْتُكُم بِآيَةٍ مِّن رَّبِّكُمْ أَنِّي أَخْلُقُ لَكُم مِّنَ الطِّينِ كَهَيْئَةِ الطَّيْرِ فَأَنفُخُ فِيهِ فَيَكُونُ طَيْرًا بِإِذْنِ اللّهِ وَأُبْرِئُ الأكْمَهَ والأَبْرَصَ وَأُحْيِي الْمَوْتَى بِإِذْنِ اللّهِ وَأُنَبِّئُكُم بِمَا تَأْكُلُونَ وَمَا تَدَّخِرُونَ فِي بُيُوتِكُمْ إِنَّ فِي ذَلِكَ لآيَةً لَّكُمْ إِن كُنتُم مُّؤْمِنِينَ 687{آل عمران/49}

إِذْ قَالَ اللّهُ يَا عِيسى ابْنَ مَرْيَمَ اذْكُرْ نِعْمَتِي عَلَيْكَ وَعَلَى وَالِدَتِكَ إِذْ أَيَّدتُّكَ بِرُوحِ الْقُدُسِ تُكَلِّمُ النَّاسَ فِي الْمَهْدِ وَكَهْلاً وَإِذْ عَلَّمْتُكَ الْكِتَابَ وَالْحِكْمَةَ وَالتَّوْرَاةَ وَالإِنجِيلَ وَإِذْ تَخْلُقُ مِنَ الطِّينِ كَهَيْئَةِ الطَّيْرِ بِإِذْنِي فَتَنفُخُ فِيهَا فَتَكُونُ طَيْرًا بِإِذْنِي وَتُبْرِىءُ الأَكْمَهَ وَالأَبْرَصَ بِإِذْنِي وَإِذْ تُخْرِجُ الْمَوَتَى بِإِذْنِي وَإِذْ كَفَفْتُ بَنِي إِسْرَائِيلَ عَنكَ إِذْ جِئْتَهُمْ بِالْبَيِّنَاتِ فَقَالَ الَّذِينَ كَفَرُواْ مِنْهُمْ إِنْ هَذَا إِلاَّ سِحْرٌ مُّبِينٌ 688{المائدة/110}

---

686. Allah—there is no deity except Him, the Ever-Living, the Sustainer of [all] existence. Neither drowsiness overtakes Him nor sleep. To Him belongs whatever is in the heavens and whatever is on the earth. Who is it that can intercede with Him except by His permission? He knows what is [presently] before them and what will be after them, and they encompass not a thing of His knowledge except for what He wills. His Kursî extends over the heavens and the earth, and their preservation tires Him not. And He is the Most High, the Most Great.

687. And [make him] a messenger to the Children of Israel, [who will say], 'Indeed I have come to you with a sign from your Lord in that I design for you from clay [that which is] like the form of a bird, then I breathe into it and it becomes a bird by permission of Allah. And I cure the blind [from birth] and the leper, and I give life to the dead—by permission of Allah. And I inform you of what you eat and what you store in your houses. Indeed in that is a sign for you, if you are believers.

688. [The Day] when Allah will say, "O Jesus, Son of Mary, remember My favor upon you and upon your mother when I supported you with the Pure Spirit [i.e., the angel Gabriel] and you spoke to the people in the cradle and in maturity; and [remember] when I taught you writing and wisdom and the Torah and the Gospel; and when you designed from clay [what was] like the form of a bird with My permission, then you breathed into it, and it became a bird with My permission; and you healed the blind [from birth] and the leper with My permission; and when you brought forth the dead with My permission; and when I restrained the Children of Israel from [killing] you when you came to them with clear proofs and those who disbelieved among them said, "This is not but obvious magic."

[186]⁶⁸⁹

لَتُبْلَوُنَّ فِي اَمْوَالِكُمْ وَاَنْفُسِكُمْ وَلَتَسْمَعُنَّ مِنَ الَّذِينَ اُوتُوا الْكِتَابَ مِنْ قَبْلِكُمْ وَمِنَ الَّذِينَ اَشْرَكُوا اَذًى كَثِيرًا وَاِنْ تَصْبِرُوا وَتَتَّقُوا فَاِنَّ ذٰلِكَ مِنْ عَزْمِ الْاُمُورِ (186)

It is interesting to see that the current situation of Muslims is mentioned in the Qurān as part of the Qadar. In other words, the treatments of the groups towards Muslims مِنَ الَّذِينَ اُوتُوا الْكِتَابَ مِنْ قَبْلِكُمْ وَمِنَ الَّذِينَ اَشْرَكُو⁶⁹⁰, are present as part of the Divine Destiny with hikmah and wisdom from Allah ﷻ. Therefore, one should not be upset, depressed, and have doubts about one's disposition in Islam. At the same one should not get distracted and lose the real purpose of life. For example, a Muslim can easily lose the focus while being too much engaged with current affairs or news.

Therefore, it is important to know where everyone stands and accordingly control one's heart. A lot of times, Muslims don't understand why people have an attitude towards them. There are problems that are caused by Muslims because of not understanding the true teachings of Islam. However, there are also realities and attitudes of others because of a person simply due to being a Muslim. The above verse and others normalize this position, realities and difference. There can be possible different reasons for this: jealousy, group arrogance, fear of losing power and position etc.

In another verse in Sûrah Maidah, it is mentioned that

قُلْ يَا اَهْلَ الْكِتَابِ هَلْ تَنْقِمُونَ مِنَّا اِلَّا اَنْ اٰمَنَّا بِاللّٰهِ وَمَا اُنْزِلَ اِلَيْنَا وَمَا اُنْزِلَ مِنْ قَبْلُ وَاَنَّ اَكْثَرَكُمْ فَاسِقُونَ (59)⁶⁹¹

One of the possible reasons as mentioned above is the logical, reasonable and inclusive stance of Islam. In other words, some ahlu kitāb does not like the positive inclusivity of Islam as the religion

---

689. 3:186 You shall most certainly be tried in your possessions and in your persons; and indeed you shall hear many hurtful things from those to whom revelation was granted before your time, as well as from those who have come to ascribe divinity to other beings beside God. But if you remain patient in adversity and conscious of Him—this, behold, is something to set one's heart upon.

690. From those to whom revelation was granted before your time, as well as from those who have come to ascribe divinity to other beings beside God.

691. Say, "O People of the Scripture, do you resent us except [for the fact] that we have believed in Allah and what was revealed to us and what was revealed before and because most of you are defiantly disobedient?"

recognizing the previous books and the messengers of Allah ﷻ with similar teachings. When a message is inclusive, then the differences or identity conflicts can be minimized among different groups. Existing differences can be situated on a positive constructive stance rather than a negative exclusive position.

[191]⁶⁹²

الَّذِينَ يَذْكُرُونَ اللّهَ قِيَامًا وَقُعُودًا وَعَلَىٰ جُنُوبِهِمْ وَيَتَفَكَّرُونَ فِي خَلْقِ السَّمَاوَاتِ وَالْأَرْضِ رَبَّنَا مَا خَلَقْتَ هَٰذَا بَاطِلاً سُبْحَانَكَ فَقِنَا عَذَابَ النَّارِ {آل عمران/191}

وَمَا خَلَقْنَا السَّمَاءَ وَالْأَرْضَ وَمَا بَيْنَهُمَا بَاطِلاً ذَٰلِكَ ظَنُّ الَّذِينَ كَفَرُوا فَوَيْلٌ لِّلَّذِينَ كَفَرُوا مِنَ النَّارِ⁶⁹³ {ص/27}

The word batil, بَاطِلاً⁶⁹⁴, can signify that in this world, in the universe and in the creation, everything has a meaning and purpose. Noting is random. There is no chaos. There is no pessimism. This word repeats in many places in the Qurān to allude to this effect. At a personal level, it is expected that the person needs to get a meaning from everything in his or her life that everything comes with a meaning, message, and purpose from Allah ﷻ. Therefore, as the person gets more close to Allah ﷻ, this self-awareness becomes more sensitive, sharp, profound and perceptive within oneself. In other words, all the externalities of this person become internal. All the externalities are internalized through interpretation of their correct meanings, الله اعلم.

This perspective can take the person to a level of thinking, reflecting, interpreting, analyzing, deducing meanings and applying. In this standpoint, one can now analyze this and similar ayahs to allude to these notions.

---

692. (3:191) [and] who remember God when they stand, and when they sit, and when they lie down to sleep, and [thus] reflect on the creation of the heavens and the earth: "O our Sustainer! Thou hast not created [aught of] this without meaning and purpose. Limitless art Thou in Thy glory! Keep us safe, then, from suffering through fire!
693. And We did not create the heaven and the earth and that between them aimlessly. That is the assumption of those who disbelieve, so woe to those who disbelieve from the Fire.
694. Aimlessly.

الَّذِينَ يَذْكُرُونَ اللّهَ قِيَامًا وَقُعُودًا وَعَلَىٰ جُنُوبِهِمْ وَيَتَفَكَّرُونَ فِي خَلْقِ السَّمَاوَاتِ وَالأَرْضِ رَبَّنَا مَا خَلَقْتَ هَذا بَاطِلاً سُبْحَانَكَ فَقِنَا عَذَابَ النَّارِ 695{آل عمران/191}

{ أَوَلَمْ يَتَفَكَّرُوا فِي أَنفُسِهِمْ مَا خَلَقَ اللّهُ السَّمَاوَاتِ وَالأَرْضَ وَمَا بَيْنَهُمَا إِلَّا بِالْحَقِّ وَأَجَلٍ مُّسَمًّى وَإِنَّ كَثِيرًا مِّنَ النَّاسِ بِلِقَاء رَبِّهِمْ لَكَافِرُونَ {الروم/8}

{ يُنبِتُ لَكُم بِهِ الزَّرْعَ وَالزَّيْتُونَ وَالنَّخِيلَ وَالأَعْنَابَ وَمِن كُلِّ الثَّمَرَاتِ إِنَّ فِي ذَلِكَ لآيَةً لَّقَوْمٍ يَتَفَكَّرُونَ 696{النحل/11}

One can analyze the word يَتَفَكَّرُونَ[697] in the Qurān. It seems that اعلم الله, all the creation with natural, social, humanities, and spiritual sciences of tasawwuf are one book to read and reflect as the word يَتَفَكَّرُونَ is especially used in different places. On the other hand, the Qurān is another book that the person should constantly go back and go back refer to is used with the word أَفَلاَ يَتَدَبَّرُونَ الْقُرْآنَ:

أَفَلاَ يَتَدَبَّرُونَ الْقُرْآنَ وَلَوْ كَانَ مِنْ عِندِ غَيْرِ اللّهِ لَوَجَدُواْ فِيهِ اخْتِلاَفًا كَثِيرًا 698{النساء/82}

{ أَفَلَا يَتَدَبَّرُونَ الْقُرْآنَ أَمْ عَلَى قُلُوبٍ أَقْفَالُهَا 699{محمد/24}

One can review the different meanings of yatadabburu[700] and yatafakkaru[701] with the understandings of cognitive science. One can refer to the desired methodology critical thinking as aimed in colleges or universities in our contemporary time.

A person is most of the time at the state of silence, not talking. The thoughts are constantly flying in one's mind as Imam Ghazali mentions similar to birds (10). When a person focuses and thinks about a matter even though he or she may forget it, the traces of that thought can be retained in short memory. If it is retrieved immediately, can remember

---

695. [And] Who remember God when they stand, and when they sit, and when they lie down to sleep, and [thus] reflect on the creation of the heavens and the earth: "O our Sustainer! Thou hast not created [aught of] this without meaning and purpose. Limitless art Thou in Thy glory! Keep us safe, then, from suffering through fire!

696. He causes to grow for you thereby the crops, olives, palm trees, grapevines, and from all the fruits. Indeed in that is a sign for a people who give thought.

697. People who give thought.

698. Then do they not reflect upon the Qurān? If it had been from [any] other than Allah, they would have found within it much contradiction.

699. Then do they not reflect upon the Qurān, or are there locks upon [their] hearts?

700. Reflect.

701. People who give thought.

the details of previous critical thinking. If not, the person can remember as an unidentified or the un-detailed way. When a similar reminder comes signaling previous thoughts or reflection, he may have some feelings or recall some portion. In this case, after these critical thinking of tafakkur and tadabbur, it is important to take notes of the critically thought subjects, so that further steps can follow.

The next step after the critical thinking and analysis, synthesis should ideally follow. In other words, the ways and methods of applying this teachings in one's life. If it is natural sciences one call this applied sciences such as engineering. Even the come phrase of "appliance" takes its source from this methodology as mentioned in oxford dictionary for the word appliance "the action or process of bringing something into operation (32)." One can also visit and review concept of the application in religious matters. In other words, if the tafakkur and tadabbur is performed with all the sciences of cosmos and the Qurān then, the Sunnah of the Prophet صلى الله عليه وسلم and the changing and contextualizing issues with time, place and people in accordance with the Qurān and the Sunnah will be the synthesis and application of these critical thinking, الله اعلم.

5

Sûrah Nisã

[34]702

الرِّجَالُ قَوَّامُونَ عَلَى النِّسَاء بِمَا فَضَّلَ اللّهُ بَعْضَهُمْ عَلَى بَعْضٍ وَبِمَا أَنفَقُواْ مِنْ أَمْوَالِهِمْ
فَالصَّالِحَاتُ قَانِتَاتٌ حَافِظَاتٌ لِّلْغَيْبِ بِمَا حَفِظَ اللّهُ وَاللاَّتِي تَخَافُونَ نُشُوزَهُنَّ فَعِظُوهُنَّ
وَاهْجُرُوهُنَّ فِي الْمَضَاجِعِ وَاضْرِبُوهُنَّ فَإِنْ أَطَعْنَكُمْ فَلاَ تَبْغُواْ عَلَيْهِنَّ سَبِيلاً إِنَّ اللّهَ كَانَ
عَلِيًّا كَبِيرًا {النساء/34}

يَا أَيُّهَا الَّذِينَ آمَنُواْ كُونُواْ قَوَّامِينَ بِالْقِسْطِ شُهَدَاء لِلّهِ وَلَوْ عَلَى أَنفُسِكُمْ أَوِ الْوَالِدَيْنِ وَالأَقْرَبِينَ
إِن يَكُنْ غَنِيًّا أَوْ فَقَيرًا فَاللّهُ أَوْلَى بِهِمَا فَلاَ تَتَّبِعُواْ الْهَوَى أَن تَعْدِلُواْ وَإِن تَلْوُواْ أَوْ تُعْرِضُواْ
فَإِنَّ اللّهَ كَانَ بِمَا تَعْمَلُونَ خَبِيرًا703 {النساء/135}

يَا أَيُّهَا الَّذِينَ آمَنُواْ كُونُواْ قَوَّامِينَ لِلّهِ شُهَدَاء بِالْقِسْطِ وَلاَ يَجْرِمَنَّكُمْ شَنَآنُ قَوْمٍ عَلَى أَلاَّ
تَعْدِلُواْ اعْدِلُواْ هُوَ أَقْرَبُ لِلتَّقْوَى وَاتَّقُواْ اللّهَ إِنَّ اللّهَ خَبِيرٌ بِمَا تَعْمَلُونَ704 {المائدة/8}

When one reviews a key word قَوَّامُونَ705 in the above ayahs one can
see the notion of establishing and being a role model for justice that the
person will face Allah ﷻ and be accountable in the application of justice.
It is a very dangerous, challenging and cumbersome task to apply justice
especially with the phrase قَوَّامِينَ لِلّهِ شُهَدَاء بِالْقِسْطِ706.

---

702. 4:34 MEN SHALL take full care of women with the bounties which God has bestowed
more abundantly on the former than on the latter, and with what they may spend out of their
possessions. And the righteous women are the truly devout ones, who guard the intimacy
which God has [ordained to be] guarded. And as for those women whose ill-will you have
reason to fear, admonish them [first]; then leave them alone in bed; then beat them; and if
thereupon they pay you heed, do not seek to harm them. Behold, God is indeed most high,
great!
703. O you who have believed, be persistently standing firm in justice, witnesses for Allah,
even if it be against yourselves or parents and relatives. Whether one is rich or poor, Allah
is more worthy of both. So follow not [personal] inclination, lest you not be just. And if you
distort [your testimony] or refuse [to give it], then indeed Allah is ever, with what you do,
Acquainted.
704. O you who have believed, be persistently standing firm for Allah, witnesses in justice,
and do not let the hatred of a people prevent you from being just. Be just; that is nearer to
righteousness. And fear Allah; indeed, Allah is Acquainted with what you do.
705. Persistently standing firm.
706. Be persistently standing firm for Allah, witnesses in justice.

Then, to put everything in perspective, the phrases immediately follow اللّٰه حَفِظَ بِمَا لِّلْغَيْبِ حَافِظَاتٌ قَانِتَاتٌ فَالصَّالِحَاتُ[707] specifically in muennes, feminine form about women to elevate their status. In other words, the women are not given a lower status.

The expression اضْرِبُوهُنَّ[708] is interpreted as "hit" in traditional understanding. Most of the English translations present this word as "beat." In English, the word beat means really abusing someone physically in its colloquial usage. A common usage of "beat to death" is an example of this in English. Here is an example of definition of "beat" from New Oxford American dictionary (21):

beat |bēt|
verb (past beat; past participle beaten |ˈbētn|) [with obj.]
1 strike (a person or an animal) repeatedly and violently so as to hurt or injure them, usually with an implement such as a club or whip: a woman whose husband would frequently beat her after becoming drunk | the victims were beaten to death with baseball bats.

So, that is a very clear mistake in translations assuming that it has the notion or understanding of hit. In classical understandings, there are interpretations to allude that it is not hit but touch or tap someone to show that you are upset.

Another interpretation is that this word does not mean hit, touch or tap but send someone for vacation to refresh oneself spiritually. Because the word اضْرِبُوهُنَّ is used in other places of the with meaning of traveling.

On another note, to eliminate any type of misunderstandings, Allah ﷻ specifically mentions only the women for their piety level فَالصَّالِحَاتُ اللّٰه حَفِظَ بِمَا لِّلْغَيْبِ حَافِظَاتٌ قَانِتَاتٌ but not the men in order to elevate their status, اعلم اللّٰه.

In this case of family disputes between different genders, husband and wife or sometimes father and daughter, when there is a potential problem the case of فَعِظُوهُنَّ[709], counseling, and advise comes as the first step in the sequence of the verse. Then, the second step having some

---

707. And the righteous women are the truly devout ones, who guard the intimacy which God has [ordained to be] guarded.
708. Then beat them.
709. Admonish them [first].

distance with the expression وَاهْجُرُوهُنَّ فِي الْمَضَاجِعِ[710] is mentioned. This can be perhaps due to the need of self-reflection in one's life with some distance of stepping out from the habitual daily personal interactions, الله اعلم. Then, the word اضْرِبُوهُنَّ comes as the last step which has a disputable stance in translations.

[78-79][711]

أَيْنَمَا تَكُونُواْ يُدْرِككُّمُ الْمَوْتُ وَلَوْ كُنتُمْ فِي بُرُوجٍ مُّشَيَّدَةٍ وَإِن تُصِبْهُمْ حَسَنَةٌ يَقُولُواْ هَذِهِ مِنْ عِندِ اللهِ وَإِن تُصِبْهُمْ سَيِّئَةٌ يَقُولُواْ هَذِهِ مِنْ عِندِكَ قُلْ كُلٌّ مِّنْ عِندِ اللهِ فَمَا لِهَؤُلاء الْقَوْمِ لاَ يَكَادُونَ يَفْقَهُونَ حَدِيثًا {النساء/78} مَّا أَصَابَكَ مِنْ حَسَنَةٍ فَمِنَ اللهِ وَمَا أَصَابَكَ مِن سَيِّئَةٍ فَمِن نَّفْسِكَ وَأَرْسَلْنَاكَ لِلنَّاسِ رَسُولاً وَكَفَى بِاللهِ شَهِيدًا {النساء/79}

Allah ﷻ creates everything according to kasb, intention, acquirement, and free will execution of the person. But one should review the reality and adab of how the position of a person should be in one's relationship with Allah ﷻ in the encounter of good and evil-looking incidents.

[85][712]

مَّن يَشْفَعْ شَفَاعَةً حَسَنَةً يَكُن لَّهُ نَصِيبٌ مِّنْهَا وَمَن يَشْفَعْ شَفَاعَةً سَيِّئَةً يَكُن لَّهُ كِفْلٌ مِّنْهَا وَكَانَ اللهُ عَلَى كُلِّ شَيْءٍ مُّقِيتًا {النساء/85}

Above ayah is another proof of the Rahmah of Allah ﷻ on people when one analyzes two key words: نَصِيبٌ[713] and كِفْلٌ[714]. Allah ﷻ gives countlessly with the Fadl and Rahmah as the word نَصِيبٌ can entail. The word nasib نَصِيبٌ can entail countless of blessings. On the other hand, the word كِفْلٌ can imply the equivalence or something exactly the same. Allah ﷻ makes

---

710. Then leave them alone in bed.
711. 4:78) Wherever you may be, death will overtake you—even though you be in towers raised high.
"Yet, when a good thing happens to them, some [people] say, "This is from God," whereas when evil befalls them, they say, "This is from thee [O fellowman]!" Say: "All is from God." What, then, is amiss with these people that they are in no wise near to grasping the truth of what they are told? 4:79 Whatever good happens to thee is from God; and whatever evil befalls thee is from thyself. AND WE have sent thee [O Muhammad] as an apostle unto all mankind: and none can bear witness [thereto] as God does.
712. 4:85 Whoever rallies to a good cause shall have a share in its blessings; and whoever rallies to an evil cause shall be answerable for his part in it: for, indeed, God watches over everything.
713. Rally.
714. A guarantee.

Adl and Justice when a person does something evil, then the word كِفْلٌ is used for equivalence and justice.

[87 & 122]⁷¹⁵

اللّهُ لا إِلَهَ إِلاَّ هُوَ لَيَجْمَعَنَّكُمْ إِلَى يَوْمِ الْقِيَامَةِ لاَ رَيْبَ فِيهِ وَمَنْ أَصْدَقُ مِنَ اللّهِ حَدِيثًا
{النساء/87}

وَالَّذِينَ آمَنُواْ وَعَمِلُواْ الصَّالِحَاتِ سَنُدْخِلُهُمْ جَنَّاتٍ تَجْرِي مِن تَحْتِهَا الأَنْهَارُ خَالِدِينَ فِيهَا
أَبَدًا وَعْدَ اللّهِ حَقًّا وَمَنْ أَصْدَقُ مِنَ اللّهِ قِيلاً {النساء/122}

When one reviews the two phrases as وَمَنْ أَصْدَقُ مِنَ اللّهِ حَدِيثًا {النساء/87}⁷¹⁶ and وَمَنْ أَصْدَقُ مِنَ اللّهِ قِيلاً {النساء/122}⁷¹⁷ then, one can realize the meaning of what the objective and absolute truth and who has the authority to relate them. In this case, the expressions mention that Allah ﷻ has the Authority of absolute and objective truth in all discourses of narrations and discourses as mentioned with the words حَدِيثًا⁷¹⁸ and علم الله اعلم, قِيلًا.

In addition, one can see in the above ayahs that Allah ﷻ presents this Absolute Truth with Full Authority about the afterlife. As the matters of afterlife are unseen and requires full belief, Allah ﷻ mentions them so that the person can reflect Who the Speaker is and accordingly ask oneself their disposition. In other words, if Allah ﷻ says and mentions it that is the final say and there is nothing more. The previous statements before these phrases as لَا رَيْبَ فِيهِ⁷¹⁹ and وَعْدَ اللّهِ حَقًّا⁷²⁰ adds more and more tak'id and emphasis as this is the truth and for sure, there is no doubt about it. One can doubt about everything but not when Allah ﷻ mentions in such an absolute and clear way, الله اعلم.

According to some tasawwufin, the difference between the ayah numbers as 122-87 = 35 can implicitly point that a person is expected to embody and understand the real meanings of these ayahs that the

---

715. 4:87 God—save whom there is no deity—will surely gather you all together on the Day of Resurrection, [the coming of] which is beyond all doubt: and whose word could be truer than God's?
4:122 Yet those who attain to faith and do righteous deeds We shall bring into gardens through which running waters flow, therein to abide beyond the count of time: this is, in truth, God's promise—and whose word could be truer than God's?
716. And whose word could be truer than God's?
717. And whose word could be truer than God's?
718. Word.
719. Which is beyond all doubt.
720. This is, in truth, God's promise.

person does not put anything above the word and pleasure of Allah ﷻ in his or her life until one dies. He or she reaches to an age of maturity to understand the realities of as

وَمَنْ أَصْدَقُ مِنَ اللَّهِ قِيلاً and وَمَنْ أَصْدَقُ مِنَ اللَّهِ حَدِيثًا. These are interpretations, Allah ﷻ knows the best yet it is important realize these realities before one dies and it is too late.

[97][721]

إِنَّ الَّذِينَ تَوَفَّاهُمُ الْمَلَآئِكَةُ ظَالِمِي أَنْفُسِهِمْ قَالُواْ فِيمَ كُنتُمْ قَالُواْ كُنَّا مُسْتَضْعَفِينَ فِي الأَرْضِ قَالُواْ أَلَمْ تَكُنْ أَرْضُ اللَّهِ وَاسِعَةً فَتُهَاجِرُواْ فِيهَا فَأُوْلَئِكَ مَأْوَاهُمْ جَهَنَّمُ وَسَاءتْ مَصِيرًا {النساء/97}

It is interesting to view these ayahs that if one is weak in a society and compromising from the essence of one's religion, then it is expected that this person should leave that place. Not leaving or abandoning this place and people cannot be an excuse but there are always exceptions, الله اعلم. The expression ظَالِمِي أَنْفُسِهِمْ[722] is critical to ponder on. They did something on themselves as an oppression when they did not make hijrah, الله اعلم.

110[723]

وَمَن يَعْمَلْ سُوءًا أَوْ يَظْلِمْ نَفْسَهُ ثُمَّ يَسْتَغْفِرِ اللَّهَ يَجِدِ اللَّهَ غَفُورًا رَّحِيمًا

The above verse mentions that the person oppresses their own selves. In four other parts of the Qurān, [2, 57], [7, 160], [9, 70], and [16:118], Allah ﷻ mentions وَلَكِن كَانُواْ أَنفُسَهُمْ يَظْلِمُونَ[724] that they in reality have been oppressing their own selves, egos, bodies in this world and afterlife. The main oppression is lying against God. When a person lies about not recognizing God truly then the person suffers in this world and in the afterlife. The type of lying can range from explicit to implicit levels. A person can explicitly lie about non-existence of the Creator. Alternatively,

---

721. 4:97, Indeed, those whom the angels take [in death] while wronging themselves—[the angels] will say, "In what [condition] were you?" They will say, "We were oppressed in the land." They [the angels] will say, "Was not the earth of Allah spacious [enough] for you to emigrate therein?" For those, their refuge is Hell—and evil it is as a destination.
722. While wronging themselves.
723. 4:110 Yet he who does evil or [otherwise] sins against himself, and thereafter prays God to forgive him, shall find God much-forgiving, a dispenser of grace.
724. But they were [only] wronging themselves.

a person can believe in God but still lie about the true understanding of God. Further, a person can verbalize the true understanding of God but may not internalize or embody it in one's actions or thoughts and still lie implicitly. Therefore, the Prophet Muhammad (ﷺ) mentions that "I am not afraid about your (Muslims) explicit lies about God but I am afraid about your implicit lies such as the acts of ostentation and showing off. "

According to some scholars, the pronoun "I" is dangerous to use, in reality there is always Allah جل جلاله and everything that follows it as a blessing, beneficial and good is from Allah ﷻ. Someone utterance expressions of "my work, I did this…." can be examples of this implicit oppression (zulm) that can spoil the sweetness of belief in Allah ﷻ for a believer, mumin. On the contrary, all the destructions, evils, bad outcomes are from the self, ego and the person. The person asks for it and then it is created for this person.

[104]725

وَلاَ تَهِنُواْ فِي ابْتِغَاء الْقَوْمِ إِن تَكُونُواْ تَأْلَمُونَ فَإِنَّهُمْ يَأْلَمُونَ كَمَا تَأْلَمونَ وَتَرْجُونَ مِنَ اللّهِ مَا لاَ يَرْجُونَ وَكَانَ اللّهُ عَلِيمًا حَكِيمًا {النساء/410}

This is an important ayah to analyze in our times. There is a lot of mischief, humiliation, oppression towards Muslims. In this regard, Allah ﷻ mentions that the people who are taking this as a task to give difficulty for Muslim are humans too. They have their grief, stress, and worries and you have the similar ones. But you have something that they don't have that you expect a reward from Allah ﷻ for your patience and the difficulties that you are going through. This itself can give a person a spiritual uplift that a person may not realize sometimes. Therefore, Allah ﷻ reminds here this very critical difference, الله اعلم.

---

725. 4:104 And be not faint of heart when you seek out the [enemy] host. If you happen to suffer pain, behold, they suffer pain even as you suffer it: but you are hoping [to receive] from God what they cannot hope for. And God is indeed all-knowing, wise.

[113]⁷²⁶

وَلَوْلاَ فَضْلُ اللهِ عَلَيْكَ وَرَحْمَتُهُ لَهَمَّت طَّآئِفَةٌ مُنْهُمْ أَن يُضِلُّوكَ وَمَا يُضِلُّونَ إِلاَّ أَنْفُسَهُمْ وَمَا يَضُرُّونَكَ مِن شَيْءٍ وَأَنزَلَ اللهُ عَلَيْكَ الْكِتَابَ وَالْحِكْمَةَ وَعَلَّمَكَ مَا لَمْ تَكُنْ تَعْلَمُ وَكَانَ فَضْلُ اللهِ عَلَيْكَ عَظِيمًا {النساء/113}

Above verse similar to others initially address the Prophet ﷺ in its specific sabab-nuzûl. In its general application, a person can establish relationship with the Qurān and examine how each ayah of the Qurān can individually affect us in our own personal lives, affairs, adventures and discourses.

In this case, the expression وَكَانَ فَضْلُ اللهِ عَلَيْكَ عَظِيمًا⁷²⁷ is very critical to ponder upon. Allah ﷻ gives each person a lot of bounties and there is a lot of Fadl of Allah ﷻ to each person. Each person knows themselves if he or she fairly reflects upon them in one's journey of life. Therefore, in the Qurān, the expression اقْرَأْ كَتَابَكَ كَفَى بِنَفْسِكَ الْيَوْمَ عَلَيْكَ حَسِيبًا⁷²⁸ {الإسراء/14} can show this point that everyone knows him or herself in reality.

With this discourse, one should really humbly put one's head down and ponder on all individual discourses in one's life and then appreciate what Allah ﷻ did all along. Then, if there are problems, or sins one should ask forgiveness from Allah ﷻ.

On another note, if the person follows truly the Qurān, the Sunnah of the Prophet ﷺ then, Allah ﷻ guides and teaches the person what he or she doesn't know as the ayah signifies وَأَنزَلَ اللهُ عَلَيْكَ الْكِتَابَ وَالْحِكْمَةَ وَعَلَّمَكَ⁷²⁹ مَا لَمْ تَكُنْ تَعْلَمُ. This perspective is also mentioned in Sûrah Alaq as

عَلَّمَ الْإِنسَانَ مَا لَمْ يَعْلَمْ⁷³⁰ {العلق/5}

In this perspective, the religion is very clear and guidelines are very clear. Nothing is mysterious or unclear, Alhamdulillah.

---

726. 4:113 And but for God's favour upon thee and His grace, some of those [who are false to themselves] would indeed endeavour to lead thee astray; yet none but themselves do they lead astray. Nor can they harm thee in any way, since God has bestowed upon thee from on high this divine writ and [given thee] wisdom, and has imparted unto thee the knowledge of what thou didst not know. And God's favour upon thee is tremendous indeed.

727. And God's favour upon thee is tremendous indeed.

728. [It will be said], "Read your record. Sufficient is yourself against you this Day as accountant."

729. Since God has bestowed upon thee from on high this divine writ and [given thee] wisdom, and has imparted unto thee the knowledge of what thou didst not know.

730. [He] taught man that which they did not know.

[146-147]⁷³¹

إِلاَّ الَّذِينَ تَابُواْ وَأَصْلَحُواْ وَاعْتَصَمُواْ بِاللّهِ وَأَخْلَصُواْ دِينَهُمْ لِلّهِ فَأُوْلَئِكَ مَعَ الْمُؤْمِنِينَ وَسَوْفَ يُؤْتِ اللّهُ الْمُؤْمِنِينَ أَجْرًا عَظِيمًا {النساء/146} مَّا يَفْعَلُ اللّهُ بِعَذَابِكُمْ إِن شَكَرْتُمْ وَآمَنتُمْ وَكَانَ اللّهُ شَاكِرًا عَلِيمًا {النساء/147}

The importance of the ikhlas, sincerity comes with the expression أَخْلَصُواْ دِينَهُمْ لِلّهِ as mentioned in the verses of Surah Zumar [2, 11, 14]. If the person has sincerity and effort, and appreciation of all the nimahs from Allah with this sincere recognition of Allah and asks the question مَّا⁷³² يَفْعَلُ اللّهُ بِعَذَابِكُمْ إِن شَكَرْتُمْ وَآمَنتُمْ, that why Allah will have the person in punishment if the person is in the sincere appreciative state with the sincere and true belief of Allah? Definitely No, because Allah knows and appreciates all those as mentioned وَكَانَ اللّهُ شَاكِرًا عَلِيمًا⁷³³.

One can analyze the word of shukr, thanking or shakirun in the below ayahs and others in the Qurān.

وَإِذْ تَأَذَّنَ رَبُّكُمْ لَئِن شَكَرْتُمْ لأَزِيدَنَّكُمْ وَلَئِن كَفَرْتُمْ إِنَّ عَذَابِي لَشَدِيدٌ⁷³⁴{إبراهيم/7}

فَتَبَسَّمَ ضَاحِكًا مِّن قَوْلِهَا وَقَالَ رَبِّ أَوْزِعْنِي أَنْ أَشْكُرَ نِعْمَتَكَ الَّتِي أَنْعَمْتَ عَلَيَّ وَعَلَى وَالِدَيَّ وَأَنْ أَعْمَلَ صَالِحًا تَرْضَاهُ وَأَدْخِلْنِي بِرَحْمَتِكَ فِي عِبَادِكَ الصَّالِحِينَ⁷³⁵{النمل/19}

---

731. (4:146) But excepted shall be they who repent, and live righteously, and hold fast unto God, and grow sincere in their faith in God alone: for these shall be one with the believers—and in time God will grant to all believers a mighty reward.
4:147 Why would God cause you to suffer [for your past sins] if you are grateful and attain to belief—seeing that God is always responsive to gratitude, all-knowing?
732. Why would God cause you to suffer [for your past sins] if you are grateful and attain to belief.
733. God is always responsive to gratitude, all-knowing?
734. And [remember] when your Lord proclaimed, 'If you are grateful, I will surely increase you [in favor]; but if you deny, indeed, My punishment is severe.'
735. So [Solomon] smiled, amused at her speech, and said, "My Lord, enable me to be grateful for Your favor which You have bestowed upon me and upon my parents and to do righteousness of which You approve. And admit me by Your mercy into [the ranks of] Your righteous servants."

قَالَ الَّذِي عِندَهُ عِلْمٌ مِّنَ الْكِتَابِ أَنَا آتِيكَ بِهِ قَبْلَ أَن يَرْتَدَّ إِلَيْكَ طَرْفُكَ فَلَمَّا رَآهُ مُسْتَقِرًّا عِندَهُ قَالَ هَذَا مِن فَضْلِ رَبِّي لِيَبْلُوَنِي أَأَشْكُرُ أَمْ أَكْفُرُ وَمَن شَكَرَ فَإِنَّمَا يَشْكُرُ لِنَفْسِهِ وَمَن كَفَرَ فَإِنَّ رَبِّي غَنِيٌّ كَرِيمٌ ٧٣٦{النمل/40}

لَقَدْ كَانَ لِسَبَإٍ فِي مَسْكَنِهِمْ آيَةٌ جَنَّتَانِ عَن يَمِينٍ وَشِمَالٍ كُلُوا مِن رِّزْقِ رَبِّكُمْ وَاشْكُرُوا لَهُ بَلْدَةٌ طَيِّبَةٌ وَرَبٌّ غَفُورٌ ٧٣٧{سبأ/15} فَأَعْرَضُوا فَأَرْسَلْنَا عَلَيْهِمْ سَيْلَ الْعَرِمِ وَبَدَّلْنَاهُم بِجَنَّتَيْهِمْ جَنَّتَيْنِ ذَوَاتَى أُكُلٍ خَمْطٍ وَأَثْلٍ وَشَيْءٍ مِّن سِدْرٍ قَلِيلٍ ٧٣٨{سبأ/16}

Sometimes, a person can ask how can one live a life without much trials and tests or hard tribulations? One of the keys is to be always in the state of shukr. In other words, the trials and tests can come to a person to remind this required embodiment in a human being. In this perspective, Sulayman as represents the worldly blessings as the prophet of Allah ﷻ but one can review in the above ayahs he as constantly mentions this notion of shukr as if to remind the people that this can be a reason why he was in that state.

A person can see the opposite example of this with the people of saba as mentioned above. Allah ﷻ gave them a lot of bounties and required them to be thankful and they did not do it. In this case, they were tested and given difficulty and the loss of the bounty.

The Prophet ﷺ was at the highest of shukr with the hamd as his name was Muhammad ﷺ. Then, with this state, the Prophet ﷺ was offered to be either a king prophet or not. He preferred humbleness and humility. With this choice and trait, the Prophet boosted his ﷺ's level next to Allah ﷻ that no other Prophet was able reach. This level is called Maqam Mahmud. The level of Hamd. This is such a level that the Prophet takes an authority of in both this world and afterlife in the Day of Judgment when no one has any say. This is all granted to him ﷺ by Allah ﷻ due this embodiment of hamd, الله اعلم.

---

736. Said one who had knowledge from the Scripture, "I will bring it to you before your glance returns to you." And when [Solomon] saw it placed before him, he said, "This is from the favor of my Lord to test me whether I will be grateful or ungrateful. And whoever is grateful—his gratitude is only for [the benefit of] himself. And whoever is ungrateful—then indeed, my Lord is Free of need and Generous."
737. There was for [the tribe of] Sabā in their dwelling place a sign: two [fields of] gardens on the right and on the left. [They were told], "Eat from the provisions of your Lord and be grateful to Him. A good land [have you], and a forgiving Lord."
738. But they turned away [refusing], so We sent upon them the flood of the dam, and We replaced their two [fields of] gardens with gardens of bitter fruit, tamarisks and something of sparse lote trees.

If the person still does not care then,

[150]⁷³⁹

إِنَّ الَّذِينَ يَكْفُرُونَ بِاللَّهِ وَرُسُلِهِ وَيُرِيدُونَ أَن يُفَرِّقُواْ بَيْنَ اللَّهِ وَرُسُلِهِ وَيقُولُونَ نُؤْمِنُ بِبَعْضٍ
وَنَكْفُرُ بِبَعْضٍ وَيُرِيدُونَ أَن يَتَّخِذُواْ بَيْنَ ذَلِكَ سَبِيلاً {النساء/150} أُوْلَئِكَ هُمُ الْكَافِرُونَ
حَقًّا وَأَعْتَدْنَا لِلْكَافِرِينَ عَذَابًا مُّهِينًا ⁷⁴⁰{النساء/151} وَالَّذِينَ آمَنُواْ بِاللَّهِ وَرُسُلِهِ وَلَمْ يُفَرِّقُواْ
بَيْنَ أَحَدٍ مِّنْهُمْ أُوْلَئِكَ سَوْفَ يُؤْتِيهِمْ أُجُورَهُمْ وَكَانَ اللَّهُ غَفُورًا رَّحِيمًا ⁷⁴¹{النساء/152}

Imān is accepting and believing all the structures and details of the faith whole.

The concept of selective belief or acceptance of the teachings of the Qurān and not the Prophet or vice versa is presented as kufr in the above verses as وَيقُولُونَ نُؤْمِنُ بِبَعْضٍ وَنَكْفُرُ بِبَعْضٍ⁷⁴². This approach is considered as the true kufr as mentioned أُوْلَئِكَ هُمُ الْكَافِرُونَ حَقًّا⁷⁴³. On the other hand, the case and attitude of people who have imān presented with وَالَّذِينَ آمَنُواْ⁷⁴⁴ بِاللَّهِ وَرُسُلِهِ وَلَمْ يُفَرِّقُواْ بَيْنَ أَحَدٍ مِّنْهُمْ.

Imān and kufur are opposites of each other. Therefore, if one exists the others cannot exist. There is no mixed state or classification of imān and kufur. A person can have the qualities of imān or kufur but it belongs to one group in classification. A person can have imān but when he or she lies then this person has the qualities of kufr. A person can have kufr but when this person is ethical and honest then this person has the qualities of imān. This notion is a fundamental concept separating the stance of mutazalites and kharijis that their stance was about the grave oppressions or sins that the person does not have imān. In the normative stance of Muslims about this topic, the person can have imān but with fisq.

---

739. 4:150 VERILY, those who deny God and His apostles by endeavouring to make a distinction between [belief in] God and [belief in] His apostles, and who say, "We believe in the one but we deny the other," and want to pursue a path in-between

740. Those are the disbelievers, truly. And We have prepared for the disbelievers a humiliating punishment.

741. But they who believe in Allah and His messengers and do not discriminate between any of them—to those He is going to give their rewards. And ever is Allah Forgiving and Merciful.

742. We believe in the one but we deny the other.

743. Those are the disbelievers, truly.

744. But they who believe in Allah and His messengers and do not discriminate between any of them.

[155-157][745]

فَبِمَا نَقْضِهِم مِّيثَاقَهُمْ وَكُفْرِهِم بَآيَاتِ اللهِ وَقَتْلِهِمُ الأَنْبِيَاء بِغَيْرِ حَقٍّ وَقَوْلِهِمْ قُلُوبُنَا غُلْفٌ بَلْ طَبَعَ اللهُ عَلَيْهَا بِكُفْرِهِمْ فَلاَ يُؤْمِنُونَ إِلاَّ قَلِيلاً {النساء/155} وَبِكُفْرِهِمْ وَقَوْلِهِمْ عَلَى مَرْيَمَ بُهْتَانًا عَظِيمًا [746] {النساء/156} وَقَوْلِهِمْ إِنَّا قَتَلْنَا الْمَسِيحَ عِيسَى ابْنَ مَرْيَمَ رَسُولَ اللهِ وَمَا قَتَلُوهُ وَمَا صَلَبُوهُ وَلَكِن شُبِّهَ لَهُمْ وَإِنَّ الَّذِينَ اخْتَلَفُواْ فِيهِ لَفِي شَكٍّ مِّنْهُ مَا لَهُم بِهِ مِنْ عِلْمٍ إِلاَّ اتِّبَاعَ الظَّنِّ وَمَا قَتَلُوهُ يَقِينًا [747] {النساء/157}

One can review above ayah around the word قَوْلِهِمْ[748] that how the words can endanger fully one's relationship with Allah ☙although he or she can have imān, or be a believer. Most of the time, the words can reflect the person's inner disposition of heart and character. For example, if we take[749] وَقَوْلِهِمْ إِنَّا قَتَلْنَا الْمَسِيحَ عِيسَى ابْنَ مَرْيَمَ رَسُولَ اللهِ to analyze one's inner disposition which can be very interesting. A person can make a sin but then publicizing it and making fun of the sacred. This, for sure, can challenge the core values of imān. In this case, one can ask: "how can one who has imān can make fun and say "we killed the prophet of God?" Here, there are two dispositions. One is if the person did not believe someone as a messenger then one can call them with different titles. For examples, one can take the case of Musaylama. There were no reported narrations from any sahabah with a similar expression of "we killed the prophet of God" although Musaylama claimed the false prophethood. In the second disposition, if a person knows and feels about the possibility of a person as the Prophet of Allah ☙with all the miracles then makes the statement of "we killed the prophet of God "then, it becomes more dangerous and scary in one's relationship with Allah ☙.

Also, from a legal point, the expression, وَقَوْلِهِمْ إِنَّا قَتَلْنَا الْمَسِيحَ عِيسَى ابْنَ مَرْيَمَ رَسُولَ اللهِ can have a problematic disposition that killing someone is illegal, prohibited and haram.

---

745. 4:155 And so, [We punished them] for the breaking of their pledge, and their refusal to acknowledge God's messages, and their slaying of prophets against all right, and their boast, "Our hearts are already full of knowledge"- nay, but God has sealed their hearts in result of their denial of the truth, and [now] they believe in but few things.
746. And [We cursed them] for their disbelief and their saying against Mary a great slander.
747. And [for] their saying, "Indeed, we have killed the Messiah, Jesus, the son of Mary, the messenger of Allah." And they did not kill him, nor did they crucify him; but [another] was made to resemble him to them. And indeed, those who differ over it are in doubt about it. They have no knowledge of it except the following of assumption. And they did not kill him, for certain.
748. Their saying.
749. And [for] their saying, "Indeed, we have killed the Messiah, Jesus, the son of Mary, the messenger of Allah."

6

Sûrah Maidah

[1-2][750]

يَا أَيُّهَا الَّذِينَ آمَنُواْ أَوْفُواْ بِالْعُقُودِ أُحِلَّتْ لَكُم بَهِيمَةُ الأَنْعَامِ إِلاَّ مَا يُتْلَى عَلَيْكُمْ غَيْرَ مُحِلِّي
الصَّيْدِ وَأَنتُمْ حُرُمٌ إِنَّ اللَّهَ يَحْكُمُ مَا يُرِيدُ {المائدة/1} يَا أَيُّهَا الَّذِينَ آمَنُواْ لاَ تُحِلُّواْ شَعَآئِرَ
اللَّهِ وَلاَ الشَّهْرَ الْحَرَامَ وَلاَ الْهَدْيَ وَلاَ الْقَلآئِدَ وَلا آمِّينَ الْبَيْتَ الْحَرَامَ يَبْتَغُونَ فَضْلاً مِّن
رَّبِّهِمْ وَرِضْوَانًا وَإِذَا حَلَلْتُمْ فَاصْطَادُواْ وَلاَ يَجْرِمَنَّكُمْ شَنَآنُ قَوْمٍ أَن صَدُّوكُمْ عَنِ الْمَسْجِدِ
الْحَرَامِ أَن تَعْتَدُواْ وَتَعَاوَنُواْ عَلَى الْبِرِّ وَالتَّقْوَى وَلاَ تَعَاوَنُواْ عَلَى الإِثْمِ وَالْعُدْوَانِ وَاتَّقُواْ
اللَّهَ إِنَّ اللَّهَ شَدِيدُ الْعِقَابِ {المائدة/2}

It is very interesting that this Sûrah starts with an order from Allah ﷻ to keep the promises and all agreements as mentioned يَا أَيُّهَا الَّذِينَ آمَنُواْ أَوْفُواْ[751] بِالْعُقُودِ. How serious is breaking a promise that Allah ﷻ starts one of the longest surahs in the Qurãn with this order, subhanAllah. Then, there are examples given. But later, another interesting point is that وَلاَ يَجْرِمَنَّكُمْ شَنَآنُ قَوْمٍ أَن صَدُّوكُمْ عَنِ الْمَسْجِدِ الْحَرَامِ أَن تَعْتَدُواْ[752], a person or a group can oppress you but this oppression should not make the person act emotionally, with the feelings of revenge and counter act but still the person should observe أَن تَعْتَدُوا[753] which is adalah, justice and proper steps of solving the problem and removing the oppression. In this regard, one of the key steps is to plan, to consult and make mashawarah with each other and ask help. The purpose of asking help and planning

---

750. 5:1 O YOU who have attained to faith! Be true to your covenants! Lawful to you is the [flesh of every] beast that feeds on plants, save what is mentioned to you [hereinafter]: but you are not allowed to hunt while you are in the state of pilgrimage. Behold, God ordains in accordance with His will.
5:2 O you who have attained to faith! Offend not against the symbols set up by God, nor against the sacred month [of pilgrimage], nor against the garlanded offerings, nor against those who flock to the Inviolable Temple, seeking favour with their Sustainer and His goodly acceptance; and [only] after your pilgrimage is over are you free to hunt. And never let your hatred of people who would bar you from the Inviolable House of Worship lead you into the sin of aggression: but rather help one another in furthering virtue and God-consciousness, and do not help one another in furthering evil and enmity; and remain conscious of God: for, behold, God is severe in retribution!
751. O YOU who have attained to faith! Be true to your covenants!
752. And never let your hatred of people who would bar you from the Inviolable House of Worship lead you into the sin of aggression.
753. Lead you into the sin of aggression.

or acting together is not to take revenge but the purpose is الْبِرُّ وَالتَّقْوَى[754], the good, the best for the sake of Allah, knowing that Allah knows what you do if you are inclined to oppress. This is so important that وَلَا[755] تَعَاوَنُواْ عَلَى الإِثْمِ وَالْعُدْوَانِ, this notion is repeated with emphasis, takid, that not to help each other and plan for something bad, evil and revenge as a group. And remember, Allah is al-Qadir, All Powerful, to take revenge for you as mentioned إِنَّ اللَّهَ شَدِيدُ الْعِقَابِ[756] and Allah's restitutions are not like yours but it is شَدِيدٌ, very powerful. So, don't worry about that part, but do your part by doing and implementing good, ethical in the times of oppression as well. With your feelings of revenge, make tawakkul to Allah as Allah is إِنَّ اللَّهَ شَدِيدُ الْعِقَابِ.

[3][757]

حُرِّمَتْ عَلَيْكُمُ الْمَيْتَةُ وَالدَّمُ وَلَحْمُ الْخِنْزِيرِ وَمَا أُهِلَّ لِغَيْرِ اللّهِ بِهِ وَالْمُنْخَنِقَةُ وَالْمَوْقُوذَةُ وَالْمُتَرَدِّيَةُ وَالنَّطِيحَةُ وَمَا أَكَلَ السَّبُعُ إِلاَّ مَا ذَكَّيْتُمْ وَمَا ذُبِحَ عَلَى النُّصُبِ وَأَن تَسْتَقْسِمُوا بِالأَزْلاَمِ ذَلِكُمْ فِسْقٌ الْيَوْمَ يَئِسَ الَّذِينَ كَفَرُوا مِن دِينِكُمْ فَلاَ تَخْشَوْهُمْ وَاخْشَوْنِ الْيَوْمَ أَكْمَلْتُ لَكُمْ دِينَكُمْ وَأَتْمَمْتُ عَلَيْكُمْ نِعْمَتِي وَرَضِيتُ لَكُمُ الإِسْلاَمَ دِيناً فَمَنِ اضْطُرَّ فِي مَخْمَصَةٍ غَيْرَ مُتَجَانِفٍ لإِثْمٍ فَإِنَّ اللّهَ غَفُورٌ رَحِيمٌ

The expression in the above ayah الْيَوْمَ أَكْمَلْتُ لَكُمْ دِينَكُمْ وَأَتْمَمْتُ عَلَيْكُمْ نِعْمَتِي[758] وَرَضِيتُ لَكُمُ الإِسْلاَمَ دِين is very important that one can see the fruits of this ayah all over the Muslim world. One can go to poor Muslim countries. In most of these countries, people are poorer compared to Western countries. In some places, they are in difficult hygienic conditions, lack

---

754. Virtue and God-consciousness.
755. And do not help one another in furthering evil and enmity.
756. God is severe in retribution!
757. 5:3 FORBIDDEN to you is carrion, and blood, and the flesh of swine, and that over which any name other than God's has been invoked, and the animal that has been strangled, or beaten to death, or killed by a fall, or gored to death, or savaged by a beast of prey, save that which you [yourselves] may have slaughtered while it was still alive; and [forbidden to you is] all that has been slaughtered on idolatrous altars. And [you are forbidden] to seek to learn through divination what the future may hold in store for you: this is sinful conduct. Today, those who are bent on denying the truth have lost all hope of [your ever forsaking] your religion: do not, then, hold them in awe, but stand in awe of Me! Today have I perfected your religious law for you, and have bestowed upon you the full measure of My blessings, and willed that self-surrender unto Me shall be your religion.' As for him, however, who is driven [to what is forbidden] by dire necessity and not by an inclination to sinning—behold, God is much-forgiving, a dispenser of grace.
758. Today have I perfected your religious law for you, and have bestowed upon you the full measure of My blessings, and willed that self-surrender unto Me shall be your religion.

of food, poor conditions of shelter and heating, one can still meet with happy people compared to some individuals in Western societies. One can argue that the same can be true in Western countries as well. I think if the same living conditions are in Western countries, the people would not tolerate these type of minimum living conditions. Therefore, kinship studies of anthropology mainly approches this hidden happiness in people's life although the level of welfare can be at minimum levels.

Some ethnographic examples of this can be for example kids playing in the mud with very unhygienic conditions, women in their traditional life style, and men with their five times engagements in the mosques can portray a very lively picture of a happy, contented and satisfied life style. Although an outsider may think that they are in horrible suffering conditions but in reality they are truly enjoying their life with the teachings of Islam, making shukr, listening to the recitation of the Qurān, and the Islamic teachings being part of their daily life on the streets and at home.

In a normative understanding, اَلْيَوْمَ اَكْمَلْتُ لَكُمْ دِينَكُمْ وَاَتْمَمْتُ عَلَيْكُمْ نِعْمَتِي وَرَضِيتُ لَكُمُ الْاِسْلَامَ دِين can allude to the notion that the teachings of Islam are perfect and there is no place of innovations, bidah [15][759]

يَا أَهْلَ الْكِتَابِ قَدْ جَاءكُمْ رَسُولُنَا يُبَيِّنُ لَكُمْ كَثِيرًا مِّمَّا كُنتُمْ تُخْفُونَ مِنَ الْكِتَابِ وَيَعْفُو عَن كَثِيرٍ قَدْ جَاءكُم مِّنَ اللّهِ نُورٌ وَكِتَابٌ مُّبِينٌ {المائدة/15}

The above ayah is interesting to allude to the fact as to how Muslims can put the means and reasons to communicate these verses with ahlu-kitāb. In one possibility, these verses can be there, but the people of the book do not reveal them. From another perspective, it could have been removed from the current versions of these scriptures. In this regard, the style or method of وَيَعْفُو عَن كَثِيرٍ[760] shows the point is not who is right or wrong but learning and benefitting from the Qurān as the latest Testament from God as mentioned with قَدْ جَاءكُم مِّنَ اللّهِ نُورٌ وَكِتَابٌ مُّبِينٌ[761]. In other words, Allah as you may call as God or Adonai strongly and nicely advises them to benefit from the Qurān, الله اعلم.

---

759. (5:15) O followers of the Bible! Now there has come unto you Our Apostle, to make clear unto you much of what you have been concealing [from yourselves] of the Bible, and to pardon much. Now there has come unto you from God a light, and a clear divine writ,
760. And to pardon much.
761. Now there has come unto you from God a light, and a clear divine writ,

[18]

وَقَالَتِ الْيَهُودُ وَالنَّصَارَى نَحْنُ أَبْنَاء اللّهِ وَأَحِبَّاؤُهُ قُلْ فَلِمَ يُعَذِّبُكُم بِذُنُوبِكُم بَلْ أَنتُم بَشَرٌ مِّمَّنْ خَلَقَ يَغْفِرُ لِمَن يَشَاء وَيُعَذِّبُ مَن يَشَاء وَلِلّهِ مُلْكُ السَّمَاوَاتِ وَالأَرْضِ وَمَا بَيْنَهُمَا وَإِلَيْهِ الْمَصِيرُ 762{المائدة/18}

One can see in the above verses the wordings of ahlu-kitāb that they use with their positions with Allah ﷻ. One can see and realize the similar wording discourses in the interactions between Christians and others. The concept of نَحْنُ أَبْنَاء اللّهِ763 can reveal their disposition of the father concept in the creed of trinity. Then, all also, in their popular usage as one can hear a lot as "we are children of God," to allude to this custom. However, Allah ﷻ corrects their wording and shows the true disposition of the person with Rabbul Alamin. This is expressed as بَلْ أَنتُم بَشَرٌ مِّمَّنْ764 خَلَقَ which can translate as "you are humans who Allah ﷻ created among other creations." Here, first humans are creations but not children or sons and daughters. Second, Allah ﷻ created other creations. So, what is special about humans that humans are making such a wrong and false claim? Third, the real value of everything becomes valuable and precious with their true value without any lies and exaggerations. If a gold has other materials inside, then it goes through a process to only have the value of gold. Similarly, human gets and receives a value when they accept that they are humans and created. Claims of divinity over humans can be similar to an adult dress on a child which can make the person appear funny.

---

762. But the Jews and the Christians say, "We are the children of Allah and His beloved." Say, "Then why does He punish you for your sins?" Rather, you are human beings from among those He has created. He forgives whom He wills, and He punishes whom He wills. And to Allah belongs the dominion of the heavens and the earth and whatever is between them, and to Him is the [final] destination.
763. We are the children of Allah.
764. Rather, you are human beings from among those He has created.

[24-30][765]

قَالُواْ يَا مُوسَى إِنَّا لَن نَّدْخُلَهَا أَبَدًا مَّا دَامُواْ فِيهَا فَاذْهَبْ أَنتَ وَرَبُّكَ فَقَاتِلا إِنَّا هَاهُنَا قَاعِدُونَ {المائدة/24} قَالَ رَبِّ إِنِّي لا أَمْلِكُ إِلاَّ نَفْسِي وَأَخِي فَافْرُقْ بَيْنَنَا وَبَيْنَ الْقَوْمِ الْفَاسِقِينَ {المائدة/25} قَالَ فَإِنَّهَا مُحَرَّمَةٌ عَلَيْهِمْ أَرْبَعِينَ سَنَةً يَتِيهُونَ فِي الأَرْضِ فَلاَ تَأْسَ عَلَى الْقَوْمِ الْفَاسِقِينَ {المائدة/26} وَاتْلُ عَلَيْهِمْ نَبَأَ ابْنَيْ آدَمَ بِالْحَقِّ إِذْ قَرَّبَا قُرْبَانًا فَتُقُبِّلَ مِن أَحَدِهِمَا وَلَمْ يُتَقَبَّلْ مِنَ الآخَرِ قَالَ لَأَقْتُلَنَّكَ قَالَ إِنَّمَا يَتَقَبَّلُ اللّهُ مِنَ الْمُتَّقِينَ {المائدة/27} لَئِن بَسَطتَ إِلَيَّ يَدَكَ لِتَقْتُلَنِي مَا أَنَاْ بِبَاسِطٍ يَدِيَ إِلَيْكَ لَأَقْتُلَكَ إِنِّي أَخَافُ اللّهَ رَبَّ الْعَالَمِينَ {المائدة/28} إِنِّي أُرِيدُ أَن تَبُوءَ بِإِثْمِي وَإِثْمِكَ فَتَكُونَ مِنْ أَصْحَابِ النَّارِ وَذَلِكَ جَزَاء الظَّالِمِينَ {المائدة/29} فَطَوَّعَتْ لَهُ نَفْسُهُ قَتْلَ أَخِيهِ فَقَتَلَهُ فَأَصْبَحَ مِنَ الْخَاسِرِينَ {المائدة/30}

In the above ayahs, one can analyze two cases around the word and concept of أَخِي[766] a familial relationship, brotherhood or sisterhood. In the first case, the case of a brother with Musa as and Harun as. They support each for good and in their relationship with Allah ﷻ. There is no destructive jealousy but helping each other to save themselves both from the displeasure of Allah ﷻ. This is encouraged and it is a positive kinship relationship when one is helping another.

On the other hand, the case of two brothers, Habìl and Qabìl. They both want to do something for the sake of Allah ﷻ. One shows jealousy, attitude and zulm, and the other shows humbleness, and taqwa. They are both kinship brothers. The jealousy presents itself at such a level that the oppressor kills the mazlûm. One brother kills the other. One can see a very similar incident in the kinship relationship of Yûsuf as with his brothers.

---

765. 5:24 [But] they said: "O Moses! Behold, never shall we enter that [land] so long as those others are in it. Go forth, then, thou and thy Sustainer, and fight, both of you! We, behold, shall remain here!" (5:25) Prayed [Moses]: "O my Sustainer! Of none am I master but of myself and my brother [Aaron]: draw Thou, then, a dividing-line between us and these iniquitous folk!" 5:26 Answered He: "Then, verily, this [land] shall be forbidden to them for forty years, while they wander on earth, bewildered, to and fro; and sorrow thou not over these iniquitous folk." (5:27) And convey unto them, setting forth the truth, the story of the two sons of Adam—how each offered a sacrifice, and it was accepted from one of them whereas it was not accepted from the other. [And Cain] said: "I will surely slay thee!" [Abel] replied: "Behold, God accepts only from those who are conscious of Him. (28) Even if thou lay thy hand on me to slay me, I shall not lay my hand on thee to slay thee: behold, I fear God, the Sustainer of all the worlds. (5:29) I am willing, indeed, for thee to bear [the burden of] all the sins ever done by me as well as of the sin done by thee: [but] then thou wouldst be destined for the fire, since that is the requital of evildoers!" 5:30 But the other's passion drove him to slaying his brother; and he slew him: and thus he became one of the lost.
766. My brother.

In both cases, Allah ﷻ mentions two cases. The first one is the ideal case as a role model between Musa as and Harun as. A positive kinship relationship can make the person in blessings in this world and afterlife. The second case is the one that humans tend to make a bad or wrong choice due to the diseases of the heart, nafs and temptations of shaytan, اللهم احفظنا من هذا امين[767].

[32][768]

مِنْ أَجْلِ ذَلِكَ كَتَبْنَا عَلَى بَنِي إِسْرَائِيلَ أَنَّهُ مَن قَتَلَ نَفْسًا بِغَيْرِ نَفْسٍ أَوْ فَسَادٍ فِي الأَرْضِ فَكَأَنَّمَا قَتَلَ النَّاسَ جَمِيعًا وَمَنْ أَحْيَاهَا فَكَأَنَّمَا أَحْيَا النَّاسَ جَمِيعًا وَلَقَدْ جَاء تْهُمْ رُسُلُنَا بِالْبَيِّنَاتِ ثُمَّ إِنَّ كَثِيرًا مِّنْهُم بَعْدَ ذَلِكَ فِي الأَرْضِ لَمُسْرِفُونَ {المائدة/32}

It is interesting to note that one of the famous verses especially today in Western discourses of explaining the exclusion of violence from Islam comes immediately after the story of Habil and Qabil. In this perspective, with first attempt and incident of killing in human history, the above ruling of Allah ﷻ has been always there in the true and unaltered teachings of the scriptures. In this perspective, religion establishes unchanging comprehensive rules and guidelines as presented here.

[35]

يَا أَيُّهَا الَّذِينَ آمَنُواْ اتَّقُواْ اللّهَ وَابْتَغُواْ إِلَيهِ الْوَسِيلَةَ وَجَاهِدُواْ فِي سَبِيلِهِ لَعَلَّكُمْ تُفْلِحُونَ[769]

This verse urges to seek means to get close to Allah and to please Allah ﷻ. The best means to get closer to someone is to be in the company of ones that this person loves. Similarly, the best way to please Allah ﷻ is to be with the ones that Allah ﷻ loves. The highest means is the Prophet

---

767. Oh Allah protect us from this.
768. 5:32 Because of this did We ordain unto the children of Israel that if anyone slays a human being unless it be [in punishment] for murder or for spreading corruption on earth—it shall be as though he had slain all mankind; whereas, if anyone saves a life, it shall be as though he had saved the lives of all mankind. And, indeed, there came unto them Our apostles with all evidence of the truth: yet, behold, notwithstanding all this, many of them go on committing all manner of excesses on earth.
769. Because of that, We decreed upon the Children of Israel that whoever kills a soul unless for a soul or for corruption [done] in the land—it is as if he had slain mankind entirely. And whoever saves one—it is as if he had saved mankind entirely. And Our messengers had certainly come to them with clear proofs. Then indeed many of them, [even] after that, throughout the land, were transgressors.

Muhammad (ﷺ) in this regard, when the person follows the teachings of the Prophet صلى الله عليه وسلم, the Sunnah. The title of the Prophet صلى الله عليه وسلم is the Loved one, (al-Habib), by Allah ﷻ. When the person imitates the role model, the Prophet ﷺ, inshAllah the genuine and practical learning will happen, which is pleasing to Allah ﷻ.

[44-49]⁷⁷⁰

{ إِنَّا أَنزَلْنَا التَّوْرَاةَ فِيهَا هُدًى وَنُورٌ يَحْكُمُ بِهَا النَّبِيُّونَ الَّذِينَ أَسْلَمُواْ لِلَّذِينَ هَادُواْ وَالرَّبَّانِيُّونَ وَالأَحْبَارُ بِمَا اسْتُحْفِظُواْ مِن كِتَابِ اللّهِ وَكَانُواْ عَلَيْهِ شُهَدَاء فَلاَ تَخْشَوُاْ النَّاسَ وَاخْشَوْنِ وَلاَ تَشْتَرُواْ بِآيَاتِي ثَمَناً قَلِيلاً وَمَن لَّمْ يَحْكُم بِمَا أَنزَلَ اللّهُ فَأُوْلَئِكَ هُمُ الْكَافِرُونَ {المائدة/44} وَكَتَبْنَا عَلَيْهِمْ فِيهَا أَنَّ النَّفْسَ بِالنَّفْسِ وَالْعَيْنَ بِالْعَيْنِ وَالأَنفَ بِالأَنفِ وَالأُذُنَ بِالأُذُنِ وَالسِّنَّ

---

770. 5:44 Verily, it is We who bestowed from on high the Torah, wherein there was guidance and light. On its strength did the prophets, who had surrendered themselves unto God, deliver judgment unto those who followed the Jewish faith; and so did the [early] men of God and the rabbis, inasmuch as some of God's writ had been entrusted to their care; and they [all] bore witness to its truth. Therefore, [O children of Israel,] hold not men in awe, but stand in awe of Me; and do not barter away My messages for a trifling gain: for they who do not judge in accordance with what God has bestowed from on high are, indeed, deniers of the truth! 5:45 And We ordained for them in that [Torah]: A life for a life, and an eye for an eye, and a nose for a nose, and an ear for an ear, and a tooth for a tooth, and a [similar] retribution for wounds; but he who shall forgo it out of charity will atone thereby for some of his past sins. And they who do not judge in accordance with what God has revealed—they, they are the evildoers! 5:46

And We caused Jesus, the son of Mary, to follow in the footsteps of those [earlier prophets], confirming the truth of whatever there still remained of the Torah; and We vouchsafed unto him the Gospel, wherein there was guidance and light, confirming the truth of whatever there still remained of the Torah, and as a guidance and admonition unto the God-conscious. (5:47) Let, then, the followers of the Gospel judge in accordance with what God has revealed therein: for they who do not judge in the light of what God has bestowed from on high—it is they, they who are truly iniquitous!

5:48 And unto thee [O Prophet] have We vouchsafed this divine writ, setting forth the truth, confirming the truth of whatever there still remains of earlier revelations and determining what is true therein. Judge, then, between the followers of earlier revelation in accordance with what God has bestowed from on high, and do not follow their errant views, forsaking the truth that has come unto thee.

Unto every one of you have We appointed a [different] law and way of life. And if God had so willed, He could surely have made you all one single community: but [He willed it otherwise] in order to test you by means of what He has vouchsafed unto, you. Vie, then, with one another in doing good works! Unto God you all must return; and then He will make you truly understand all that on which you were wont to differ. 5:49 Hence, judge between the followers of earlier revelation in accordance with what God has bestowed from on high, and do not follow their errant views; and beware of them, lest they tempt thee away from aught that God has bestowed from on high upon thee. And if they turn away [from His commandments], then know that it is but God's will [thus] to afflict them for some of their sins:70 for, behold, a great many people are iniquitous indeed

بِالسِّنِّ وَالْجُرُوحَ قِصَاصٌ فَمَن تَصَدَّقَ بِهِ فَهُوَ كَفَّارَةٌ لَّهُ وَمَن لَّمْ يَحْكُم بِمَا أَنزَلَ اللّهُ فَأُوْلَئِكَ هُمُ الظَّالِمُونَ {المائدة/45}

It really needs deep pondering and reflecting in order to derive and interpret the changing conditions of the person, the people and incidents. If one for example reviews the identity dynamics of ahlu kitāb, in this case for example, yahud, the combining term for everyone including Muslims is the trait of الَّذِينَ أَسْلَمُوا[771]. Then, the specific identity words are mentioned as لِلَّذِينَ هَادُواْ وَالرَّبَّانِيُّونَ وَالأَحْبَارُ[772]. First, group identifier as yahud then, the terms of rabbani and ahbar. They may have similar correspondence in Muslim literature but, the Qurān does not mix these referrals such as :

لَوْلاَ يَنْهَاهُمُ الرَّبَّانِيُّونَ وَالأَحْبَارُ عَن قَوْلِهِمُ الإِثْمَ وَأَكْلِهِمُ السُّحْتَ لَبِئْسَ مَا كَانُواْ يَصْنَعُونَ. {المائدة/63}[773].

From another perspective, the same text sometimes can be read differently at different times by different people. In this perspective, the yahud are praised in the Qurān as the "guided" ones. Existing categories such as rabbani and ahbār are praised categories. The topic of fulfilling the responsibility of being a rabbani or ahbār is a separate topic.

وَقَفَّيْنَا عَلَى آثَارِهِم بِعَيسَى ابْنِ مَرْيَمَ مُصَدِّقًا لِّمَا بَيْنَ يَدَيْهِ مِنَ التَّوْرَاةِ وَآتَيْنَاهُ الإِنجِيلَ فِيهِ هُدًى وَنُورٌ وَمُصَدِّقًا لِّمَا بَيْنَ يَدَيْهِ مِنَ التَّوْرَاةِ وَهُدًى وَمَوْعِظَةً لِّلْمُتَّقِينَ {المائدة/46}

وَلْيَحْكُمْ أَهْلُ الإِنجِيلِ بِمَا أَنزَلَ اللّهُ فِيهِ وَمَن لَّمْ يَحْكُم بِمَا أَنزَلَ اللّهُ فَأُوْلَئِكَ هُمُ الْفَاسِقُونَ {المائدة/47} وَأَنزَلْنَا إِلَيْكَ الْكِتَابَ بِالْحَقِّ مُصَدِّقًا لِّمَا بَيْنَ يَدَيْهِ مِنَ الْكِتَابِ وَمُهَيْمِنًا عَلَيْهِ فَاحْكُم بَيْنَهُم بِمَا أَنزَلَ اللّهُ وَلاَ تَتَّبِعْ أَهْوَاءهُمْ عَمَّا جَاءكَ مِنَ الْحَقِّ لِكُلٍّ جَعَلْنَا مِنكُمْ شِرْعَةً وَمِنْهَاجًا وَلَوْ شَاء اللّهُ لَجَعَلَكُمْ أُمَّةً وَاحِدَةً وَلَكِن لِّيَبْلُوَكُمْ فِي مَآ آتَاكُم فَاسْتَبِقُوا الْخَيْرَاتِ إِلَى الله مَرْجِعُكُمْ جَمِيعًا فَيُنَبِّئُكُم بِمَا كُنتُمْ فِيهِ تَخْتَلِفُونَ {المائدة/48} وَأَنِ احْكُم بَيْنَهُم بِمَا أَنزَلَ اللّهُ وَلاَ تَتَّبِعْ أَهْوَاءهُمْ وَاحْذَرْهُمْ أَن يَفْتِنُوكَ عَن بَعْضِ مَا أَنزَلَ اللّهُ إِلَيْكَ فَإِن تَوَلَّوْاْ فَاعْلَمْ أَنَّمَا يُرِيدُ اللّهُ أَن يُصِيبَهُم بِبَعْضِ ذُنُوبِهِمْ وَإِنَّ كَثِيرًا مِّنَ النَّاسِ لَفَاسِقُونَ {المائدة/49}

---

771. Who had surrendered themselves unto God.
772. Deliver judgment unto those who followed the Jewish faith;58 and so did the [early] men of God and the rabbis.
773. Why do the rabbis and religious scholars not forbid them from saying what is sinful and devouring what is unlawful? How wretched is what they have been practicing.

It is interesting to review above ayahs in the light of the interactions with ahlu-kitāb. It is important to understand the position of ahlu-kitāb today when Allah ﷻ in the Qurān mentions their expected position. In the traditional understanding وَلْيَحْكُمْ أَهْلُ الإِنجِيلِ[774] is interpreted that Allah ﷻ previously ordered them to follow their book, Injīl (33). The same notion was presented in the previous ayah as مَن لَّمْ يَحْكُم بِمَا أَنزَلَ اللّهُ فَأُوْلَٰئِكَ هُمُ الْكَافِرُونَ {المائدة/44}

[55-57][775]

إِنَّمَا وَلِيُّكُمُ اللّهُ وَرَسُولُهُ وَالَّذِينَ آمَنُواْ الَّذِينَ يُقِيمُونَ الصَّلاَةَ وَيُؤْتُونَ الزَّكَاةَ وَهُمْ رَاكِعُونَ {المائدة/55} وَمَن يَتَوَلَّ اللّهَ وَرَسُولَهُ وَالَّذِينَ آمَنُواْ فَإِنَّ حِزْبَ اللّهِ هُمُ الْغَالِبُونَ {المائدة/56} يَا أَيُّهَا الَّذِينَ آمَنُواْ لاَ تَتَّخِذُواْ الَّذِينَ اتَّخَذُواْ دِينَكُمْ هُزُوًا وَلَعِبًا مِّنَ الَّذِينَ أُوتُواْ الْكِتَابَ مِن قَبْلِكُمْ وَالْكُفَّارَ أَوْلِيَاء وَاتَّقُواْ اللّهَ إِن كُنتُم مُّؤْمِنِينَ {المائدة/57}

The above set of verses differentiate two groups of people. One group is taking Allah ﷻ as their main concern in their life styles. The other group is taking and preferring a life style other than Allah ﷻ such as materialism etc. In this regard, although the value system of both groups may have a lot of similarities, in their essence, there will be a main and basic system in terms of their motivation or intention of the individual. Therefore, there would be clashes sometimes understanding, communicating and empathizing with each other. In this regard, Allah ﷻ mentions that the notion of waliy as إِنَّمَا وَلِيُّكُمُ اللّهُ وَرَسُولُهُ وَالَّذِينَ آمَنُواْ[776]. Even among the ones who have imān, there would be spectrum of different people who may not embody the imān in the same way. Then, these criteria explain for the embodiment of who should be a true waliyy for the person to be الَّذِينَ يُقِيمُونَ الصَّلاَةَ وَيُؤْتُونَ الزَّكَاةَ وَهُمْ رَاكِعُونَ[777]. Because, there are a lot of

---

774. Let, then, the followers of the Gospel judge
775. 5:55 Behold, your only helper shall be God, and His Apostle, and those who have attained to faith—those that are constant in prayer, and render the purifying dues, and bow down [before God]: (5:56) for, all who ally themselves with God and His Apostle and those who have attained to faith—behold, it is they, the partisans of God, who shall be victorious! 5:57 O you who have attained to faith! Do not take for your friends such as mock at your, faith and make a jest of it—be they from among those who have been vouchsafed revelation before your time, or [from among] those who deny the truth [of revelation as such]—but remain conscious of God, if you are [truly] believers.
776. Behold, your only helper shall be God, and His Apostle, and those who have attained to faith.
777. Those that are constant in prayer, and render the purifying dues, and bow down [before God].

Muslims who cannot differentiate this basic premise between these two groups. In other words, even among Muslims one should be selective who to choose as a waliyy.

[59-60][778]

قُلْ يَا أَهْلَ الْكِتَابِ هَلْ تَنقِمُونَ مِنَّا إِلاَّ أَنْ آمَنَّا بِاللّهِ وَمَا أُنزِلَ إِلَيْنَا وَمَا أُنزِلَ مِن قَبْلُ وَأَنَّ أَكْثَرَكُمْ فَاسِقُونَ [779] {المائدة/59} قُلْ هَلْ أُنَبِّئُكُم بِشَرٍّ مِّن ذَلِكَ مَثُوبَةً عِندَ اللهِ مَن لَّعَنَهُ اللّهُ وَغَضِبَ عَلَيْهِ وَجَعَلَ مِنْهُمُ الْقِرَدَةَ وَالْخَنَازِيرَ وَعَبَدَ الطَّاغُوتَ أُوْلَئِكَ شَرٌّ مَّكَاناً وَأَضَلُّ عَن سَوَاء السَّبِيلِ {المائدة/60}

Above is an interesting ayah to show possible psychology of some of the ahlu-kitāb why they have problems with Muslims as mentioned هَلْ[780] تَنقِمُونَ مِنَّا إِلاَّ أَنْ آمَنَّا بِاللّهِ وَمَا أُنزِلَ إِلَيْنَا وَمَا أُنزِلَ مِن قَبْلُ. The message of Islam being logical, reasonable and inclusive can bother and cause hate and jealousy for some people although it is very reasonable. It is reasonable because the Qurān puts forward all the similarities with Bible and Torah to minimize and remove the negative identity barriers which prevents benefitting from each other. In other words, although a person may not do something harmful to others the position being good and ethical can bother some people who have spiritual diseases. Another example of this is the case between Habìl and Qabìl. One did not do anything to another but the other still wanted to kill him, Alllahu A'lam.

---

778. 5:59 Say: "O followers of earlier revelation! Do you find fault with us for no other reason than that we believe in God [alone], and in that which He has bestowed from on high upon us as well as that which He has bestowed aforetime?—or [is it only] because most of you are iniquitous?"
5:60 Say: "Shall I tell you who, in the sight of God, deserves a yet worse retribution than these? They whom God has rejected and whom He has condemned, and whom He has turned into apes and swine because they worshipped the powers of evil: these are yet worse in station, and farther astray from the right path [than the mockers].
779. Say, "O People of the Scripture, do you resent us except [for the fact] that we have believed in Allah and what was revealed to us and what was revealed before and because most of you are defiantly disobedient?"
780. Do you resent us except [for the fact] that we have believed in Allah and what was revealed to us and what was revealed before.

[65-66]⁷⁸¹

وَلَوْ أَنَّ أَهْلَ الْكِتَابِ آمَنُواْ وَاتَّقَوْا لَكَفَّرْنَا عَنْهُمْ سَيِّئَاتِهِمْ وَلأَدْخَلْنَاهُمْ جَنَّاتِ النَّعِيمِ {المائدة/65} وَلَوْ أَنَّهُمْ أَقَامُواْ التَّوْرَاةَ وَالإِنجِيلَ وَمَا أُنزِلَ إِلَيهِم مِّن رَّبِّهِمْ لأَكَلُواْ مِن فَوْقِهِمْ وَمِن تَحْتِ أَرْجُلِهِم مِّنْهُمْ أُمَّةٌ مُّقْتَصِدَةٌ وَكَثِيرٌ مِّنْهُمْ سَاء مَا يَعْمَلُونَ {المائدة/66}

Above is another ayah about when and how to ensure minimizing the trials in this dunya and have a life with possibly less trials. So, the first step is to follow the guidelines of the dīn as mentioned with وَلَوْ أَنَّهُمْ⁷⁸² أَقَامُواْ التَّوْرَاةَ وَالإِنجِيلَ وَمَا أُنزِلَ إِلَيهِم مِّن رَّبِّهِمْ.

Second, the believers can demonstrate the traits of ungratefulness like others sometimes. Allah ﷻ gives the person so much but still the person is in the state of depression, pessimism and questioning instead of being in the state of gratefulness and shukr. This concept is constantly mentioned in the Qurān.

As the person is in the state of shukr even in the difficult situations, then Allah ﷻ promises to increase what is already given. The constant state of shukr and hamd can be achieved by pondering what one already has. This can be called muraqaba, looking to oneself for all the bounties of Allah ﷻ and realizing the necessity of constant shukr and hamd to Allah ﷻ.

One of the traits that make the Prophet ﷺ as the person of embodying this gratefulness and shukr is that he ﷺ never complained what we normally complain in our lives. An unpleasant food, environment or people are some examples of this when, even who we consider good people can complain. Or, if we take it further, for example, hunger is one of the cases that make people lose their real self and become ungrateful, mean and angry. The Prophet ﷺ did not complain but maintained most of his life with hunger without complaining but still being grateful and in shukr to Allah ﷻ.

---

781. 5:65 If the followers of the Bible would but attain to [true] faith and God-consciousness, We should indeed efface their [previous] bad deeds, and indeed bring them into gardens of bliss; (5:66) and if they would but truly observe the Torah and the Gospel and all [the revelation] that has been bestowed from on high upon them by their Sustainer, they would indeed partake of all the blessings of heaven and earth. Some of them do pursue a right course; but as for most of them—vile indeed is what they do!

782. And if they would but truly observe the Torah and the Gospel and all [the revelation] that has been bestowed from on high upon them by their Sustainer.

[67]⁷⁸³

يَا أَيُّهَا الرَّسُولُ بَلِّغْ مَا أُنزِلَ إِلَيْكَ مِن رَّبِّكَ وَإِن لَّمْ تَفْعَلْ فَمَا بَلَّغْتَ رِسَالَتَهُ وَاللّهُ يَعْصِمُكَ مِنَ النَّاسِ إِنَّ اللّهَ لاَ يَهْدِي الْقَوْمَ الْكَافِرِينَ {المائدة/67}

As most of the ayahs at their specific sabab nuzûl address the Prophet صلى الله عليه وسلم, in its generalizability they address all the Muslims until the day of Qiyamah. The above ayah alludes to the difficult task of balance in one's relationship with others with the intention of making dawah, explaining about the religion. Sometimes a person can be in a very hard thought process of what to explain first and how to deliver it. On one side, there is the responsibility of not delivering the message and on the other side due to problems in delivery of the message, there is the possibility of making people turn away from the teachings of the religion due to one's method. Sometimes, a person can also have a fear of losing something while in the position of delivery of the divine message to others. It happened in the past and will continue to happen. In this regard, Allah ﷻ gives assurance that when a person has a sincere trust to Allah ﷻ then, the ayah follows as وَأَللّهُ يَعْصِمُكَ مِنَ النَّاسِ⁷⁸⁴.

[78]⁷⁸⁵

لُعِنَ الَّذِينَ كَفَرُواْ مِن بَنِي إِسْرَائِيلَ عَلَى لِسَانِ دَاوُودَ وَعِيسَى ابْنِ مَرْيَمَ ذَلِكَ بِمَا عَصَوا وَّكَانُواْ يَعْتَدُونَ {المائدة/78}

It is interesting to see that there are specifically two names mentioned: Isa as and Dawud as. Isa as is the person that Christians expect most benefit in terms of their religious affiliation. Yet, Isa as makes la'nah to them who makes shirk and kufr to Allah ﷻ for their not genuine and altered religious dispositions. In the case of Dawud as, there is the expectation of Jews that messiah would be from the descent of Dawud as and there is a lot of renderings and preparation about it among them. In both cases,

---

783. 5:67 O APOSTLE! Announce all that has been bestowed from on high upon thee by thy Sustainer: for unless thou doest it fully, thou wilt not have delivered His message [at all]. And God will protect thee from [unbelieving] men: behold, God does not guide people who refuse to acknowledge the truth.

784. And God will protect thee from [unbelieving] men.

785. 5:78 THOSE of the children of Israel who were bent on denying the truth have [already] been cursed by the tongue of David and of Jesus, the son of Mary? this, because they rebelled [against God] and persisted in transgressing the bounds of what is right.

the person or people expect the most benefit from the benefactors but they themselves turn away from them. This should be very devastating and disappointing. One of the hikmahs of these verses is that it is really expected for them to reconsider their disposition, الله اعلم.

BIBLIOGRAPHY

1. Vahide, S. *The Collection of Light* . s.l.: ihlas nur publication, 2001.
2. Sirhindi, Ahmad. *Maktubat Imam Rabbani Shaykh Ahmad Sirhindi Faruqi*. s.l.: Maktabah Mujaddidiyah (www.maktabah.org), 2008.
3. Al-Bukhari, M. *The translation of the meanings of Sahih Al-Bukhari*. s.l.: Kazi Publications, 1986.
4. Demirci, Muhsin. *Tefsir Tarihi (History of Exegesis of Quran)*. Istanbul: ifav, 2010. pp. 34–38.
5. As-Suyuti, Jalal ad-Din. *Gateway to the Qur'anic Sciences*. s.l.: Turath Publishing, 2017.
6. Kumek, Y. *The Noble Quran: Selected Passages From Al-Quran Al-Kareem With Interpreted Meanings*. Buffalo, New York: Medina House Publishing, 2020.
7. Kumek, Yunus J. *Practical Mysticism: Sufi Journeys of Heart and Mind*. Dubuque: Kendall Hunt, 2018.
8. Razi, M. *Mafatih al-Ghayb known as al-Tafsir al-Kabir*. Cairo: Dar Ibya al-Kutub al-Bahiyya, 1172.
9. Muslim, A. *Sahih Muslim (translated by Siddiqui, A.)*. s.l.: Peace Vision, 1972.
10. Al-Ghazali, M. *Ihya 'Ulum al-Din* . s.l.: Dar al-Fikr, 2004.
11. Kasir, Ibn. *Tafsir al-Qur'an al-Azim*. Beirut: Dar al-Ilm, 1982.
12. Bukhari, Muhammad Ibn Ismail. *Moral Teachings of Islam: Prophetic Traditions from Al-Adab Al-mufrad*. s.l.: Rowman Altamira, 2003.
13. Taftazani, At. *Sharhu Taftazani*. p. 69.
14. Aristotle. *Aristotle's Metaphysics*.
15. Kumek, Yunus. *Revealing Pearls and Diamonds: Selected Duas of Rasulullah saw*. s.l.: Medina House Publishing, 2019.
16. Arabi, Ibn. *Al Futuhat Al Makkiya*. s.l.: Dar Al-Kotob Al-Ilmiyah.
17. Raymond D. Berendt, Edith L. R. Corliss, Morris S. Ojalvo. *Quieting A Practical Guide to Noise Control*. s.l.: University Press of the Pacific, 2000. pp. 1–2.

18. Dawud, Abu (Sulaiman bin Ash'ath). *Sunan Abu Dawud.* riyadh: Darussalam, 2008.
19. Laney, Marti Olsen. *The Introvert Advantage: How to Thrive in an Extrovert World.* s.l.: Workman Publishing Company, 2002. p. 41.
20. Majah, Ibn. *Sunan Ibn Majah.* s.l.: Darus-Salam, 2007.
21. Oxford, University Press. Oxford Dictionaries. [Online] 2016. [Cited: 2016.] http://www.oxforddictionaries.com/us/definition/american_english/say.
22. Hanbal, Ahmad B. *Musnad Imam Ahmad Ibn Hanbal.* s.l.: Dar-Us-Salam Publications, 2012.
23. Shafi, Muhammad. *Ma'ariful Qur'an.* s.l.: maktaba-e Darul-Uloom, 2005. pp. 129–131. Vol. 1.
24. Al-Marghinani, Burhan Uddin Abu Al-Hasan Ali Ibn Abu Bakr Ibn Abdul Jaleel Ar-Rashidani. *Al Hidayah Sharh Bidayat Al-Mubtadi.* Beirut, Lebanon: Dar Al Hadith.
25. Al-Wahidi, Imam Ali Ibn Ahmad. *Alwajizu fi tafsiriil kitabil Aziz.* s.l.: Darul Qalam & Dar Shamia.
26. Tirmizi, M. *Jami At-Tirmizi.* s.l.: Dar-us-Salam, 2007.
27. Al-Hakim. *Mustadrak.* p. 1/612.
28. Hibban, Ibn. *As-Sahih.* pp. 4/612, 6/411.
29. Bolelli, Nusraddin. *Balagatul Arabiyya.* s.l.: ifav, 2009.
30. Ibrahim Kalin, John L. Esposito. *Islamophobia The Challenge of Pluralism in the 21st Century.* s.l.: Oxford University Press, USA, 2011. p. 192.
31. Maturidi, Abu Mansur Al. *Ta'wilat Ahl As Sunnah.* s.l.: Dar al Kotob al ilmiyyah,.
32. Oxford, University Press. Oxford Dictionaries. [Online] 2016. [Cited: 2016.] http://www.oxforddictionaries.com/us/definition/american_english/.
33. Thalabi, Abu Ishaq. *Al-Kashaf wal bayab.* Beirut: DKI, 2004.
34. Mojaddedi, Jawid. *The Wiley Blackwell Companion to the Qur'an.* s.l.: Wiley, 2017. p. 120.
35. AbdulFadl, Muhammad. *Lectures on Quran.* 2019.
36. Baghawi, Husayn. *Tafsir al-Baghawi al-musamma Ma'alim al-tanzil.* Bayrut: Dar al-Ma'rifah, 1987.
37. Ehrman, Bart D. *Misquoting Jesus The Story Behind Who Changed the Bible and Why.* s.l.: HarperOne, 2009.

38. Janney, Rebecca Price. *Then Comes Marriage? A Cultural History of the American Family.* s.l.: Moody Publishers, 2010. p. 108.
39. Rebeca Mejía-Arauz, Barbara Rogoff. *Children Learn by Observing and Contributing to Family and Community Endeavors: A Cultural Paradigm.* s.l.: Elsevier Science, 2015. p. 54.
40. Cox, R.R. *Schutz's Theory of Relevance: A Phenomenological Critique.* s.l.: Springer Netherlands, 2012.
41. O., Dr. Meggie. *LBGT issue from the Perspective of a ObGyn Specialist.* [interv.] Y. Kumek. March 17, 2016.
42. Zamakhshari, Abu Kassim. *Tafsir al-Kashaf.* Beirut: DKI, .
43. 'Imadi, Abu Al-Su'Ud Muhammad Ibn Muhammad Ibn Mus. *Tafsir abi al-su'ud, aw, irshad al-'aql al-salim ila mazaya al-qur'an al-karim.* s.l.: Turath For Solutions, 2013.
44. al-Ghazali, Abu Hamid. *The Quran and Its Exegesis (translation by Helmut Gatie).* s.l.: Oxford: Oneworld, 1996.
45. *Psychology and Light: The Effects of Light on Mental Functions.* Muensterberg, Hugo. 1916, Scientific American, Vol. 82, p. 406.
46. Shaykh Muhammad Nazim Adil Al-Haqqani, Shaykh Muhammad Hisham Kabbani. *Muhammad, the Messenger of Islam His Life & Prophecy.* s.l.: Islamic Supreme Council of America, 2002. p. 141.
47. Nasafi, I. *Tafsirul Nasafi.*
48. Ma'lūf, Luwīs. *Al Munjid Arabic Dictionary.* s.l.: Dar Al mashriq, 2000.
49. Shushmaruk, Peter. *Magnetic Universe.* s.l.: Lulu.com. p. 62.
50. Hauck, Dennis William. *The Complete Idiot's Guide to Alchemy.* s.l.: Alpha Books, 2008. p. 201.
51. Bizony, Piers. *How to Build Your Own Spaceship The Science of Personal Space Travel.* 2009. p. chapter 3.
52. *Surah Abasa.* Yener, M. s.l.: New Hope.
53. Pinna, Simon de. *Chemical Reactions.* s.l.: Gareth Stevens Pub. p. 32.

AUTHOR BIO

Dr. Kumek had classical training in Islamic sciences from the respected Shuyûqh/Teachers of Turkey, India, Egypt, Yemen, Somalia, Morocco, Sudan, and the United States. He stayed and studied classical Islamic sciences in Egypt and Turkey as well.

In his Western training, education and teaching experience, Dr. Kumek has acted as the religious studies coordinator at State University of New York (SUNY) Buffalo State and taught undergraduate and graduate courses in religious studies at SUNY at Buffalo State, Niagara University, Daemen College and Harvard Divinity School. Dr. Kumek also pursued doctorate degree in physics at SUNY at Buffalo published academic papers in the areas of quantum physics and medical physics. Then, he decided to engage with the world of social sciences through social anthropology, education, and cultural anthropology in his doctorate studies and subsequently, spent a few years as a research associate in the anthropology department of the same university and subsequently, completed a postdoctoral fellowship at Harvard Divinity school. Some of his book titles include sociology through religion, religious literacy through ethnography, selected passages from the Qurãn, selected passages from the Hadith (titled as Rasulullah ﷺ) and selected prayers of the Prophet Muhammad ﷺ (titled as Pearls and Diamonds). Dr. M. Yunus Kumek is currently teaching on Muslim Ministry and Spiritual Care at Harvard Divinity School.

ACKNOWLEDGMENTS

I would like to thank all my unnamed teachers, friends, and students for their input, ideas, suggestions, help, and support during and before the preparation of this book.

I would like to thank Dr. David Banks, faculty of the Department of Anthropology, State University of New York (SUNY), Sister Toni Hajdaj, Sister Umm Aisha, Dr. AbdulAhad, Br. Ali Rifat and His wife Sister Yildiz at-Turki, Sheikh Dr. Omar of Maryland al-Hindi, Sheikh Tamer of Buffalo, and Sheikh Ali of Hartford Seminary, Sisters Asya Hamad, Amina Osman, and Fatima Samrodia of Darul-Ulum Madania of Buffalo, Mufti Hussain Memon of Darul-Ulum Canada and Imam Khalil Qadri of Islamic Center of Niagara Frontier (ISNF) for all their editing, suggestions and comments.

I want to also thank the team of Medina House Publishing in all their preparations and efforts at all stages of this book especially Br. Murat, Br. Khalid (Halit), Br. Mehmet (Matt) and Sister Karen.

Lastly, I would like to thank all of my family members for their patience with me during the preparation of this book.

We ask Allah ﷻ to accept all our efforts with the Divine Karam, Fadl, and Grace but not with our faulty and limited efforts deeming rejection. اللَّهُمَّ صلِّ عَلى سَيِّدِناَ وَ حَبِيْبِنَا وَ مَوْلَانَا مُحَمَّد.

INDEX

www.ingramcontent.com/pod-product-compliance
Lightning Source LLC
Chambersburg PA
CBHW052126270326
41930CB00012B/2775